THE TRUE STORY OF ROY FITZGERALD
WHOSE GLITTERING LIFE AS ROCK HUDSON
MADE HIM A SCREEN IDOL—AND ONE OF THE
MOST TRAGIC FIGURES IN RECENT MEMORY.

Whether arranged or not—"If you knew the number of arranged marriages in this town," Robert Stack said with a laugh—it seems quite probable that Rock did care for Phyllis Gates, enjoyed her company, and even held hopes that the marriage would be a success. Such things, after all, do happen, even in Hollywood. The boy who'd never had a real family was still yearning for one. It is unwise to assume that just because the marriage was arranged, and Rock was a homosexual, that there was no affection at all between him and Gates. Thirty years later he assured Marc Christian that there had definitely been a relationship between them— one that was both physical and emotional. Marriage, however, had destroyed it, he said. Jimmy Dobson, Rock's long-time vocal coach, agreed. "Roy told me he had really loved this person, and I believed him."

If true, the failure of his marriage illuminates a problem Rock had throughout his life with all his emotional relationships. Living together—domestically—was equated in his mind with lack of sexual interest. The pursuit, the chase, the romantic preliminaries were what entranced him. . . .

IDOL
ROCK HUDSON

THE TRUE STORY OF
AN AMERICAN FILM HERO

Jerry Oppenheimer
and Jack Vitek

BANTAM BOOKS
TORONTO • NEW YORK • LONDON • SYDNEY • AUCKLAND

*This low-priced Bantam Book
has been completely reset in a typeface
designed for easy reading, and was printed
from new plates. It contains the complete
text of the original hardcover edition.*
NOT ONE WORD HAS BEEN OMITTED.

IDOL: ROCK HUDSON

*A Bantam Book / published by arrangement with
Villard Books*

*PRINTING HISTORY
Villard Books edition published May 1986
Bantam edition / February 1987
Book of the Month Club, July 1986
Nostalgia Book Club, July 1986
Movie/Entertainment Book Club, July 1986
Troll Book Clubs, August 1986*

*Excerpts of this book appeared in Ladies Home Journal,
August—News America Syndicate, September—The Star,
September*

*All rights reserved.
Copyright © 1986 by Jack Vitek and Jerry Oppenheimer.
Library of Congress Catalog Card Number: 86-11142
Cover photograph by John Bryson/SYGMA
This book may not be reproduced in whole or in part, by
mimeograph or any other means, without permission.
For information address: Villard Books, 201 East 50 Street,
New York, NY 10022*

ISBN 0-553-26680-2

Published simultaneously in the United States and Canada

*Bantam Books are published by Bantam Books, Inc. Its trade-
mark, consisting of the words "Bantam Books" and the portrayal of a rooster, is registered in U.S. Patent and Trademark
Office and in other countries. Marca Registrada. Bantam
Books, Inc., 666 Fifth Avenue, New York, New York 10103.*

PRINTED IN THE UNITED STATES OF AMERICA

KR   0 9 8 7 6 5 4 3 2 1

Judy Oppenheimer assisted in the conception, reporting, writing, and organization of this book. It could not have been completed without her superb journalistic skills, tireless dedication, and invaluable insights.
—*Jerry Oppenheimer*

I would like to thank my wife, Susan, for her wise counsel and enduring support through the countless crises that researching, writing, and collaborating on a book of this sort involved.
—*Jack Vitek*

ACKNOWLEDGMENTS

The authors would like to thank the following people for their insights, guidance, remembrances, generosity, and candor: Jay Allen, Julie Andrews, Lou Antonio, Army Archerd, Jane Ardmore, Jim Bacon, Solly Baiano, Fredda Dudley Balling, Marty Baum, Pat Boone, Marcia Borie, Pat Broeski, Richard Brooks, Jim Brown, L. Z. Brown, Beth Burr, Lewis John Carlino, Carleton Carpenter, Allan Carr, Marc Christian, Mary Clark, Yanou Collart, Maybelle Conger, Patrick Cotter, George Crepus, Bud Davis, Jerry Davis, Samson De Brier, Fred de Cordova, Jimmy Dobson, Dr. Dominique Dormont, Charlie Earle, Leslie Easterbrook, Blake Edwards, Alan Eichler, George Englund, Edward Z. Epstein, Jon Epstein, Sylvia Fine, Bob Finkel, Nello Fragasi, John Frankenheimer, Dave Freyss, Lou Friedman, Michael Gordon, Greg Gorman, David Greene, Seli Groves, Joyce Haber, Uta Hagen, Randa Handler, Estelle Harmon, Jimmy Hawkins, Dr. Thomas Hewes, Burt Hixson, Kim Hunt, Darlene Ilg, Ed Jenner, Salome Jens, Betty Kimble, Richard Lamparski, Piper Laurie, Liberty, David Lipton, Jerry London, Mary Anita Loos, Dorothy Malone, Dorothy Manners, Jim Matteoni, Armistead Maupin, Juliet McGrew, Pat McGuire, Joe Morella, Dick Morris, Ed Muhl, Stan Musgrove, Lori Nelson, Ralph Nelson, Christian Nyby III, Willem Oltmans, Joe Pevney, Debbie Power, David Ragan, Tony Randall, John Randolph, Bruce Redor, Mark Reedall, Larry Rentz, Dick Richards, George Robotham, Leigh Rutledge, Peter Saldutti, Gus Schirmer, Stanley Shapiro, George Sherman, Lou Sherrell, Randy Shilts,

Dave Shumacher, Linda Simon, Gordy Smith, Robert Stack, Susan Stafford, Leonard Stern, Elaine Stritch, Gary Sweat, Father Terry Sweeney, Sue Terry, Kevin Thomas, J. Lee Thompson, Bobby Troup, Jack Trux, Mamie Van Doren, Peter Van Gelder, Dr. Paul Volberding, Earl Weirich, Ray Weise, Matthew West, Jane Wilkie, Mac Williams, Jeannie Wolf, and Lee Wood.

The authors would also like to thank Patricia Barlow and Val Virga for their help and guidance in photo research.

The authors have respected the wishes of those who asked that their names not be mentioned.

CONTENTS

PROLOGUE

Ten-thirty in the morning, October 2, 1985. Mortuary employees Larry Rentz and Chris Kremins placed the wasted body of screen idol Rock Hudson—covered and strapped to a gurney—into the back of their unmarked van. Ninety minutes earlier, Hudson had died in his sleep, the ravaged victim of Acquired Immune Deficiency Syndrome, at age fifty-nine.

Rentz got behind the wheel and was slowly maneuvering the van out of Hudson's garage when he spotted Tom Clark, the dead actor's longtime friend, running toward the makeshift hearse. Pale, distraught, and visibly shaken, Clark insisted that he sit next to the body on the ride to the crematory.

Clark was determined to protect Rock in death—as he had tried to in life. His major concern was that a photographer might try to take a last photo of Rock and sell it to one of the tabloids, as had happened with Elvis and John Lennon. Clark did not want the world to see how Rock looked in death. Rock had already suffered too many indignities over the last months; Clark wanted to make certain there would be no more.

A mob of reporters and photographers—more than a hundred strong—had gathered outside the front gate of Hudson's Spanish-style Beverly Hills estate. A media death watch had been in effect since early summer, when the news was revealed that Rock had AIDS, a fatal virus that was primarily striking homosexuals. The revelation had catapulted the disease and Hudson's secret life out of the closet.

Clark hauled a chair into the back of the van so that he could sit next to Rock's body. With the help of the two men from the mortuary, he placed long bath towels over the van's rear and side windows to block probing camera lenses.

Security people, sent over by Rock's friend Elizabeth Taylor, tried unsuccessfully to clear a path for the van through the media horde. Photographers attached themselves like leeches to the front bumper, flashing pictures through the windshield—all but blinding Rentz and Kremins in the front seats. In back, Clark hid his face with his hands and tried to shield the body bag.

Other reporters and photographers started pounding on the doors, shouting questions at Rentz and Kremins. Rentz feared they would smash the windows or pull off the door handles. He had overseen numerous celebrity removals over the years, but none had been as violent as this. He thought of a lynch mob. Huddled in back, Clark feared someone might break through the rear doors and pull out the body.

Finally, after about fifteen minutes, Rentz managed to maneuver the van through the mob and onto Beverly Crest Drive. Reporters and photographers jumped into cars and tailgated the van down the hill to the treacherous San Diego Freeway. Rentz, fearing an accident, was headed to the mortuary office in North Hollywood, where he had to drop off the death certificate and get the paperwork necessary to authorize the cremation.

At the office, the van slowed as Kremins jumped out to get the documents. Rentz asked Clark if he wanted to get in the front seat. "Hell, no!" Clark yelled. "I don't want pictures taken of me, either." Rentz told Kremins to call ahead to the crematory to have the police waiting to handle the media people who were following the van. Six cars were still in pursuit when Rentz entered the Ventura Freeway, heading east toward the Grand View crematory in Glendale.

During the ride, Clark told Rentz how upset he was by the press. "I can't see why they can't let him rest in peace. He's dead. What else is there?" Clark said.

The police had not arrived by the time Rentz pulled up

at the crematory. As he got out of the van, two photographers tried to push past him to get into the vehicle. Clark yelled at them. Rentz pushed them aside. A fistfight almost ensued, but the police arrived in time to avoid any more violence. Rentz moved the van next to the small, Spanish-style crematory building.

"I'll wait here," Clark said shakily. He watched as Rentz removed the body and wheeled it inside the building. There were no more photographers around. Tom Clark had managed to do one last favor for his friend.

PART I

CHAPTER ONE

Beginnings

His looks would always attract attention, and the day of his birth—November 17, 1925, at two in the morning—was no exception. Roy Harold Scherer, Jr., who as Rock Hudson would one day render women around the world breathless, caused a few gasps that day too in Winnetka, Illinois, a small North Shore town outside Chicago. Although his weight was a modest five and a half pounds, it was stretched out over an incredible twenty-seven-inch frame. It had been a long, difficult birth for Katherine Scherer, a fact she never let her son forget. As late as 1976, when he was fifty-one, he told director Ralph Nelson what a large baby he'd been. "He said he was an only child—she never wanted to go through it again," said Nelson. Rock had told Nelson he weighed thirteen pounds at birth—he was never above bending a tale a bit to improve it. But the story was based on the truth, and the truth was obviously one that had been imprinted strongly.

Katherine Wood Scherer, known as Kay, was of Irish-English descent; her husband, Roy, Sr., was of Swiss-German stock. Although Kay had been raised a Catholic and Roy, Sr., a Lutheran, there was no conflict. Religion was not terribly important to either family. Later, Roy, Jr.'s Aunt Hedwig Wood secretly took the boy to be baptized in the Catholic faith—without telling his mother.

Roy, Jr., was born into a large, boisterous, loving, extended family. Kay's parents and four brothers lived

3

nearby. Roy, Sr.'s parents had a six-hundred-acre farm a few hours away in Olney, Illinois. Several of his eight brothers and sisters lived in the area; his sister Pearl, a nurse, had been on hand for Roy's birth. Roy, Sr., was an automobile mechanic, making a modest but decent income. Kay, a large, vibrant woman, spent her days with her young son. In the summer little Roy stayed at his grandparents' farm.

It was an idyllic existence. Unfortunately, it lasted less than five years. Only the lucky escaped the Depression, and the Scherers were not lucky. Roy, Sr., lost his job and was unable to find work. His pride crumbled. His ability to be a man, to take care of his wife and son, was taken away. Finally, desperate, he told his wife he had to leave. He would go to California, the golden land, and try to start again. Maybe after he was settled, he would send for them.

"There was family gossip that she was so devoted to Roy that she ignored her husband, and that's why Scherer left," said Ed Wood, one of Roy's cousins.

Little Roy was staying at his grandparents' farm when his father left home. He did not see him go. When Kay came to take him home, she told the little boy that his father would be coming back soon. For several years, she continued to assure him his father would be back, while Roy waited, helpless.

With her husband gone and money scarce, Kay moved back with her parents. Her brother John, his wife, Hedwig, and their four children had already moved in. Hard times had hit them all. Kay began working, first as a waitress and baby-sitter, then as a telephone operator. Roy, who until then had lived in a small family, receiving his parents' complete attention, found himself at age five living in a very different environment. His fun-loving father was gone; his mother was strained and preoccupied. All the adults seemed burdened, concerned with adult problems. Tempers were short in the small, crowded house. No one had much time for him. He was an amiable, noncomplaining child, and worked hard to fit in. Children abandoned at a young age often think they are to blame in some way, and decide that if they are very good, no one will leave them again. Roy was a very good boy.

Kay was not just giving her son empty assurances. She actually believed her husband would come back. He had written her from California a couple of times, and she felt sure they would be together again eventually. After two years of working, living with her parents and her brother's family, she took matters into her own hands. She saved up enough money to buy her husband a bus ticket for the trip from Los Angeles to Chicago, and sent it. Roy, Sr., mailed it back, saying he couldn't accept it.

Kay was more determined than ever; she had to try to improve her life. Packing a few things, she boarded the bus for California with her son. She knew that once they saw Roy, Sr., face-to-face, everything would change. It was just a matter of taking direct action. A strong-willed woman, Kay felt sure she was doing the right thing by asserting herself. Her husband would come back and they would be a family once again. Roy sat quietly on the bus during the long ride, excitement racing through him. They were going to find Daddy and bring him home.

It didn't work out that way. Kay was able to find Roy by tracking him down to his last address. Roy, Jr., was able to see and touch his father for the first time in two years. But Roy, Sr., refused to go home with them. Kay boarded the bus back, deeply upset, lost in her own misery. She needed to figure out how to handle her life, now that her last attempt to save her family had failed. She had been so sure she could control the outcome, yet it had backfired. She was too involved in her own grief to pay much attention to the small boy sitting next to her, and she had no more reassurances to offer anyway. He stared out the window silently. He was only seven, and deeply confused. He had found his father, only to be abandoned again. How could he understand? Was it something he had done, or the way he looked? He had been powerless to change anything.

He was to grow to strong, handsome manhood and eventually be idolized by millions, but the feelings he had on the bus ride home from California—the inadequacy, the sorrow—he would carry within him forever. Spurred on by his mother, he had dreamed and hoped for two years. But his father had seen him, actually held him in his arms, and yet refused to come back. The pain would always be a part of him. In later years many fans commented on the haunting sadness in his eyes.

After returning to Winnetka, Kay was officially divorced within the year. Shortly afterward she married a tall, handsome ex-marine, Wallace Fitzgerald. It seemed a wise decision at the time: married, she could finally leave her parents' house and resume her life as an adult. Her new husband had promised to adopt Roy, whose name became Roy Fitzgerald. Marriage meant a husband for her and a father for her boy.

But Kay's streak of bad luck was not over yet. The marriage went bad almost from the start, although she was to hold on, grimly tenacious, for eight years. Divorced women were rare in the Midwest in the thirties and were viewed as slightly soiled. A good woman managed to stay married no matter what. Kay had already been a victim of this sort of bigotry in her own family. One of her brothers, Charles, had married a very religious woman after his first wife died. When she refused to associate with Kay, the family began to splinter. Another divorce would be unthinkable.

And so Kay stayed with Fitzgerald, who was a tough, macho boozer with a bad temper he rarely tried to curb. Unused to children and jealous of anyone who had a claim on his new wife, he had it in for Roy from the beginning. Roy was growing up too soft without a father, he announced to Kay. He issued strict directives, in the best military manner. Roy was to stop kissing his mother good night—he was too old for that. He was to get rid of any toys Fitzgerald deemed too childish. He was to speak when spoken to, obey orders, and stay out of the way as much as possible. Fitzgerald knew how to handle insubordination: with the back of his hand.

"He was a drunk," said Ed Wood bluntly. "He used to beat Roy and Katherine."

Roy was now nearly nine. When his father had left and refused to come back he had been terribly confused. Now at least he was clear on one thing: he hated Fitzgerald with all his heart, and did his best to stay away from the house. That was his hobby when he was young, he once told a reporter—staying away from the house.

His feeling for his stepfather was so intense it would reverberate through the years. An avid, indiscriminate movie fan, he was never able to stand one star: Errol Flynn. Flynn's moustache and dashing manner reminded him too much of Fitzgerald, he said.

Early in the marriage, Fitzgerald took his new wife and stepson on a visit to his home state, Maine, where he was determined to introduce Roy to a New England fish dinner. "I remember how gray all the food looked, the oysters and other shellfish. He forced me to eat and I kept getting sick. Later, he took me on a roller coaster and I was sick again," Roy recalled years later. He was never able to eat seafood again.

Kay's loyalties were torn between her new husband and her son. Since she wanted very much for the marriage to work, she allowed Fitzgerald to have his own way in disciplining Roy much of the time. After all, she believed the boy needed a father. When things got too explosive at home, she ran to her mother, and, when her mother died two years after the remarriage, to her brother John's family. Betty Kimble, one of John's daughters, who was two years older than Roy, remembered many times when her aunt and cousin would hide out at their house for a few hours, or days, until Fitzgerald's temper cooled. "They had a rough time of it," she said.

At such times, Kay and Roy would feel more like co-conspirators fleeing a common enemy than like mother and son. Yet, sooner or later, Kay would inevitably return to her husband. It was demoralizing for Roy, and must have felt like a repeated betrayal by the person closest to him, the one who was supposed to protect him.

Years later Kay was to say that she herself had never had any trouble disciplining her son. All you had to do, she confided, was to tell him he was stupid. That upset him so much, it was enough to bring him into line. It would be decades before psychiatrists spread the word about the dangers of such an approach. In the thirties and forties, the best discipline was the one that worked—and this did.

Of course, there were repercussions. After he rose to stardom, many colleagues were to notice Rock Hudson's lack of confidence, so remarkable in a world-famous celebrity, especially in the entertainment field, where egos flourish like crabgrass. They had not met the adults who raised him.

Kay had another phrase she used with her son. Betty Kimble remembered her saying it, and so did Rock. In fact, in his last interview, a few months before his death, he was to mention it one final time. "She used to say, 'Don't do anything to make me ashamed,'" he said. "If that doesn't make a young boy think twice!"

"He could do what he wanted, as long as he didn't disgrace my husband or me," Kay once said in an interview. At the time she was giving her son this instruction, her husband was drinking heavily and beating him often. The injustice must have been clear to Roy, but he didn't protest. He buried any anger he felt toward his mother.

Throughout his life, he continued to face the world with a calm demeanor, no matter what might be going on under the surface. "What I have is this outward peace," he once said. "I can be dying inside, but my discomfort doesn't show much."

One rare sign of his inner turmoil was his nail-biting, which began in his childhood and lasted his whole life. Many years later a friend, journalist Armistead Maupin, noticed a deep groove running across Rock's thumb. Rock himself passed it off as a "war injury," said Maupin, but later Rock's longtime friend Tom Clark set Maupin straight. Rock had caused the groove himself by constantly rubbing his thumb with the nail of his forefinger.

Roy had come into the world an easygoing, amenable child. He was an easy target for controlling adults. In different ways, both Kay and Fitzgerald were controllers. Unfortunately, Roy was trained well. For the rest of his life, he displayed a deep-seated passivity, an almost fatalistic docility, strikingly at odds with the image he presented to the world—that of a competent, all-American man.

He had learned the lesson in childhood, where it served him well. After all, what better defense can a young boy construct against an abusive stepfather than compliant passivity? How else to deal with abandonment, pain, deprivation than by stoic acceptance—a studied lack of response? A child has few options. But the trait followed him into adulthood, as learned passivity has a tendency to do. Then it proved to be less useful. In fact, it worked against him. His passivity enabled him to be used, often poorly, by the studio system for nearly twenty years, and by agents and friends. At times he must have felt he was wrestling an unseen enemy, when, in fact, what held him down most—what kept him from achieving what he longed to achieve—were actually the very shackles he had wrapped around himself years before for survival. Forced as a child to accept the hand he'd been dealt, he continued to accept it, long after he could have stepped in to change the cards himself. The lesson had been learned too well.

Roy began to work at part-time jobs from the time he was ten, delivering newspapers, then groceries, later caddying at a local golf course. The money was needed at home. Since Fitzgerald was often out of work, Kay's job as a telephone operator was the only steady income. But need wasn't the only reason for Roy's labors: working was another excuse to stay away from home.

Fitzgerald, who had an ex-marine's respect for a uniform, any uniform, insisted that Roy join the Boy Scouts to help make a man of him. Not unexpectedly, the boy hated it—the regimentation, the lack of freedom, but most particularly the uniform itself. Whenever he could, he skipped meetings to hang around with his friends.

After Kay's marriage to Fitzgerald, Roy began to look outside his home for family. Friendships are important to any boy, but they became doubly important to Roy. It was with other boys that he found the acceptance, the safe haven he no longer had at home. For the rest of his life, he looked to friends for family life.

Two boys, Jim Matteoni and Pat McGuire, became his closest friends as he moved into adolescence. The Triumvirate, they called themselves. Then as now, Winnetka was considered one of the fanciest of Chicago's suburbs, an enclave of wealthy families. Both of Roy's friends, like him, were from lower-middle-class families, which set them apart from the country-club set.

"It was a very upscale community," said Bud Davis, who was in Roy's class at New Trier High School. "Probably not as pretentious as today, but still . . . There were the ins and the outs, and the cliques." For the rest of his life, Rock Hudson despised anything that smacked of elitism or snobbery. Many of his friends came from lower-middle-class backgrounds like his own.

Kay, however, had more of an upwardly striving nature. She wanted the best for her son and saw no reason why he shouldn't hobnob with Winnetka's finest. She had little use for either Jim Matteoni, whose father ran a local restaurant, or Pat McGuire, and kept her eye out for a higher-class playmate.

Ed Jenner, who came from one of the wealthiest families in town, seemed to fit the bill. Jenner, a small boy, looked up to Roy, who had once defended him against a group of bullies. Kay pushed the friendship for all she was worth, inviting Jenner over to spend the night several times.

Roy, as always a good boy, did what his mother wanted, but he was uncomfortable with the friendship. The difference in status, the contrast between his house and Jenner's mansion, was too acute. The Fitzgeralds lived on the grounds of Horace Mann Elementary School in a tiny one-story red brick house that consisted of a pullman kitchen, a small living-dining area, and two cramped bedrooms. Roy's room had only a bed, a bureau, and a lamp. Ed Jenner's home sat on ten acres, with a swimming pool and several servants.

It was overwhelming for Roy. "Is this candelabra really silver?" he would ask. "You really have a baby-grand piano?"

The worst humiliation came one night at Roy's house, when Kay was trying to get the two adolescents to go to bed. Kay, never known for her tact, warned Ed that before he got into bed he should wrap a towel around him. Roy blanched, but his mother sped on, disregarding him. Roy, she told his friend, was a habitual bed wetter. Without the towel Ed was sure to get soaked in the night.

Roy never had Ed over again. Soon after, Ed left for boarding school at age fourteen. Years later, he reappeared on the edition of "This Is Your Life" that featured Rock Hudson. When Ralph Edwards planned the segment in the early fifties, he asked Kay to submit a list of boyhood friends. Kay conveniently forgot about Jim Matteoni and Pat McGuire (Matteoni was included at the last minute). But high on the list was Ed Jenner, whose friendship with her son she had worked so hard to orchestrate. Her son was already a nationally known star, but Kay was still doing her best to control his life.

As a young teen-ager, Roy fell in love with movies and the theater. His friendship with Jim Matteoni, which continued the rest of his life, was sealed over a Danny Kaye film, *Up in Arms*.

"We saw that movie perhaps fifteen times," said Matteoni, now a music teacher and father of three. "Danny Kaye would do some nonsense patter in his movies, using silly little words and expressions. Roy and I memorized them and would repeat them over and over and burst into laughter. It was like a private joke between us."

The two boys realized they liked to laugh at the same things and would often travel seventy miles by streetcar and bus to towns like Gary and Whiting to see certain movies.

All three boys—Roy, Jim, and Pat McGuire—hung around the Threshold Players, a small theater group in Winnetka, offering their services as prop boys and gofers. They loved working behind the scenes. Roy was fascinated by the makeup, the costumes, the lights.

"I think one of the reasons Roy became so enamored of the movies and the stage was as a way to escape the pressures and hardships at home," said Matteoni. "It was pure fantasy and escapism for him."

Also, it was fun. In one season, the Threshold Players produced a romantic play, *The Dove and the Hero*, that featured the deathless line "I'm the best damned caballero in all Mehico." For weeks, his friends remember, he used the line every chance he got.

Undoubtedly, even then, Roy was harboring dreams of becoming an actor. But he never told his friends. The whole idea seemed too much of a fantasy. It wasn't something you said out loud, he later explained, not then, not in Winnetka, not if you didn't want to be laughed at. Even at that age, Roy had gotten into the habit of keeping certain things to himself, especially if he felt others wouldn't understand. But it was clear to his friends how much he loved the world of theater.

As Matteoni said, "Roy was more taken by the whole thing than either me or Pat. The glamour lasted in him longer than it lasted in us."

All three boys attended New Trier High School, an enormous education mill that is, even today, the largest high school in the country. Roy distinguished himself neither by academics nor by sports, although he did spend a brief season with the swim team. The competition for roles in school-play productions was fierce; Roy never made it. Charlton Heston had a leading role in most of the plays. Roy spent his time after school working at his part-time jobs and hanging out with his pals. He managed to teach himself piano and learned to play a mean boogie-woogie. He and Jim, who was a music buff, spent hours at Winnetka's Community House practicing and composing tunes. At one point, the two boys even cut a record, which Matteoni kept for years. It featured Rock singing a ditty to Jim's piano accompaniment about a racehorse who took opium. The boys haunted secondhand shops, looking for records to add to their collections, a passion they shared.

Roy, Jim, and Pat often got together with Roy's teen-age cousins. "We had a ball together," Betty Kimble said. "We didn't know there was a Depression, didn't know about family problems. We just had fun. Sleigh rides in winter, skating parties, sledding, swimming in the summer, beach parties at Lake Michigan, back-to-school parties. Whenever there was an excuse." Roy would often play the piano at parties. "I don't know if he ever had any lessons; he picked it up by ear. We thought he was good."

As the boys began to date, girls became a part of their social lives. Roy, said Matteoni and McGuire, seemed as interested as they were. When the boys pawed through copies of Thorne Smith novels to look at the sexy sketches that accompanied them—the closest thing to a *Playboy* layout available back then—Roy seemed just as eager as his friends. No one in Winnetka—not family, not his closest friends—ever believed Roy was homosexual, even in later years, when the rumors began drifting back. Betty Kimble is satisfied with her own explanation: "He liked girls then. It was in the navy that he changed."

Roy had already learned at an early age not to make waves and to keep his deepest feelings private. It seems natural to assume he would conceal sexual feelings as well, particularly if they fell outside the norm in any way. He had even hidden his acting ambitions because it seemed a strange thing for a regular guy to be interested in—and Roy was as eager as any adolescent to be seen as a regular guy. He was aware very early of the importance of protective coloration. Adolescence is a time of sexual awakening, but if Roy was conscious of any sexual feelings toward men, he kept them pushed down far below the surface. It was the beginning of a lifetime habit. He would always do his best to keep his sexual inclinations very private, even with close friends. He later told Marc Christian, a lover, that he had known about his nature when he was eight. It was the year, oddly enough, that his mother had met and married Wallace Fitzgerald.

In the high-school social scene, Roy was a success. He dated several girls, and even went steady. He loved to jitterbug and was in demand as a partner. Roy was beginning to shoot up in height, way past his friends, and his looks were attracting more and more attention. "He was always gorgeous," said Kimble. "Handsome George, my mother always called him."

"We didn't have much on our minds besides girls and fun," said McGuire. "We didn't have much idea of a future. For all we knew, we would end up operating punch presses in a factory somewhere." Jim's parents were more demanding; of the three, he was the only decent student.

All three boys took part-time jobs wherever they could get them. One job Roy loved was working as an usher at the

Teatro Del Lago, a local movie house. It meant wearing a uniform, just as the Boy Scouts had, but this one—maroon with gold braid and brass buttons—he wore proudly.

One fall Roy and Pat found work with an awning company, removing awnings from the lakeside summer homes of the wealthy and packing them up for storage. "It was a nasty job," McGuire recalled. "It was cold up there on the North Shore by then, and your hands hurt." The boys were supposed to label the awnings carefully, but disgusted with the job, they just threw them into the warehouse, unlabeled. The next summer the owner was faced with a pile of anonymous awnings. "I don't know what we had on our minds," said McGuire. "The guy was talking to himself about that for two years."

The summer before Roy entered eleventh grade, he went to visit his father in California—for the first time since he was seven. Though Roy Scherer, Sr., had remarried, he had kept in touch with his first family at least sporadically. Roy initially planned to stay with his father and attend high school in California, but he changed his mind and returned to Winnetka. He missed his friends; he did not feel comfortable with his father's new family; and besides, the atmosphere back home had changed. Kay had finally taken the step she had avoided for so long—divorce. Wallace Fitzgerald, for eight years the bane of Roy's existence, was gone. Years later, in Los Angeles, Kay would marry Joe Olsen, a retired Winnetka civil servant. Their marriage would be a success.

Back in Winnetka, Roy and his pals continued to hang out and to make the usual teen-age forays into the world of adulthood. They all had their driver's licenses by now, which meant a certain freedom—generally, the freedom to drive to another town and pick up a six-pack. Kay had been horrified when she discovered Roy with a cigarette at age twelve and a beer a year later; but by the time he was sixteen, Kay's influence was receding. With Fitzgerald out of their lives, Kay and Roy were forging a new relationship. Roy was no longer a little boy; he now topped Kay by several inches. More and more, she treated him as an adult. After all, he was the man in the house now.

"We did all the usual things," said McGuire. "We altered birthdays on driver's licenses, all that sort of thing." For the most part, the drinking consisted of beer only. McGuire remembers the time they actually got hold of real liquor: a bottle of rum and one of gin. It tasted so bad they had to choke it down—with beer, of course. "We drank it because we thought it was the smart thing to do," he said. They didn't go out of their way to repeat the experience.

Only Jim Matteoni graduated with their class; both Roy and Pat, whose involvement with academia was minimal, were forced to return for an extra semester. "We were just a couple of dumb kids who didn't know what to do with themselves," McGuire said.

The outside world, however, was beginning to close in. Roy had turned sixteen a month before Pearl Harbor. The Triumvirate—Roy, Pat, and Jim—held a summit meeting, and decided there was only one thing for a red-blooded man to do: enlist. Preferably in the army air corps or marines, the most romantic outfits.

Chests out and voices lowered to seem older, the three lined up at the recruiting stations, only to be thanked and dismissed with patronizing grins. "We'll see you after graduation, boys," said the recruiters; and they went home, abashed. When she heard about it, Kay was horrified. Roy was the only man in her life now; how could he even think of deserting her?

After finishing school in 1944, Roy immediately joined the navy. Even Kay understood the necessity, with the draft board breathing down his neck. Pat put off enlisting for a few months, and was drafted. Jim, slightly younger, stayed out a little longer, but he too eventually wound up in the navy. Roy went through boot camp at the Great Lakes Naval Base, a half hour from home. Kay visited him every weekend.

Roy's first post after training was less than exotic—the Naval Air Station at Glenview, Illinois, a short ride from Winnetka. Working behind the scenes, Kay had managed to exert control. Using the excuse of hardship, she arranged for him to be stationed near home. Shortly afterward, she too showed up at the base, working as a telephone operator. Each night mother and son would go home to Winnetka, except when Roy had guard or other special duty. Kay had already lost two men, to divorce. She was determined to hold on to this one.

Her machinations almost landed Roy in the soup. While home one night, he developed a bad cold that swiftly escalated into a serious respiratory infection. He was too sick to return to the base, yet terrified to call his C.O. to tell him what had happened. After all, it was wartime and he could be court-martialed.

He finally called Jim Matteoni for advice. Jim came over right away, and stayed all day long, cracking jokes to cheer Roy up. He told Roy his one priority should be to get back to Glenview as soon as possible; he had no urge to visit a friend in the brig. The next morning, Roy, still sick, squared his shoulders and returned to face the punishment.

Luckily there was none. His company commander took one look at the sick seaman and told him to check into the hospital. Roy's brief AWOL was forgotten.

At one point, Roy and Jim hitchhiked to Scott Field, near St. Louis, where Pat McGuire was stationed. Pat remembered the time well. According to him, Roy was the only one of the three to distinguish himself that weekend by ending up in bed with a woman. "I don't remember what she looked like, but I'm sure she was pretty attractive, because Roy wasn't given to running around with skags. It wasn't the first time something like that had happened, either." Around his buddies, especially Pat, Roy played "macho man" to the hilt.

After six months at Glenview, Roy was shipped to the Philippines. Kay had run out of strings to pull. Roy was looking forward to it. It meant a chance to see a little of the war and to be on his own for once. On his way out, he stopped in Los Angeles to visit briefly with his father, who was now running an appliance store.

In the South Pacific, Roy was put to work as an airplane mechanic, a job for which he had little natural talent. Later he told interviewers that one day on the job he had revved up both engines on one side of a plane, which had then veered off the runway, chopping a smaller plane to bits with its propellers. No one had told him that wasn't the way to do it. Whether or not the story is true, he was not much of a success as a mechanic and was soon transferred to laundry duty, where he served out his term.

"Best job in the navy," he told Hollywood gossip-columnist Hedda Hopper later. "The cooks have to have their whites washed all the time. So you tell them, 'If you want better service, I've got to have better food.' You get it. Also, the officers give you liquor for taking care of their uniforms. And an energetic guy can pick up forty or fifty bucks a week just by going through the pockets of dirty uniforms."

On Christmas Day, 1945, Roy sent a note to Pat, then stationed at Chanute Field, in Rantoul, Illinois. He had just turned twenty. The tone—tough, swaggering, full of braggadocio—will be familiar to any parent of adolescent sons.

Dear Rugged,
What a day. Christmas, etc., and I am sweating my balls off. Yesterday I laid out in the sun and got burnt to shit.

Christ, buddy, you sure are lucky to be so close to home. When I hadn't heard from you in so long I thought you'd be on your way out here to pay me a little visit. But no, there you are, only a hop, skip and a jump from home.

Telling you about the gook ass would take a ten-page letter, so I'd better wait until I come home. I figure I'll be home about April or May. I have 24 points now, and it goes up three-quarters of a point a month. I certainly don't expect to be home before that time. If it's after that time, I'll probably commit suicide.

There was a party at my Dad's house in L.A. and I had to put him to bed. I had a girl there. We went out in the car in the garage . . . [Description deleted by McGuire].

Well, I've shot the shit enough, so I'd better

sign off. It's no use wishing you a Merry Christmas. You probably will be having the time of your life. I'm not.

As ever
Roy.

P.S. Why the fuck don't you send me a picture, you bastard?

In 1946 Roy was back in Winnetka, a couple of routine Pacific War Theater ribbons under his belt, honorable discharge in tow. He had no plans and was in no rush to make them. While Kay worked at her telephone operator's job, Roy spent an aimless year collecting his eighty dollars a month from the government (the amount due every unemployed veteran) and hanging out with Jim and Pat, also back home. The three friends enjoyed their freedom from the disciplines of school and service. They knew, though, that it couldn't last forever.

"When Roy came back from the war, he was a little older but still just a naïve kid," said Matteoni. "We both were. I remember us talking about the fact that we were now going to have to come to some decision about what we were going to do with our lives."

When the government checks stopped coming, Roy got a job as a mailman. Jim had enrolled at the Chicago Conservatory of Music and was busy with his own concerns. Roy had a sense of waiting for his life to take off. He looked like a man—six-feet-four, muscular, strikingly handsome—but he had yet to assert himself. Just as he had in high school, he was hanging around Winnetka, hoping that something wonderful was about to happen.

Passivity had never been part of Kay's nature. She could see that her son was at a crossroads and needed some direction. Determinedly, she seized the reins. She asked the telephone company for a transfer to Pasadena and got it. They were moving to California, she announced to Roy.

Roy was ready. He quit his mailman job on the spot. When Roy gave notice at the post office, the postmaster, Arthur Klepfer, was upset. He was losing a good man. Help wasn't that easy to get.

"Well, you'll never work for the post office again," he told Roy angrily.

Not many years later, Arthur Klepfer declared Roy's birthday, November 17, Rock Hudson Day at the Winnetka Post Office.

California meant his father, sunshine, the possibility of college. It also meant something he could hardly even admit to himself he was still dreaming about—Hollywood.

In Los Angeles, Roy started by working for his father, selling vacuum cleaners door to door. Shy and hesitant with strangers, he made a botch of it almost instantly. Next, he made a few desultory attempts to enroll at the University of Southern California on the GI Bill. They were interested only in B-plus students, however, and in high school Roy had considered himself lucky when he got a C. He took a job driving a truck for Budget Pack, hauling dried beans and macaroni, and moved into a rooming house in Westlake Park with two other truck drivers. He kept in close touch with Kay, phoning her daily and occasionally taking her with him on the road.

Instead of drying up in the hot sun, Roy's dreams of being a movie actor intensified in California. He had always been an avid reader of movie magazines, and it was from this fount of wisdom that he drew up his game plan for breaking in. All his life he had been told he was handsome enough to be in the movies. He decided he would just make himself available for discovery; it was that simple. After all, that was how all the stars had done it.

So one afternoon between deliveries, the tall, handsome, fresh-faced young man parked his truck near the back gates of one of the major studios. Dressed in his driver's outfit of khaki, with the Teamsters' Union badge, he leaned up against the truck for an hour, smoking one cigarette after another. Nothing happened. A few days later, he repeated the experiment, nervous, terribly embarrassed, but still hopeful.

"Believe it or not, I was so naïve I believed all those stories about people being discovered. Maybe it sounds foolish, but that's what I did," he admitted later. During interviews, he often alluded bitterly to the tales of movie-star discoveries made on the street or in a drugstore. "No one is discovered that way, no one," he said. He had believed the myths, and felt they had made a fool of him. He would carry a grudge against the myth makers for life, and was especially annoyed by the tales they constructed about his own break-in. He had been, they said, a mailman discovered on his route; a truck driver who had been spotted by a studio exec. Rock knew the truth. It wasn't that easy.

As it turned out, though, it wasn't all that hard, either. Since Los Angeles was a very different place from Winnetka—here, no one thought you were weird if you wanted to be in the movies, anything but—Roy had started telling some of the other truck drivers about his ambition. A few of them gave him some advice: if he was serious about this thing, he should have professional photos taken and mail them out to agents and studios. Roy dutifully posed for pictures, five shots for twenty-five dollars, and sent them off. He even bought a suit—his first—to wear in case he was called in for an interview.

"I'd never owned a real suit. My idea of getting dressed up was to put on a sports coat and a red satin tie," he said. "The suit was so big for me that when the pants were taken in, the two hip pockets were next door to each other."

Still there was no response. Finally, one driver who knew someone in radio told Roy he had heard through his friend that Selznick Studio was casting. Roy drove over in his truck and left his photo at the studio reception desk. The next day he received a call.

"I put on that awful suit and kept the appointment. It was September 1947," said Roy. Rock Hudson was about to be born.

When he walked into the studio, he was directed to the office of a talent scout named Henry Willson. Willson was behind the desk as Roy entered the room. Short, a bit pudgy, nattily dressed, Willson cocked his head to one side and glanced up from under his heavy brows to eye the striking young man in front of him. Roy—nervous, bumbling, positive he was about to knock over a chair any minute—met his gaze. It was a moment neither man would ever forget.

"I don't think anything important ever happened to me until I walked into Willson's office that day," Roy later said. The little man behind the desk coolly examining him was to be the motivating force in making him a movie star.

At age thirty-six, Willson, who was doing a brief stint as talent scout for Selznick, was already known in the trade as an agent's agent. "A man from the East," actor Robert Stack described him, and it seemed to sum him up. There was little of the rugged, hard-hewn West about him, and a great deal of the effete, refined East, where he had been raised. He spoke in an affected, drawling voice and gave perfectly appointed dinner parties: the wine was always at the right temperature, the candles burning at the proper length. "He was a man of taste, a man who liked things done well," said Estelle Harmon, acting coach at Universal. "He liked to dress well, have fine wines." His own favorite drink on these occasions was a glass of champagne with a single floating strawberry.

"He was an elegant character," said Carleton Carpenter, an MGM song-and-dance man. "That was part of being an agent. Part of it all was for flair and for show. That's part of the fabric of being an agent. But he seemed a little dandified, a little put on. A little pseudo-elegant."

Henry Willson was homosexual and went to no particular trouble to hide the fact. "At a time when most were in the closet, Henry was not," said Harmon. Others were even more blunt. "He was gay," said one former fan-magazine editor. "This was well known in the industry."

In fact, he came close to parading his predilection, his voice and style reflecting the manner of refined, witty Edwardian gentlemen made so popular by Oscar Wilde. His face, however, belied such delicacy: it was heavy, strong-featured, with more than a little hint of Edward G. Robinson around the mouth. A tough, shrewd face, belonging to a tough, shrewd man.

Willson, at the time Roy Fitzgerald came into his office, was in the business of manufacturing stars. Not talent necessarily—talent could muddy the process. When the navy trained frogmen, they looked for men who had never learned to swim. What Willson preferred was to take good-looking young people—men, generally—who were raw, eager, and open to instruction, and turn them into industry pay dirt. He looked for potential—good looks, charisma, magnetism—but even more than that, he looked for malleability. Someone who would turn himself over completely and allow Willson to mold him.

Willson was a controller, like Roy's mother and his stepfather; a master controller, in fact. But unlike the adults who had ruled Roy's early life, this man was offering something exciting in exchange: a chance to see his dreams come true. It is too simple to describe Willson as predator, Roy as prey. If so, the fox in this case had been waiting most of his life for the hound to show up. Still, this is how many see it.

"It's awful when dirty old men get ahold of a young boy who is innocence abroad," said actress Dorothy Malone, in discussing Rock's relationship with Willson.

A number of people, looking back, have concluded that Willson had a lot to do not only with Rock Hudson's success but with his homosexuality as well. It would make for a dramatic tale, fit for the movies, if it were so, but such things are rarely, if ever, possible. One's sexual compass points are set in childhood, and deeply ingrained. A person can no more be converted to homosexuality than to hetero-sexuality.

Although he represented a few women stars—Lana Turner, Natalie Wood—Willson was best known for his large collection of would-be male stars and was almost always seen around town with a few of them in tow. Some of the men were gay and others were not. The industry cognoscenti assumed he was sleeping with some of his clients.

"Willson was notorious for having these good-looking guys who couldn't do anything but be good-looking," said Dick Morris, who was moving up at Universal as a writer, producer, and director. "They were all just kind of pinups. They came to him after a while. Every little farmboy who thought he was good-looking came to him. He got a lot of publicity for having this stable of good-looking young boys.

"You'd see Henry around town. Lots of times he'd just be in the company of three or four of those boys. He'd go to nightclubs and places. A lot of time the boys got a bad reputation of being one of Henry's boys."

"He held court with all his finds gathered at his feet," said a fan-magazine editor. "And he promised them stardom. Henry had the power in this town to do it. He could get them into the business by reason of that power.

"Henry wasn't a handsome man, but he was very charming. He wasn't swishy or effeminate, but he was homosexual, and a predatory one at that. He liked attractive young men. He made money from promoting them, and he had affairs with some of them."

"Henry cared a great deal about his young attractive male clients," said Harmon. "I'm not saying they were his lovers; he just cared about them a lot. He was totally devoted to being an agent. Day and night was related to them. When he finished his day, he'd either have a group over to his house for a party or take them out somewhere." She remembered running into him often at a restaurant called Frascatti's. Willson would stand close to the piano, surrounded by his handsome clients.

His first step in the process of transforming his clients into stars—raw meat into gold—was to change their names. This branded them forever as one of his clients, since Willson's names were known throughout the business. Willson was responsible for turning Art Gelien into Tab Hunter, Francis McGowan into Rory Calhoun, Robert Moseley into Guy Madison, Merle Johnson into Troy Donahue. Julia Turner became Lana; Marilyn Louis, Rhonda Fleming. Whatever else you could say about his names, they certainly stuck in the mind—which was, of course, the point.

"I always gave a green actor the gimmick of a trick name to help him get known while he was learning his trade," Willson told an interviewer. "I named Guy Madison for a signboard advertising Dolly Madison cakes. All that boy thinks about is food. Tab Hunter's name came because I couldn't think of anything to tab him."

Everyone knew about Willson's names. For years

Humphrey Bogart and his cronies played an ongoing parlor game in which they tried to top them. The best they could come up with was Dungg Heep.

Willson didn't always hit the mark. One of his favorite handles was Yale Summers, which he tagged to no fewer than three actors (reportedly there is still at least one kicking around). Sadly, the name never caught on. Later in his career he named an actor John Smith. "I just got tired," he explained.

With Roy Fitzgerald, Willson was to surpass himself. "I tried to think of something strong and big," he said. "Rock of Gibraltar. Hudson came from the Hudson River, for no reason. I knew that was it. Rock Hudson."

Roy hated the name from the beginning. "I have trouble pronouncing it," he once said, deadpan, to a reporter, who took him seriously. He resisted changing his name legally until he was fifty-four, and did it then only to simplify his business affairs. The signature on his will is Roy H. Fitzgerald. All his life he felt the name was ridiculous, that it made him an easy butt for critics; how could anyone take a Rock Hudson seriously? But he did not voice these feelings until years later. When Willson presented him with his new name, he gulped and swallowed it down. Like a good boy.

On the day in September 1947 that Roy walked into Willson's office, the two began a complicated relationship that lasted nearly twenty years. Close, intense, it operated on many levels: agent-client, mentor-protégé, puppeteer-puppet, teacher-student, father-son. Willson exerted a powerful influence over Rock Hudson, who regarded him with mixed emotions—gratitude, loyalty, respect, irritation, finally rebellion. There was more than a little fear mixed in, too, in the early years. Dick Morris, who became a friend of Rock, recalled an incident when Rock deliberately dodged Willson.

"We went to a movie at Grauman's Chinese Theater. All of a sudden Rock jumped back behind a pillar.

"'What is it?' I asked.

"'It's Henry!'

"We peeked around the pillar and, sure enough, it was Willson. He looked like he was looking for someone. I always had the feeling he had followed Rock there. Willson would stalk Rock."

The relationship between this agent and his client was a complex blend. It was financial, social, and emotional, and it seems highly probable it was sexual as well. Willson certainly implied as much to others, including Estelle Harmon. Over the years, Willson let his relationships with many of his other clients slide while he attended to his primary concern, Rock Hudson. It made sense. No one else had risen to the same heights as the awkward young man from Winnetka. But it seems likely Willson was involved emotionally, too. When Rock ended the relationship finally and irrevocably in the mid-sixties, Willson was by all reports genuinely crushed. It was a wound he never recovered from.

But the prospect of a bitter ending was the last thing in Willson's mind the day Roy walked into his office. This beautiful, glowing, towering example of young manhood was exactly what he was looking for. The story, often told, is that Willson's first move was to ask Roy whether or not he could act. When he said no and turned to go, the agent surprised him. "Good. Sit down," he commanded. "I think I can do something for you." In later years, Rock got sick of the story and insisted it was the last thing he would have said. After all, he wanted to act; that was why he was there.

In truth, though, he had no idea of how to go about it. His reading for Willson that day was terrible. But the agent was undaunted. "Only twice in my life have I asked young people I was interested in to read to me," he said. "And both times, thank God, I didn't let what I heard influence me. And they turned out to be Lana Turner and Rock Hudson."

Roy had no experience. He slouched. His voice was high, thin, and bore the unmistakable stamp of the Midwest. He was completely unpolished—but such incredible raw material. Willson made his decision on the spot: he would handle his career. Roy had only to put himself completely in Willson's control. Roy leaned over the desk and the two shook hands.

The agent was as good as his word. Within a few days he had Roy read with actor Mel Ferrer, and then took him to meet producer Walter Wanger. Both men were skeptical about his chances. Unfortunately, Willson had instructed his young find to tell Wanger he was twenty-four instead of twenty-one. In Wanger's office, scared and flustered, Roy forgot. When Wanger asked his age, he turned to Willson. "How old am I?" he said. Wanger was not impressed.

But Willson was determined. This boy was going to be a star. All he needed was a little work, and Willson now launched into trimming his newest client into shape. He arranged for Rock to have voice and diction lessons with Lester Luther, drama lessons with Florence Cunningham. Rock continued to drive a truck during the day, but it didn't bother him. At last, something was happening in his life. Willson paid for most of the lessons.

Cunningham worked unceasingly with Rock, trying to make his voice deeper, fuller. Years later, Rock insisted nothing had helped until he came down with a bad case of laryngitis, which persisted for two weeks. It had come, apparently, as a direct gift from God. When he returned to the drama coach, his voice had suddenly become deep and thrillingly resonant. "I recommend it to any young actor," Rock said, laughing.

Throughout 1948, Willson continued to parade Rock in front of a number of directors and producers, with scant luck. No one was biting. Another agent might have become discouraged, but Willson was undaunted. He knew their luck would break eventually, and it did. With a director named Raoul Walsh.

Walsh was known as a tough guy who preferred to handle other tough guys. He had the look of a seasoned war veteran, a look enhanced by the black patch he wore over one eye. In fact, he had lost the eye when a jackrabbit flew through the windshield of his car during a jaunt around Palm Springs, but as always in Hollywood, image had supplanted reality. Walsh looked tough and acted tough— so he was.

Willson had Rock dress in jeans for the interview. He knew Walsh did a lot of westerns. Rock read, nervously as usual, then stood uncomfortably, waiting for the verdict. Walsh stared at him for a long time, walking around him slowly so as to view him from every angle. "He is green," Willson admitted.

Walsh nodded slowly. "Green but ripe," he said. He continued to stare at Rock, who was trying hard not to slouch. "At the very least, he'll be good scenery."

Willson let out his breath. Walsh, he knew, was hooked.

Rock now had two sponsors—Henry Willson and Raoul Walsh. Things were definitely looking up. Walsh, the story goes, asked Rock the first day he met him in his office if he rode a horse. When Rock said he did, Walsh nodded sagaciously and offered him a small part in a movie he was making about air cadets.

The movie, of course, had no horses at all. Maybe a horse would have helped. As it was, Rock's screen debut in *Fighter Squadron* was hardly auspicious. "Green but ripe," Walsh had pronounced him in his office that first day, glancing over Rock's lengthy frame the way a man in a different industry might eye a likely shipment of produce. On his first film, no one was arguing about the green. His one line, admittedly something of a tongue twister, was "You've got to buy a bigger blackboard," and it was one Rock never forgot. It took him, he later told reporters, some thirty-eight tries to get it right. Always eager to please, he had tried the line every possible way—"You've got to get a *bigger* blackboard"; "You've got to get a bigger *blackboard*"; even "*You've* got to get a bigger blackboard"—but somehow the perfect delivery eluded him. In fact, most times the line came out "You've got to get a bligger backboard," he admitted.

"He was very nice, very shy, and of course he didn't know what the hell he was doing because it was his first movie," said Robert Stack, who had the leading role in the film. "Very, very handsome, but it was a man's picture, so nobody paid a hell of a lot of attention to him."

The film was about P47 pilots, and was based on a real-life incident from World War II. The event involved a pilot swooping down and picking up another pilot who had been shot down, then piggy-backing him out. "I played the pilot who flew the thing down and flew Eddie O'Brien out," said Stack. "The P47 pilots took it very seriously because it had actually happened. They invited us to a get-together. Up till then I had thought it was just a lot of nothing motion-picture making."

As the director, Walsh was the one responsible for Rock's being on the set, but he made no attempt to break in the young actor gently.

"At one point Rock was in the middle of the scene without anything to do; he just kind of stood there. And Raoul said, 'Jesus Christ, you're standing there like a goddamn tree—get out of the middle of the shot, for Chrissake, or stand sideways so you don't block everybody,'" Stack said. Walsh was "this rough tough guy who was hardly a director of boudoir romances." The actor laughed, remembering Walsh's brief attempt to direct him in *Fighter Squadron's* lone love scene.

"He said, 'Okay, now, this is the love scene.' I said, 'I know that, Raoul.' He said, 'Okay, now. You two . . . okay, look . . . ahh, the hell with it. She's a girl, you're a guy, play the damn scene.'

"That's pretty much the way he directed. He was better at blowing up oil wells and tanks."

Walsh's offhand treatment of Rock during the shooting was not particularly unusual. "It was the way they brought up young actors," said Stack. "It was done with love, but a kind of irony. Raoul would never let anybody know he had sponsored Rock. I remember my first screen test. They stick you on one of those chairs that spin, turn you around and say, 'Okay, show me the profile. Oh, Jesus, look at that nose. Spin around. Well, the back isn't so bad.' I was ready to punch them out, but this is what they did to all the young actors." It was a process not unlike that of basic training, with gruff-but-kindly-underneath-it-all sergeants doing their best to whip raw recruits into shape. The object was still winning, but in a very different kind of war.

Rock's first role may not have brought him much attention, but he still found it exciting. He made sure his pals back in Winnetka knew about it.

"The movie was nothing more than a potboiler, but it dazzled me," said Pat McGuire. "There was the big boy, right up on the screen. I thought, This can't be. This isn't going to last. You'd better make a buck while you can, pal.

"I didn't think he could do it," McGuire mused. "Really, he was kind of a shy guy. But he did."

Rock let Kay know about the film, too, but in an indirect way. He had never told his mother he wanted to be a movie star, any more than he had told his friends.

What he did, he said later, was take Kay to see *Fighter Squadron* one evening—without saying a word. He waited tensely for his "bigger blackboard" moment to unroll on the screen. After it did, Kay turned to him. "Is that you?" she said. When he nodded, she made only one comment: "Save your money."

It was a story Rock liked to tell in interviews, and he did so often. It was a perfect example of his sly, self-deprecating humor. Yet the last time he told the story, in August 1984, it came out differently. It was colder. "When I took her to that movie, she had no idea. She thought I was still driving a truck. None of her business. I was over twenty-one. I'll do what I damn please."

Rock had worked eight weeks, at $125 a week, on *Fighter Squadron*. Now Walsh signed him to a personal contract that guaranteed him forty more weeks at that rate, whether he worked or not. In the interim, Walsh used him for odd jobs. Hollywood correspondent Jim Bacon recalled seeing Rock chauffeuring Walsh around town during this time.

Walsh, like Willson, was convinced Rock was going to make it, despite the *Fighter Squadron* fiasco; he too put money into Rock's acting training. "It's a strange thing," he said. "A lot of youngsters come onto a set like gangbusters. This kid is quiet. If he doesn't know what he's talking about, he keeps his mouth shut. But there's something about him, a humility, a sincerity. He's going to make it."

Rock continued to take acting lessons. At Walsh's insistence he kept his hair fairly long. "You never know when you might be asked to be in a western," Walsh said. Either Walsh or Willson forked over money for him to get seven teeth capped, thus removing his only imperfection, two crooked eyeteeth. And both men continued to display their product to various studio bigwigs around town. Finally, they found a taker—Universal Studios. Rock was sold to the studio over-the-counter for $9,700, approximately the amount the two men had invested in his career.

A highly excited Rock called his friend Jim Matteoni. "One night the phone rang and it was Rock on the line. There was a lot of noise in the background, so it was hard to hear him. He told me he was at a party. He told me he had just been signed to a contract. He wasn't really sure what was going to happen next, except that he was going to go to school at the studio."

Universal, having just merged with International Pictures, was on an improvement kick. The studio's new head, William Goetz, formerly chief of International, and son-in-law of the powerful Louis B. Mayer, had announced they were going to stop cranking out B-pictures and make a play for the more sophisticated palate. To that end, they had set up a rigorous actor's training program, and were hiring a number of young new players they hoped would turn into the stars of tomorrow. A number of them actually did: Rock Hudson, Tony Curtis, Jeff Chandler, Piper Laurie, Mamie Van Doren, Hugh O'Brian, Barbara Rush.

Universal in those days had an almost farmlike atmosphere. Located five miles north of Hollywood, the studio sprawled over 230 acres. Dick Morris remembered seeing rabbits along the pathways. "It was like a little town in those days," said Mamie Van Doren. "We even had our own post office."

Rock was signed to a $125-a-week contract with Universal in 1949. The studio system, as it existed then, had its sharp pluses and minuses. Young contract players like Rock and the others who came on board around the same time were given a modest salary and rigorous training in nearly everything: acting, singing, dancing, horseback riding—in fact, in anything the studio heads thought might come in handy. Since Universal was doing a lot of swashbuckling pictures then, Rock also got his share of fencing lessons; if the part demanded it, he would be able to swashbuckle with expertise. Every studio had its specialty.

At Metro, the joke was that every new contract player had to be given swimming lessons, because sooner or later, you were sure to find yourself spouting water alongside Esther Williams.

"The big kicker in this profession is the chance, the look-Ma-no-hands, give me the chance, I can do it," explained Robert Stack, who did his time at 20th Century–Fox. "But in the process, it was like sending a kid to school. They used to teach you things. They taught Rock, Tony Curtis, all the guys at Universal, how to do everything from juggling to dancing to sword fighting, to tumbling to riding a horse. They prepared them, like you'd prepare a girl for a debut. Prepared them to become potential movie stars." At least Rock had one advantage: he had already seen, even occasionally ridden, a horse on his grandparents' farm. Tony Curtis, on the other hand, fresh from the Bronx, had his first encounter with a horse on Universal's back lot.

Fred de Cordova, for many years producer of the "Tonight" show, was a director at Universal at the time Rock was signed on. He looked back on the studio system with fondness:

"They did try to supervise your life to some extent. But by the same token, it was then the only game in town. It was the only way to learn the business. You learned how to fence, to box, to dance. They really groomed you. Not, believe me, to make you a decent or better person—but to make you available for almost anything. If you played in a football picture, you could throw a football. They really tried to make you a rounded performer.

"I believe that if you were to take a vote in town, all of us who were around then really preferred it that way to the way it is today."

Rock himself echoed this statement only months before the end of his life. "I had it lucky," he said in April 1985. "Any kinds of lessons were free—drama, diction, voice, ballet, sword fighting, gymnastics. Go out and pay for that now! Where and how do these kids learn and still make a living today?"

The intensive training, the public exposure, the chance at the big one—these were the pluses. What the studios demanded in return was simple: subservience.

Contract players were expected to give up nearly all their time, their choices, often their right of free speech, their choice of mate, even, in some cases, their very personality. In return, they were groomed, cosseted, trained, and given a chance at stardom.

Many rebelled. Stack remembers being placed on suspension periodically, every time he refused to do a picture his studio wanted him to do. Piper Laurie eventually rebelled completely against the restraints and left. One might even argue that the more independent, creative, and adult an actor was, the more he wanted to flex himself, the more trouble he would have fitting into the studio system.

Rock too eventually came to resent the system, to chafe against its restraints. But he was to stay with it for close to twenty years. Despite the immense strain on his freedom, despite some of the ridiculous demands the system made on him as an actor and a human being, he never rebelled. The child who had never given his mother any trouble was to become the perfect studio contract player— eager, willing, uncomplaining. The boy who had longed for a family throughout his childhood had found a semblance of one in Hollywood, at Universal. True, it was a family that demanded one stay in a state of perpetual adolescence—and pliable adolescence, at that—old enough for some things, not old enough for others. But it was Rock's family and perhaps in the end no worse than most.

Piper Laurie, then only seventeen, was signed at Universal at almost the exact time Rock was, and the two made a screen test together. Each of the new players made a series of tests with various people so the studio could evaluate their strengths and weaknesses.

The test with Rock and Piper came from a screenplay called *Thunder on the Hill* and was memorable only because of one line Laurie had to say. "It was so hilarious I've never gotten it out of my head. Whenever we would meet we'd quote that stupid line. Even today it makes me giggle."

What the diminutive redheaded Laurie had to do was stare up at Rock with quiet intensity and say, "I love you like this, all stirred up with fire in your eyes." It was too much for them. They could barely get through the scene without cracking up.

Despite this, Piper Laurie's memories of life under contract to the studio focus on the dark side of the system.

"In those days Metro and Fox had more interesting projects, more interesting people. I don't know why we were there [at Universal]." Despite Goetz's announcement that Universal was getting out of the B-picture racket, the studio continued to crank them out.

What the young Laurie objected to was not the professional training but the rest of the demands made on the players. "They were manufacturing these young movie stars. When we weren't making movies, we were in school or on the road promoting the movies. We were told before going on these trips or being interviewed that we had to act a certain way, dress a certain way, say certain things, and not say certain things. No cigarettes or drinks were shown in photographs. You could not discuss politics.

"It was all very prudish and reactionary. We couldn't be ourselves. That was one of Rock's problems all his life. He was manufactured from the day he got out there and he was under that pressure his entire life."

"I was told what to do for twenty-five years," he was to say, many years later. "And I've had it."

Laurie feels she was one of the lucky ones. "I got fed up with it and left. Rock was unlucky in that he stayed long enough to get the big break and he was under their influence for such a long time. I'm sure Rock felt he would have been betraying all those people who had been responsible for his success [if he had left]." Rock's sense of loyalty was one of the strongest traits of his nature—even when that loyalty was not in his own best interest. There was no doubt he felt loyalty to Universal. Throughout his life, he would speak of his obligation to them. It was many years before Rock would feel he had the right to turn down a picture; in fact, not until the *Pillow Talk* era of his career.

The training and coaching were only part of the highly refined studio process for turning young players into stars.

Just as important—perhaps even more so—was the way in which they used the press, which in Hollywood in 1949 meant the fan magazines.

"The studios would give phony parties where actors would blow up balloons and wear funny hats. They'd do all those things for the fan magazines," said Robert Stack. "It was a whole different world then." The studio would encase a young actor in an image of its own making, instruct him in how to behave in order to keep that image alive, go to infinite pains to construct situations in which that image was exposed, favorably, to the fan magazines—and then sit back smiling, a benevolent corporate deity.

The fan magazines cooperated fully. "In those days, all publicity was good publicity," said Dorothy Manners, a fan-magazine writer for many years.

The studios were always looking for gimmicks to promote their performers. Piper Laurie, despite her years as a respected actress, is still remembered by industry old-timers as the girl who ate flowers. Universal, straining for novelty, had set up several photo sessions in which Laurie was forced to work her way through a plateful of roses.

"It was awful," said the actress flatly, undoubtedly remembering some of her less than satisfying lunches at Universal. "It was very unhealthy, especially when it happened to young people who didn't know what the hell was happening to them."

Pinup pictures too were the order of the day—for both male and female players. So many male actors were forced to pose in bathing suits that columnist Sidney Skolsky coined a term for them: the "beefcake brigade." Rock appeared so many times in so many poses, he eventually earned a special accolade: he was called the "Beefcake Baron." It was a tag that neither the critics nor the public would ever let him forget.

In many ways it was unhealthy, as Laurie said, and perhaps even dangerous. Some, of course, managed to emerge intact from the system—Laurie herself lived at home and had a strong, stable family that approved her ultimate decision to quit the studio. She later emerged as an actress, not a rose chomper. Stack came from a long line of performers. In addition, he had been a world-class Olympic athlete as a teenager. Since nothing, even Hollywood, could match that early adulation, he emerged relatively unscathed.

But for others—not so strong, perhaps; not so grounded—the studio system took its toll. Dramatically in the case of Marilyn Monroe or Judy Garland. More quietly—but still effectively—in the case of Rock Hudson.

Any resentment or regrets about the studio system, any disappointment about its ultimate effect on his life and talent, would not surface until far in Rock's future. At the beginning, back then at the dawn of the fifties—a decade that would see him rise to the very top of box-office stardom—there was nothing but exhilaration. Gangly, awkward Roy Fitzgerald—the shy, lonely, fatherless boy from Winnetka, Illinois—had signed a contract with a major motion-picture studio. The movie fan who had spent hours fantasizing about the men and women he saw on the big screen was actually on his way to becoming a movie star himself. In some ways it was probably the happiest time of Rock's life.

"I was a terrific movie fan," Rock admitted to a friend several years later. "I used to see almost every movie. My favorite actor was Spencer Tracy. I'd think of Lana Turner and I couldn't sleep. I was torn three ways as a kid—Lana Turner, boogie-woogie, and food. There were very few movie stars I didn't like."

Of course, signing on as a contract player did not mean instant stardom. In the beginning and for quite some time thereafter, in fact, it didn't even mean you could be in a movie.

"For twelve months I didn't appear in a picture—not even a walk-on role," Rock later said. "But each morning I had a riding lesson. I took a dancing lesson every day. There were lessons in fencing, posture, and diction."

As two new kids on the block, he and Laurie struck up an instant friendship. "He was just a warm, overgrown kid who loved to eat and laugh," she remembered. "He'd come to my parents' house, and the first thing my mother would do was put food on the table and he'd gobble it up."

The relationship was strictly of the big brother-kid sister variety, though looking back, Laurie thinks she might have felt a stray yearning occasionally. At twenty-four, Rock was startlingly handsome. "I didn't have romantic feelings, but that doesn't mean I couldn't have," she said a bit wistfully. "I grew up not having brothers, so it was so wonderful having a relaxed, open relationship with somebody who was beautiful and who loved to laugh so much."

To Laurie, a Los Angeles girl, Rock could seem at times "somewhat naïve, small-townish." His mother, Kay, whom Rock had brought to the studio, struck her the same way.

"She was a very large, rather plump, tall woman—extremely shy but warm and sweet. She seemed to me like the perfect fairy-tale mother, a good cook and homemaker," she said. Rock's manner with her was "respectful and friendly. It seemed a nice relationship—on the surface anyway. One never knows."

There were nice parts about the early days at the studio that Piper Laurie remembers with affection, and most of them revolved around the woman who was the chief acting coach at Universal: Sophie Rosenstein. "She was wonderful, and close to all of us," said Laurie. Rosenstein and all the other acting coaches "were all sort of paternal and maternal. They made us feel safe and taken care of."

"Warm and magnificent," were Rock's words for Rosenstein. "I owe her a lot more than I can say."

Rosenstein was in her forties, a petite brunette married to actor Gig Young. Through her acting class, she was the one mainly responsible for whipping the new Universal players into shape. A warm, caring woman, Rosenstein soon became surrogate mother to her brood, who treated her as a confidante. "There were always rumors going around that someone's option wasn't going to be picked up," said Dick Morris. "Sophie would reassure them and tell them it wasn't going to happen. She really wanted to help these young people."

Rosenstein knew she had her work cut out for her with Rock. "His biggest asset is stamina," she said. "His biggest failing is shyness. It's torture for him to get up and act before an audience, even the workshop audience of other young players. He talks too fast and he slouches. But he's learning and he's willing. He'll make it."

Later Rosenstein added that Rock "never had any vanity and was always willing to learn. Sincerity was the hardest thing he had to learn—to mean the lines he was saying."

Though Rock had barely scraped through New Trier High School, he now found himself working harder at the various Universal courses—particulary Rosenstein's—than he had ever worked in his life.

"You really had to be on your toes," said Mamie Van Doren, a young player who was eventually hawked as Universal's answer to Marilyn Monroe. "The people who survived were the ones who really worked at it. I was a worker and Rock was too."

The directors and producers at Universal were in no hurry to put the new stable of players to work in pictures, preferring to trust more seasoned performers. Rosenstein tried to remedy the situation. She produced showcases featuring her brood, to give them a chance to show the studio what they could do. One of the skits was "Pals," a musical western written by Dick Morris.

Rock auditioned eagerly for "Pals" but lost out to Tony Curtis. Morris was convinced Rock was incapable of carrying a tune. The rebuff rankled for years. In 1965 Hudson inscribed a picture to Morris with the words "So you thought I couldn't do 'Pals'?" When Morris heard Rock had collapsed in the Ritz in Paris, in July 1985, he sent off a cable: GET OUT OF BED AND COME HOME AND LET'S DO "PALS."

"Pals" did turn out to be a lucky skit for the players who starred in it, Curtis and Laurie. As a result, both were cast in their first leading roles in a movie called *The Prince Who Was a Thief*. Rock had to wait a bit longer for his chance.

He did, however, begin to appear in tiny roles on the screen. Over the next four years, he played a huge spectrum of roles, mostly brief ones, nearly all forgettable. Among them: a bomber pilot, a detective, a soldier, a football player, an Indian chief, an Arab, a convict, a prizefighter, a brassiere salesman, a gambler, a sea captain, a soda jerk, a frontier marshal, and a gunman.

Stack explained, "If there was an opening, they'd look

down the contract list, and if someone wasn't working, that was the guy who played that part. How wrong you were for the part didn't matter. It was a strange repertory system. You fell into things you were not necessarily born for. You learned a lot of strange things."

Stack's favorite example of glorious miscasting was when 20th Century—Fox, his own studio, cast the unmistakably Anglo Robert Wagner as a curly-haired Greek in *Beneath the Twelve-Mile Reef.* Rock himself felt he was a complete failure as an Indian, a part Universal had him play more than once.

"I knew I didn't look right for it," he told an interviewer years later. "I'm too English-looking. Furthermore, I'm too tall. The fact that you make up darker and wear a wig doesn't help you to resemble an Indian. I couldn't even keep my wig on. It kept blowing off when I rode horseback."

Wrong or right for the part, though, Rock did his job. He took his obligation to the studio seriously. Very soon he had impressed everybody with his diligence and cooperative spirit, his eagerness to please. At no time throughout his long career would anyone ever accuse Rock of being a prima donna. Everybody liked him—directors, producers, and actors. At the beginning of his career, very few, however, were impressed by his talent. It was obvious to everybody that Rock Hudson had a long way to go. In fact, a number of directors began to suspect that the kid just didn't have it.

"I directed one of the first things he did when he came to Universal," recalled Joseph Pevney, who spent a number of years under contract to Universal as a director, and later worked with Rock in several films.

Filmed and released in 1950, the movie was *Shakedown,* the story of a con-artist photographer who faked publicity shots to build up his career. Howard Duff had the lead; Rock's part was somewhat smaller.

"We needed a doorman to open a door for Brian Donlevy, I think it was," said Pevney. "He gets out of a car, goes into a nightclub. It was just an exterior shot and we needed a doorman to open the door."

The studio volunteered Rock's sevices; Pevney will

never forget them. "I had to show Rock about eight times how to open the door. He was a southpaw, and the door had to be opened from the right-hand side, for the camera angle."

Even his costume caused problems. "He was six-foot-four, and to get a wardrobe was quite a job. Normal wardrobe is for a six-footer." Finally a doorman's costume of the proper size was dug up and Rock managed to open the door. "I think he also said, 'Good evening, sir,'" Pevney added. "It took quite a number of rehearsals." Rock, he said, was "very nice, willing and eager, but . . ." And he shook his head.

George Sherman, also directing at Universal at that time, had his first working encounter with Rock shortly afterward, in the movie *Tomahawk*. His memory of Rock's ability in those early days is strikingly similar to Pevney's.

Rock had been cast in a small part—actually, a very small part—as a trooper. The movie, a western starring Van Heflin, was shot on location in Rapid City, South Dakota. Rock's first entrance was simple: he was to run into a room where Van Heflin and another actor were lying on the ground chewing rawhide and announce, "Mr. Bridger, Colonel Carrington wants to see you in his office right away."

There was only one problem. Every time he attempted to bring it off, he would trip on a wagon wheel and sprawl on the floor. Again and again Rock would rush in, blurt out the line, and trip over the wagon wheel—over and over, as the afternoon wore on, while the actors continued to lie on the floor, chewing rawhide between snickers, and Sherman's temper mounted.

Every evening the studio checked in with the director to see how the actors were doing. That night they called and asked about Rock. It was the wrong question. "I'll tell you how he's doing. He's a clumsy bastard who can't stay on his feet!" Sherman roared.

Still, Sherman remembered the young actor fondly as cooperative and willing. "We finally got it," he said.

Actually, Sherman's most distinct memory of filming *Tomahawk* is the movie troupe's arrival at the hotel in Rapid City. "We were shocked—the lobby and the street were filled with young girls. We thought maybe they were there for Van Heflin, but they were all there for Rock Hudson. It was amazing. He walked into the lobby and they just stormed him, clamoring for his autograph." Rock, he said, seemed very embarrassed by the incident.

At that time Rock had been with the studio for a scant two years and had turned in a number of minor, forgettable performances on a par with his doorman and trooper roles. It is possible that teen-age girls across the land had noticed his appeal, even in a doorman's suit, but it is much more likely that Universal had set up the whole thing. They routinely staged this sort of publicity stunt for young hopefuls, and in fact did do it for Rock on at least one other location shot early on in his career.

Fred de Cordova, who directed three early pictures Rock was in—Here Come the Nelsons, Peggy, and The Desert Hawk, in 1950 and 1952—described the young actor as "affable, interested, charming, and insecure. He was never sure he was doing a scene right. I can recall him saying on a number of occasions, 'Can we do that again? I know you said print it, I know we're a little behind schedule, but I know I can do it better.'

"In one or two cases you did, but usually you were working on a fairly tight schedule. I would say, 'If we're on the same set tomorrow we can look at the rushes, and if you still feel that way we'll give it another shot.'"

Rock's main ambition then, de Cordova felt, was not just to keep the job—he wanted to be a good actor. "This entire batch of Rock Hudsons and Tony Curtises were all guys who had enormous desires to be something better than they were at that moment. This sometimes made you irritated. . . . In those days you weren't involved, at least I wasn't, in heavy moviemaking. You did your best."

The movies with Rock that he directed, de Cordova cheerfully admitted, were no better than they had to be—The Desert Hawk, for instance, which saw Rock cast as an Arab, was a prime example of the "sand and tits" genre then wildly popular with the studio. "It wouldn't have gotten him an Academy Award," said de Cordova wryly. "Nor would my direction."

Rock, then, for the first few years, did little to cover

himself with glory—and he was well aware of it. In an interview years later, he mused: "When I first saw myself on film in the dailies, I thought, My God. What a clumsy, tongue-tied galoot I was. I find my old movies very embarrassing. I was so incredibly bad. I had no experience, no expression, no thoughts. The odd thing is that I thought I was overacting. Now I can see I wasn't doing a damn thing, just standing there, looking helpless. I was in a lot of B-movies, that was my training. All my mistakes are on celluloid."

"He never felt that any of his work was any good," said Piper Laurie.

Furthermore, he was well aware that his roles were not the best. "I remember once he came up to me and he was all painted with war paint. He said, 'Oh, God, I can't stand these Cochise roles,'" said Mamie Van Doren.

It was obvious to everyone at Universal that Rock's career was not taking off in the way Tony Curtis's was. In fact, Piper Laurie claims that at one point during those early years Rock came perilously close to being dropped by the studio.

"All he was doing was playing these little bit parts, really stupid things. I guess they thought he didn't really have it. They had a lot of other men then like Jeff Chandler and Tony Curtis." Rock, she said, was aware of the possibility that Universal might drop his option, and was very upset about it. "He was very unhappy, really very depressed. He expressed it to me. It was real depression, real anxiety. More than anxiety."

Laurie couldn't stand to see her good friend so miserable. Unknown to Rock, she decided to see what she could do to help. "I was luckier earlier on than him, because they worked me a lot in so-called starring roles, even though they were really stupid. So I had the ear of an important producer there." Without letting anybody know what she was up to, Laurie made an appointment with the producer (whom she refused to name)—and proceeded to plead for her friend at length. Finally, impressed by the little redhead's tenacity and loyalty, the producer agreed to give Rock a decent part in an upcoming movie.

Laurie never told Rock about her intervention. "It

would seem so self-serving," she said. In fact, her determination may have saved Rock's neck at Universal. The producer knew the actress was speaking as a friend and colleague, but he knew something else as well: Piper Laurie was also an American teen-ager. And it was the response of American teen-age girls that would ultimately make Rock Hudson a star.

Perhaps Piper Laurie's stand had something to do with it, perhaps not, but it was around this time that things began to pick up a bit for Rock. *The Iron Man*, in 1951, starring contract player Jeff Chandler, was one of the first movies in which Rock played an actual secondary lead, as a prize-fighter. Joseph Pevney directed. When Universal producer Aaron Rosenberg first suggested Rock for the part, Pevney, the memory of Rock as a doorman still sharp in his mind, was first dismissive, then horrified.

"You can't do that to me," Pevney pleaded when Rosenberg's suggestion began to look more like an order. "He's a southpaw! Jesus, give me an actor, for crying out loud."

"Joe," said Rosenberg patiently, "he's going to be a star someday."

"Aaron," said Pevney, "I'll wait."

Rock did get the part, and even Pevney was impressed with his dedication. "They had to take him down to the gym and train him to use his right hand to throw a punch. He had to learn how to fight as a right-hander, which is very difficult. But he worked hard, he did a good job, and even got some nice notices. It was the largest role he'd played up till that time. It was a good role for him, and he did well with it."

For the most part. The film had a sprinkling of comedy in it, and "he was not too adept at comedy at this point. He didn't know how to read the lines yet."

The Universal trainer, Frankie Van, took Rock in hand. "He needed a lot of deltoid development. Across the shoulders. And bigger forearms. But his legs and his rear were perfect. When he came in, he couldn't recognize a pair of boxing gloves. In six weeks I had him down to 191 pounds from 202, and he was more like Gene Tunney than Gene Tunney," Van boasted.

Rock was nothing if not thorough in his preparations. Once he was in a corner, between rounds, trying to act winded. "We put bloody makeup on, and he sat in the corner before I rolled the camera, and he exhaled and inhaled very quickly in order to get the breathy quality he wanted—and all of a sudden he froze, his eyes rolled back and he fainted. He just collapsed," said Pevney.

"An actor," he added approvingly, "trying to do a good job."

Sophie Rosenstein died in the early fifties and was replaced at Universal by Estelle Harmon, who now runs a private acting school in Los Angeles. Harmon's memories of Rock are warm. "I had the advantage. Sophie had done the preliminary work with Rock. Originally, Sophie's early notes only saw him as a big, handsome, stumbling kind of actor. But by the time I saw him, I thought he had some skills, some presence.

"He was always very shy. But he had a quality on the set that was working by the time I met him. I could see this young man, though they might have hired him because he had exceptional good looks, also had a flavor and a flair and an instinct for acting."

Harmon held an acting class three times a week for the young contract players. In addition, she had private tutoring sessions with each player. "It was an excellent program. I remember they told me if we created even one star, it would pay for the whole program." Since her students at the time included Rock, Tony Curtis, Barbara Rush, Dennis Weaver, Jeff Chandler, and Hugh O'Brian, the studio more than won its bet.

Harmon felt she may have been the first to recognize the possibility of using Rock in a comedy. "He was a handsome hunk, and they were playing him that way. But he and I began to see the possibility of his comedy skills, which nobody had realized."

Harmon continued the practice Rosenstein had begun of staging showcases featuring the Universal contract players. The productions were staged not only for Universal producers but also for producers and directors from other studios, in the hope of encouraging loan-outs.

"The scene I had Rock do was from *Fourposter*, which surprised everyone," said Harmon. His partner was a contract player named Susan Cabot. It was the first time anybody had seen Rock in anything funny—and according to Harmon, he acquitted himself well. A quarter-century later he did the same scene on stage, in the musical version of the play, *I Do! I Do!* with Carol Burnett, who at one time took private lessons from Harmon.

Harmon remembered the young Rock as being someone who "went out of his way for the underdog." At times, as Rock's star rose higher and higher, "I saw him do extraordinary things. If an actor was having trouble on the set, he'd do everything he could to help them. Even for a bit player—he would do things like flub his line on purpose, so the other actor would have another chance." At one point during her career at Universal, Harmon came into conflict with one of the big executives. "Rock was on my team all the way.

"Rock was really bright, but because he was shy and didn't talk up, some people early on thought he wasn't." Rock's personality was in sharp contrast to that of Tony Curtis, she remembered. "Tony was very outgoing, very energetic, very much a clown. Rock was quieter. Maybe Tony thought he was standoffish, but he was really just shy." As Harmon remembered it, the two did not get on together "at all." The "Pals" episode, of course, had not exactly cemented their friendship.

One of Rock's problems in his new life as actor—a problem that was to remain with him until the end—was the problem Harmon referred to as "the enemy": stage fright.

"I remember once giving him some Shakespeare to do in class, and he just disappeared for about a week!" she said. "But when he finally came, everyone in class was startled at the power, sensitivity, and understanding."

Piper Laurie painted a disturbing picture of one of Rock's bouts with stage fright, which actually seemed serious enough to qualify as outright phobia. She witnessed it at one of the showcase productions. Wandering backstage, waiting to go on, she saw her friend—tall, handsome Rock—literally sobbing with fear.

"I thought he was not going to make it. It was the most pathetic case of stage fright I've ever seen in my life. Now, I was scared—but this was pathetic. Here was this huge man, crying. I tried to be as comforting and supportive as I could, and he made it . . . but I was really struck by this great vulnerability in such a big man. I never experienced anything like that."

"Fright is one of the worst things in the world," Rock would say years later. "A terrible feeling, like a disease you can't control."

Harmon worked with Rock to ease the problem, and feels she had some effect. "There are procedures," she said. "Number one, becoming terribly aware of what's being communicated by your fellow actors . . . picking up body language, facial expression, tone of voice. It takes a lot of your mind to become alert to that. Rock was able to develop that perception, and that helped his concentration not be just on himself."

Then, too, there are exercises—an actor plays his role as if he were an ape, or sings it, so that when he finally just needs to perform the role as written, it becomes easy.

But performance fear was something Rock was never entirely able to eliminate from his life. Years later, when Harmon had left Universal and had her own acting school, Rock, then a superstar, dropped by one of her workshops and spoke to a class of young actors.

"Tell me, Mr. Hudson," one young actor said. "When do you stop being tense in front of groups?"

Rock laughed and raised his arm so the class could see the heavy streaks of sweat on his shirt. "I'll let you know," he said.

The young players at Universal were encouraged to spend any free time watching other actors. Rock was extremely impressed with the veteran actor Tyrone Power and tried to be on the set whenever he was working, although he was too shy ever to say anything to him. Several years later, in the last year of Power's life, the two men became good friends.

When Power appeared in a stage production of *John*

Brown's Body, Rock and a friend went to see it. Power recognized Rock from Universal and invited him to watch the show from backstage.

It was one of Rock's first experiences watching from the wings, and he was mesmerized. He watched eagerly, hoping to learn anything he could. What he got was a lesson in reality he would never forget. From where he was seated, he was in a prime position to see Dame Judith Anderson waft offstage after a particularly magical burst of poetry and, while the applause was still ringing from the rafters, hawk up phlegm and spit it copiously on the floor. It made an indelible impression: thirty years later he was still telling the story. More than twenty years after seeing Power in the play, Rock himself performed on stage in *John Brown's Body*, with his good friend Claire Trevor.

Despite the excitement of being with a major motion-picture studio, Rock's early years at Universal were lonely in many ways. He was, as Piper Laurie said, small-townish—used to the easy friendliness of a Midwest community. Even in the fifties, Hollywood was far from being a small town.

"I've found making lots of friends here not easy," he admitted in an interview with Hedda Hopper in 1952. "At first I just didn't seem to click. Guess everybody thought I was another square from the Midwest."

There were a few pals—like Piper Laurie, Dick Morris, singer-dancer Carleton Carpenter—but for the most part, his social life, such as it was, was engineered by Henry Willson.

Willson kept a tight reign over Rock's life, day and night. Rock was still his property, and Willson was not about to let him loose. He certainly did not intend to leave Rock's social life to chance. The social scene in Hollywood was too important. It was necessary for a client to meet the right people, be seen in the correct setting, go out with the right starlet. All these things were closely related to one's career, Willson knew. He was not just an agent. Long before the term had been coined, Willson was a "personal manager."

Undoubtedly Henry Willson was the one responsible for introducing Rock to Vera-Ellen, an established star. The fan-mag tale was that they met at Ciro's, where Willson encouraged Rock to cut in on her on the dance floor. Soon the two were reported to be officially dating, although it seems probable the relationship was never more than a friendship.

Rock and Vera-Ellen pulled off one publicity coup that hit all the papers: they showed up at the Press Photographers' Costume Ball dressed as Oscars, complete with plastic heads and prop swords, their bodies completely covered with gold paint. (A rather dangerous prank, as the movie *Goldfinger* one day made clear.) They were an instant hit. It may, of course, have been Rock's idea, but one senses the fine hand of Henry Willson behind the exhibition.

The fan mags made hay with the Rock–Vera-Ellen relationship. For many years, the traumatic breakup of his supposed love affair with her was cited as the reason he was marriage-shy. It was the difference in their salaries that had broken them up, bleated the sob sisters—Vera-Ellen, after all, was an established star, Rock only a beginner. Other than a high-school romance, this had been the only love of Rock's life, they assured their audiences, and his heart had been quite broken.

However, his comments to Hedda Hooper in the 1952 interview made the relationship seem more lukewarm. Asked why the two hadn't married, Rock said simply, "I couldn't make up my mind. Why get involved in something of which you're not sure?" The two of them were still good friends, he added, even though Vera-Ellen was now going with another man. "Had dinner together the other night," he commented casually. Shortly afterward, Vera-Ellen's life took a tragic turn: in 1954 she married a millionaire, Victor Rothschild, and after the death of their only child, who was three months old, spent the rest of her life—until her death from cancer in 1981—as a recluse.

Mamie Van Doren remembered going on an arranged date with Rock to the Photoplay Awards early in her career. Universal's public-relations department had assured her she'd have no problems fighting him off.

"They told me he was gay. They said I didn't have to

worry about anything." Van Doren had donned an ornate beaded dress for the occasion.

But Rock in the flesh was not quite what she had been told to expect. "He was very macho. I thought, God, for all the things I've heard about him, he doesn't seem to be that way." After the evening out, she invited him into her home for coffee. Rock made a pass at her and they ended up necking, though it didn't go any further. The next morning Van Doren's mother came down to breakfast and found beads from the dress all over the floor.

"She said, 'Look at all the beads!' And I told her, 'Well, he surprised me.'" Van Doren was convinced that if she had permitted it, they would have ended up in bed together. However, she had her own career to think of. "How did I know he wasn't going to go back and tell the public-relations department that I was an easy lay?"

Jimmy Dobson, who was to work as Rock's vocal coach for nearly twenty-five years, recalled first meeting the young actor around this time: "He was very shy, very reserved. He didn't know how handsome he was. He didn't realize he was a good-looking guy. I asked him once if he knew how handsome he was and he said, 'Oh, come on, I'm ordinary-looking.'"

Rock had little time for socializing during his first years with the studio, Dobson said. "I would read all these fan-magazine stories about whom he was dating and with whom he was having a big romance. The truth was that, except for publicity purposes, he was too busy to do anything. He was taking acting lessons, riding lessons, fencing lessons, dancing lessons, and making about five films a year. Now, how much time does that leave?

"When you're doing a film, you're up at four-thirty in the morning. You get home at ten-thirty at night, you study your lines and go to bed. It was a real tough life and he wanted it. He was devoted to his art. He knew exactly what he wanted: he wanted to be a movie star."

When Rock did have an occasional evening away from studio obligations and Willson-orchestrated social engagements, he liked to spend it with a few friends at home, very informally. He had a studio apartment in the Hollywood Hills and enjoyed giving small dinner parties. Carleton

Carpenter remembered nights at Rock's place, singing around the piano or playing games—Monopoly, word games. "Games, music, and good talk," said Carpenter. "We were sort of quiet and dull, to tell the truth."

Rock also liked to hang out at the old Hamburger Hamlet on Sunset Strip, Carpenter recalled. "I'd play the piano and he'd be singing."

"He didn't like to be alone," said Dick Morris. "I think that became more and more so as he grew older. Rock could be very moody. He'd be high and giddy, and then he'd be very morose." Rock, Morris felt, had "a boyish temperament. A little immature."

Rock became good friends with a cute blond script girl named Betty Abbott—who was the niece of Universal's top comedian, Bud Abbott—and with starlet Marilyn Maxwell. Naturally, both friendships were reported in the press as hot-and-heavy romances. Rock kept his actual sexual involvements very quiet. But Hollywood is a very small town in many ways. By the fifties most Universal executives were aware that Rock was homosexual. He wasn't the first, nor would he be the last.

Universal's youngest contract player, Lori Nelson, who was signed at sixteen, had a number of double dates with Rock to help generate publicity for him—but she knew he was gay. "At first it was hearsay at the studio, and then it was common knowledge," she said.

Still, Nelson believes that Rock's feelings for Betty Abbott and Marilyn Maxwell were genuine. "I thought maybe they were really affairs . . . maybe Rock was bisexual in those days. Betty was absolutely crazy about Rock."

Nelson thought of Rock as a big brother—and he once came to her rescue when she had a youthful confrontation with director Douglas Sirk. During the filming of *All I Desire* with Barbara Stanwyck, Sirk lost his temper with Nelson, and she ran crying to her dressing room.

"I wouldn't come out," Nelson recalled. "No one knew what to do with me. They called my mother, but she wasn't home. Then somebody suggested Rock. They remembered that we were good friends."

Rock wasn't at the studio that day, but when someone

called him about the problem, he made a special trip in to try to help Lori. "He came and talked to me, explained to me what it was Sirk was trying to do," Nelson recalled fondly. "He got me back on the set. I don't think anybody else could have done that."

At Universal, with *The Iron Man* under his belt, Rock was beginning to feel slightly more secure about his future. The immediate danger of being dropped seemed to have passed, and it looked as if the studio was committed to keeping him around, at least for a while. With that in mind, he continued to work hard, uncomplainingly doing what he was told, no matter how ridiculous some of the roles were. He was aware of how silly most of the movies were—off set and even on set, director and cast would often be rendered hysterical by some of the lines they were forced to say. Rock himself never forgot gazing into a woman's eyes and saying with gravity, "Unga bunga wunga," in the Indian epic *Taza, Son of Cochise*. The woman was Barbara Rush, and for the rest of their thirty-year friendship, Rock addressed her as Unga Dos Tres. But he did what was required. Rock Hudson was beginning to understand what it took to become a movie star.

"He recognized the machinery of being a movie star," said Stack. "He was willing to do his time. The bottom line was, he was a pro—a guy who shows up on time, knows his lines, isn't a pain in the hoo-haw."

Perhaps the studio was beginning to recognize his professionalism, and finally decided to give him a real chance. Or perhaps they were swayed by the sudden growth in fan mail, which had started pouring in around the time Rock, clad only in boxer shorts, appeared on the screen in *The Iron Man*. The very epitome of dashing young masculinity, the actor struck a chord not only with teen-agers but with women of all ages. Universal executives knew they'd be fools to ignore the phenomenon.

At any rate, sometime in 1953, four years after he'd signed his original contract with Universal, Rock Hudson was given the chance he had been waiting for. He was given the lead in *Magnificent Obsession*. It was the movie that would make him a star.

CHAPTER TWO
Romantic Idol

Magnificent Obsession is a tearjerker, one of the granddaddies of the genre. Originally made in 1935 with Robert Taylor and Irene Dunne, the film had been responsible for catapulting Taylor to stardom. Now one of the Universal executives, probably William Goetz, decided it was time to dust it off and give it another shot.

According to Joseph Pevney, the project was first offered to Loretta Young and John Forsythe. "I had just done another tearjerker with Loretta called *Because of You*," Pevney recalled, although his memory is a little shaky on this point—the movie may have had another title. "Weak little picture, but Loretta loved it, and it was a woman's picture, and it started a whole new ballgame at Universal, which hadn't been doing any tearjerkers. They had been doing adventure stories, stuff like that.

"This movie didn't cost any money, it went out and did very well. So the studio heads came down to see me. Mr. Goetz wanted me to do this *Magnificent Obsession* with John Forsythe and Loretta. A tearjerker in the same category, where Loretta cries a lot, it would have been a hell of a movie. They dug it up for Loretta."

Loretta Young, however, refused. "She said, 'Joe, what do you want to do a remake for? You don't have to do remakes.'" And so Pevney, to his eternal sorrow, turned it down.

"Since the executives couldn't get who they wanted,

the next best thing was getting Rock and Jane Wyman, whose career wasn't doing too well at that point," said Pevney.

Others remember the situation differently. They claim that Rock had been tapped for the lead in the picture from the very beginning. After all, there could hardly exist a better vehicle than Magnificent Obsession for packaging and presenting a new heartthrob. The movie, from the Lloyd Douglas novel of the same name, tells the tale of a careless young playboy who accidentally blinds a young widow and then not only woos her but goes to medical school, becomes a surgeon, and ultimately operates on her to restore her sight. Pure, unadulterated soap opera, and box-office dynamite for two generations.

Studio head Ed Muhl personally insisted on casting Rock as the male lead in Magnificent Obsession.

"Rock was very ready and Jane Wyman graciously agreed to accept Rock as her leading man," recalled Muhl. "Twenty years before, I was already at the studio when it borrowed Robert Taylor, an unknown from MGM, to play the same role opposite Irene Dunne. The role established Taylor also. It would have been stupid of me to have forgotten that."

When Rock realized the part was his, he was thrilled and terrified. He'd be working with Jane Wyman, an established star, and Douglas Sirk, a respected Danish-born director, who had had a successful career in pre-Nazi Germany before coming to the United States. Rock had worked under Sirk two years back in Has Anybody Seen My Gal?, playing the secondary role as Piper Laurie's soda-jerk boyfriend. But this would be different. This time he would be the star.

Sirk, according to one source, balked at doing the remake at first, telling producer Ross Hunter he was afraid they might be buried under it. After mulling it over for a few days, he changed his mind, having realized, prophetically, that "maybe this goddamn awful story could be a success." Both Sirk and Hunter had gotten to know and like Rock during his years at Universal, and felt it was time the kid had a real chance.

Rock spent the last days before shooting began trying desperately to relax—to eat right, sleep right—so he'd be in the best possible condition for the job.

One day he went to the beach, where he saw small boys paddling about in inner tubes. It looked so peaceful and appealing that he got a tube himself, blew it up, and climbed on.

For a long moment he floated blissfully. Then the ocean reasserted itself. "I'm a big guy," he said a year later, "and I had no idea of the buoyancy of that thing." Within minutes he was farther out than he had ever planned to be, riding the crest of the waves, a cork on the high seas. When a big breaker rolled in, he was helpless. He was thrown in the air and slammed down onto the beach, smashing his collarbone.

A friend remembers Rock calling from the hospital, sobbing, not from pain but from fear that his big chance might have been swept out to sea along with the inner tube. Rock refused to let doctors put a cast on him, despite their warnings that, without it, he would be bothered for many years by pain, and that the bone would probably not heal straight. (It didn't.) The movie was all-important, not his physical well-being. Rock went home aching, but without the cast. It was not the last time he would put a job before his health. He did it many times throughout his career, even in the last months of his life.

Jane Wyman, whom Rock had never met, turned out to be a warm, gracious lady who went out of her way to put the young actor at ease. She sensed his nervousness and spent time working with him away from the set. Gradually Rock gained confidence.

When the movie was released, thousands of teen-age girls had no trouble at all deciding what was magnificent about it: its leading man, Rock Hudson. Their mothers were not unmoved either. Since the Jane Wyman character is distinctly older than the man, the film fueled housewife fantasies across the country. Now the letters began pouring into the studio in earnest. Seen today, *Magnificent Obsession* has its laughable moments, but it is surprisingly touching all the same. Rock's acting was not of Academy

Award caliber, yet something about the young actor—a decency, a sincerity, an urge to please—spilled out over the screen. And, of course, there was no ignoring those spectacular good looks. Fans raved about his eyes: there was a hidden sadness in them that went to their hearts, a sadness that any one of them would have given their eyeteeth to assuage. One young fan wrote that she had tried to describe them to her mother for hours, without success. The best word she could come up with, finally, was *brown*. A teenager in Lexington, Kentucky, said she cried all night because of the "heartbreak and sorrow" she saw in Hudson's eyes.

Universal executives noted the reaction and made a corporate decision: henceforth, every Rock Hudson picture would include a scene in which he gazed soulfully into a woman's eyes. Noting the fans' thrilled response to his height, they also decided that all Rock Hudson movies should have at least one shot of the big actor overfilling a doorway.

Rock himself saw the movie for the first time at a sneak preview in Encino. It was an emotional moment. "I fled the theater before the film was over. I knew, I knew, and I knew I had to get out of there before the lights went on." What he knew was that he was no longer Rock Hudson, contract player—from here on in, he was a movie star.

The remake was successful beyond Universal's wildest dreams, earning ten times more than the original. The studio pocketed five million dollars, gave Rock a new contract, a sizable raise, and a larger dressing room.

With the release of *Magnificent Obsession*, the details of Rock's life became endlessly fascinating to millions of American women, and the fan magazines began to churn out story after story. "Will Rock Hudson Put Career Ahead of Matrimony?" blared the headline over a Louella Parsons exclusive. Parsons tweaked the young star about his relationship with Betty Abbott, whom he had taken to the gala premiere. "Are you going to marry her? She's a very pretty girl," cooed the gossip columnist.

Rock was noncommittal. "I have to work on my career and get somewhere. Then it could be. My mother likes Betty, and she has been very good to me."

The movie had made Rock the country's number one heartthrob, and the studio and fan mags were going to capitalize on it. Every story that came out added to the picture. Rock Hudson had to be shown first, not as an actor, not as a person with various interests—but as a man who loved women.

"He believes in fun babes," one columnist noted. "Not babes with messages. He believes in a good-night kiss on your first date. He's leery of two careers in one marriage, but feels the future Mrs. H. should be hep to show biz. Some vow that script girl Betty Abbott fills the bill. . . ."

More and more, the fan mags weren't content to leave it at that. Rock was approaching thirty. No man in America during the mid-fifties was unmarried when he was thirty. When, they pleaded again and again, was he going to take the step?

It could not have been easy for Rock. He'd had no real experience with duplicity before. In so many ways, he really was the simple, fun-loving, decent, sincere guy portrayed by the press. He was handsome, he was virile, he was boyish, just as they said. It's just that he was not heterosexual. The industry was aware; his friends, men and women, knew. Yet his fans across the country—those plain, decent real-life women so much like those in his own family—did not. Another, more sophisticated man, whose roots were not forged in Winnetka, would not have cared, perhaps, about the deception. Rock cared; it haunted him for the rest of his life.

Stardom, however, did bring its advantages—better treatment from the studio, more money, new friends. Rock went to Ireland to film *Captain Lightfoot* and was able to indulge in a European tour on the side. Pictures of Rock and Betty Abbott enjoying the old country were duly released, but the cognoscenti knew the truth: Henry Willson, widely rumored to be his lover from the beginning of Hudson's career, was present throughout the tour. This fact later came back to cause both men grave difficulty.

Rock's salary was steadily going up. It hovered around

$350 a week for a long time, until he happened to charm the wife of studio head William Goetz at a party. She and some other wives raved about Rock, and Goetz raised his salary to $1,000 a week, according to a story Willson told. After *Magnificent Obsession*, his salary was raised to $1,250 a week.

With his newfound prosperity, Rock bought his first house. It was one of the most important purchases of his life.

"As far back as I can remember, I have lived in other people's houses," he told a reporter. "When I was a kid, during the bad times when money was scarce, we lived with our relatives.

"Then later there was a succession of landlords with rented houses and rented apartments, and never a place I could call my own.

"But now at last I have my own house with a hearth and a latch string and a winding garden path. And it gives me a nice comfortable feeling, a real feeling of belonging."

It was a two-bedroom house of split redwood built to resemble an early Pennsylvania Dutch farmhouse. Though the house was only four years old, it had a mellow feel to it. Its shaded pathway from the front to the back was cushioned with aromatic pine needles.

The ceiling had exposed hand-rubbed beams. The floor was teak, made from hand-pegged, randomly sized boards. The cabinets were rubbed fruitwood. There was a breakfast nook, a walk-in bar, and a windowed dining alcove. Rock was on a hill and had a good view from all angles. The kitchen had an electric revolving spit.

One bedroom had a split Dutch door; the other Rock turned into a den. One of his first pieces of furniture was an antique player piano. There was only one bathroom—and no pool. Rock was thinking seriously of adding one, but since he lived on a fairly steep slope, it would have been outrageously expensive to dig one.

His house had a patio laid out of redwood rounds. The door to the garage, which housed his flashy convertible, worked with a push-button on his dashboard—a big deal in those days. The button opened the door when he was a hundred yards away. The garage closed automatically when his rear fins were clear.

Rock used the device to escape his fans, who would follow him from the studio gates. He would lead them on, then he would run up the hill quickly, stop, kill his lights, and suddenly sprint up his winding driveway through the automatic doors.

Rock always had a very masculine taste in furnishings. People always remarked on it, and it showed up in his first house. While making *Captain Lightfoot* in Ireland, he had been impressed with the furnishings of an old inn. He brought back some antique whiskey barrels to make into lamps.

There were three things his house would never have, he vowed. He would never have fringe, doilies, or drapes. He had lived in feminine households all his life, and those days were over.

Yet all was not perfect in paradise. Universal, which had waited so long to give Rock his chance, was not about to share him. Not long after *Magnificent Obsession* broke box-office records all over America, Metro-Goldwyn-Mayer offered Universal one million dollars to have Rock star in *Ben Hur*, according to Ed Muhl, who was Universal's chief production executive at the time.

"We rejected the possibility of lending him at all for that picture," recalled Muhl. "Rock was obviously very well established by that time, but it was more important to us to have him for our own pictures.

"Rock, or anyone else, was never loaned for the sole purpose of making money," says Muhl.

There is at least one indication that Rock was beginning to get a little worried about his career at this point. He'd made the big splash—yet nothing much seemed to have changed. Rather than blame the studio, he began to have second thoughts about Henry Willson.

"He came to see me one day—and he was not too happy about his career," said Joseph Pevney. "He didn't think Henry was doing him that much good. He asked me what he should do."

Pevney attempted to soothe him. After all, he reminded Rock, Henry had been the one who had discovered him, given him his name and launched his career. Willson was loyal to a fault, and had been in Rock's corner from the start. What was the problem?

Rock said that he'd like to be doing more important things. He felt Willson was not using his clout as an agent to do the best for him. "He's just not getting me anywhere— I'm not going anywhere in my career," Rock complained. He thought Willson should have been pestering the studio to allow him to do loan-outs, so he could broaden his experience.

The solution was simple, Pevney said. "All you've got to do is have a meeting with him and tell him exactly what you want. And if he doesn't produce it—dump him!"

Whether or not Rock ever confronted Willson is unclear. Rock never had an easy time standing up to authority figures, and Willson had been controlling much of his life for several years. Not until two years after *Magnificent Obsession* did he finally get an outside picture deal. When he did, it was, as far as Rock was concerned, the deal of his life: the leading role in Warner Brothers' *Giant*.

Early in 1955, Rock discovered that director George Stevens was considering him for the leading role in his upcoming spectacular, *Giant*. He had seen Rock's work in *The Lawless Breed* and was definitely interested. Universal would have to agree to the loan-out. Rock began to campaign for the part, with Willson's help. The film, a sweeping panorama of Texas (the giant of the title) based on the Edna Ferber novel, would undoubtedly be the movie of the year.

Rock was ecstatic when he was told he had the job and that Universal had agreed to let him do it. "They had to scrape me off the ceiling," he said. "Every actor in town wanted that part. Everybody—Gable, Alan Ladd, Cooper."

William Holden, in particular, was convinced he had the inside track—until Stevens took him aside and told him he had decided to cast Rock. The part demanded that the actor age twenty-five years, and the director felt it would be easier to age a younger star than to make a slightly older star look younger. Holden, upset, went to the Universal steambath room to cool down—only to run into his young rival, clad in a towel, trying his best to make his six-foot-four-inch frame invisible. Holden was a perfect gentleman. Gripping his own towel around his waist, forcing his lips into a grim smile, he congratulated Rock. "I wish you a lot of luck; it's a very good role," he said tightly.

Rock knew it. No sooner had he heard of his great good fortune than he began to have cold feet. Never before had he worked with a director of Stevens's stature. Nervously, he began to ask other people what it was like to work with him. "They said, 'You can do anything you like as long as you make yourself into a ball of putty and put yourself in his hands. Just let him take care of you,'" said Rock.

Nonetheless, Rock approached the role of Bick Benedict, the wealthy Texas rancher, with trepidation. Not only would he be portraying a more fully developed character than ever before (Bick is prejudiced, snobbish, materialistic, yet appealing and ultimately heroic), he would have to age twenty-five years in the film—although, as he later joked, "working with Stevens is an aging process in itself—he's so thorough."

Estelle Harmon, his Universal acting coach, who helped coach him for the part, described one of Stevens's approaches with the actor: "Stevens had tools and techniques for getting what he wanted from actors. In one scene, where Rock first goes to the home of Elizabeth Taylor, he's supposed to feel enormously awkward, lost, and embarrassed. Apparently Rock wasn't pulling it off the way he wanted. So Stevens finally sent just about everybody home, expressed great impatience, and put Rock at a little table with no actors around him—so that he actually did begin to feel horribly uncomfortable, awkward, and that he was disappointing everybody. And the quality that Stevens was looking for came out."

Rock and Elizabeth Taylor, his co-star, hit it off at

once—but he was never friendly with James Dean, the other star. Dean was an Actors Studio graduate. His background was the antithesis of Rock's studio training, and Rock was alienated by Dean's occasional on-set tantrums. It was the traditional reaction of the dutiful older child to the antics of the spoiled-brat youngest. Even after Stevens dressed Dean down in front of the cast and Dean's behavior improved, Rock never warmed to him. Rock and Taylor spent most of their time together during the shooting. Taylor eventually became close to Dean. When the younger actor was killed in a car crash before the film was completed, she broke down completely. To Rock's horror, Stevens insisted she come to work the next day. She sobbed throughout the scene, which Stevens was forced to film from behind her head.

The film was as massive and unending as the state of Texas, and garnered good reviews from every quarter; Rock himself received an Academy Award nomination, the only one of his life. For the rest of his career he thought back on the experience proudly. He once admitted he had seen the movie forty times after its release.

It was, he said much later, better than any part he had been given before or since. "I flat-out loved it. A marvelous role." But attending the premiere in New York was an unnerving experience.

"It was the first time a movie I was in was ever premiered. So I was impressed—thrilled. Outside the theater were thousands of people. Traffic was blocked. All of that. And I thought, My God, I'm in this movie. Playing one of the leads. Jesus, it was exciting. Then I sat there in my seat—and I was booed throughout the film."

It wasn't until the end of the film, when Bick has a fistfight with a man even more bigoted than he is, that the boos turned to applause, and Rock realized something: "The audience was reacting to the character. Not to me, but to Bick."

Before the release of *Giant*, a dark shadow fell over Rock's career. *Confidential*, the sleaziest magazine of them all, had begun nosing around, gathering information about the young star's private life. The trip to Europe with Henry Willson had stirred their interest, since Willson was known in the industry to be homosexual. Earlier in Rock's career, his sexuality had held no interest for *Confidential*—they went after stars, the bigger the better. Now, when Rock was being touted as America's new number one heartthrob, such a story was too good to resist.

According to several reports, Henry Willson knew he had to act fast to prevent the story from coming out, and so he did. *Confidential* was nipping at his heels, threatening to muddy the reputation of his top client. Rock was poised on the brink of true stardom—a lot of hopes were resting on *Giant*. Willson, it is reported, made a deal: he would give them some sort of story about another client if they would kill the story on Rock.

Parade magazine, in an item published after Rock's death, named one Willson client. *People* named another and then later retracted it.

In May 1955, there was a story in *Confidential* on Rory Calhoun, reporting that as a teen-ager he had once gone joyriding. The story was hardly sensational, and it even included an interview with a kindly priest who had supposedly set Calhoun straight.

Four months later, in September 1955, there was a story in *Confidential* that was exceptionally nasty. It concerned another Henry Willson client, blond he-man Tab Hunter. The article dealt with Hunter's arrest for disorderly conduct at a party five years earlier, before Hunter's career had been launched.

The story that Willson threw one of his clients to the wolves to preserve Rock Hudson's reputation is now part of Hollywood mythology. There is no way to document what really happened. Rock, said Jimmy Dobson, Hudson's longtime vocal coach, never discussed it. "Henry never tried to protect anybody but himself. He may have been protecting his interest in Rock, but not Rock personally. Willson wouldn't have told Rock what he was doing. Never."

Willson had managed to fend off *Confidential*, but he

knew there was only one way to end the rumors of Rock's homosexuality—or at least shut them up for a time. Rock, he realized, had to get married. And fast. Luckily, Willson, the great arranger, didn't have to look very far for a candidate. In his own office was a young woman secretary who was attractive, bright, unattached. Her name was Phyllis Gates, and in November 1955, she became Mrs. Rock Hudson.

Shortly before the marriage, Rock called Jim Matteoni in Winnetka to tell him he was dating a secretary. Both Matteoni and his wife found the call somewhat strange. Rock never talked about the women in his life.

The wedding itself was arranged at the last minute. Rock called Matteoni at 2:00 A.M., November 11, to tell him about it and to ask him to fly out immediately to serve as best man. The Matteonis were delighted. They packed and rushed to the airport. The ceremony was performed later that day in Santa Barbara. Rock's mother and her husband, Joe Olsen, were unable to attend, since Olsen was recovering from surgery. Rock had often joked to the press that he would marry when he was thirty; in fact, he was only six days off. His thirtieth birthday was November 17.

Willson formulated an elaborate plan to maximize press coverage for Rock by making the nuptials appear to be secret, thus whetting the appetites of reporters and fan-magazine editors. The agent made sure certain reporters knew the wedding had been moved up ten days from the announced date. He also added intrigue to the proceedings by having the wedding party drive sixty miles north to Ventura at the end of the day to get the license.

Fan magazines duly reported that Rock, driving his 1955 Buick convertible, got a ticket for doing 75 in a 50-mile-per-hour zone while racing to the Biltmore Hotel in Santa Barbara, where the wedding took place. One fan-magazine writer painted a romantic picture: the bride and groom standing near a crackling fireplace, the roar of the Pacific surf outside, and Rock slipping a beautiful diamond on Phyllis's finger. It was a simple Protestant ceremony, conducted by a Lutheran minister, the Reverend Nordahl Thorpe.

There was one offbeat note, however—the all-American couple asked the minister to omit the word *obey* from their vows. Otherwise, they promised to love and honor each other. Willson made sure the hotel photographers shot the couple cutting the wedding cake—and the pictures were distributed to the press shortly after the ceremony.

The Matteonis never considered the possibility that there was anything bogus about the match. "To our knowledge that marriage was done out of sincerity. If it was done otherwise, they sure fooled hell out of us," Matteoni said.

Rock, he knew, had always expressed fear of marriage, a fear he had assumed grew out of Rock's reaction to his mother's bad experiences. But Hudson had always been intensely curious about it as well, asking the Matteonis question after question about their own relationship whenever he visited them.

"He would ask me how easy it was to get along with a woman in such an intimate situation as marriage. He asked whether our marriage really worked as well as it seemed to on the surface. Some of the questions were graphic, and Gloria and I were taken aback." As the years passed, Rock stopped asking the questions.

Exactly how much masterminding Willson needed to do to arrange the marriage is difficult to determine thirty years later, but it was undoubtedly substantial. "I did think Rock needed a Mrs. Hudson," Willson admitted later. "I gave Rock a nice background on Phyllis Gates. Beforehand, I'd told her all about Rock. The next time we were all together, I asked them both to lunch. After that, they started dating and eventually got married." Details—including a Jamaica honeymoon—were arranged by Willson.

Arranged or not—"If you knew the number of arranged marriages in this town," Robert Stack said with a laugh—it seems quite probable that Rock did care for Phyllis Gates, enjoyed her company, and even held hopes that the marriage would be a success. Such things, after all, do happen, even in Hollywood. The boy who'd never had a real family was still yearning for one. It is unwise to assume that just because the marriage was arranged, and Rock was a homosexual, that there was no affection at all between him and Gates. Thirty years later he assured Marc Christian that there had definitely been a relationship between them—one that was both physical and emotional. Marriage, however, had destroyed it, he said. Dobson agreed. "Roy told me he had really loved this person, and I believed him."

If true, the failure of his marriage illuminates a problem Rock had throughout his life with all his emotional relationships. Living together—domesticity—was equated in his mind with lack of sexual interest. The pursuit, the chase, the romantic preliminaries were what entranced him.

Jane Ardmore, a movie-magazine writer who frequently interviewed Rock during his early career, feels strongly that Rock would not have gone cold-bloodedly into an arranged marriage just to save his reputation.

"I think he felt there was a reason for marrying her other than just saving his career. Maybe he thought that the marriage would be a safety valve for him."

Ardmore also interviewed Gates after the marriage. "I felt very sorry for her," she said. "It was a bad spot to be in."

Whatever Rock's feelings—or those of Phyllis Gates—the fan mags had no ambivalence. Rock's new marriage made good copy, and endless space was devoted to paeans to the happy new couple, complete with quotes from Rock too fulsome to be believed, testifying to his happiness.

One fan magazine proudly displayed a card Rock had written Gates on the occasion of their six-month anniversary. "You've got a half—want to try for one?" it said in its entirety. Within less than a year, there would be rumors of a rift.

Meanwhile, Rock continued to work hard, appearing in two more Douglas Sirk pictures, *Written on the Wind* and *Battle Hymn*. Sirk was a warmly encouraging director, with a European gift for hyperbole. Years later, with his typical self-deprecating humor, Rock told a friend about one of their exchanges. Sirk had called him at home, in the middle of a dinner party, to rave about the work he was doing in their current movie.

"He kept giving me compliments, about how great I was," Rock told director Lou Antonio. "And I knew I had to say something back, just as nice, but all these people were standing around me." Finally, squirming with embarrassment, Rock managed to blurt out his reply, with all the eloquence he could muster. It was, in toto, "Well, ditto, darn it, Doug."

Robert Stack was loaned out to Universal to make *Written on the Wind*. Rock was to make an impression on him that would last forever.

"You could see right away that mine was the flashy part," said Stack. "It dealt with emotions like fear and madness—it was the best part since *Lost Weekend*. The guy is drunk, goes psychotic, beats his wife—it's an actor's dream." It was, in fact, the best part in the picture, a part that could hardly fail to earn the actor an Academy Award nomination.

"Any actor—almost any other actor I know in the business—given the power position he had at the studio, with a loan-out actor coming in—would have gone up to the head of the studio and said, 'Hey, look, man, I'm the star—you cut this guy down or something.'

"But he never did. I never forgot that. He never said a word, not a peep. He let the part go completely. He was in a position of power, and didn't misuse it. It was my only Academy nomination." It was not in Rock to play the demanding star, loudly proclaiming his rights and desires. Throughout his life he was attentive and sensitive to the needs of other performers. Unfortunately, this generosity and lack of ego, which made him so popular with his peers in the industry, could also work against him. Rock had a hard time voicing any demands, ever, no matter how legitimate they were, which is why Universal was able to control him for so many years.

In the mid-fifties, when Rock's box-office appeal was rising to its height, Universal did their best to hawk him to the masses as the "Beefcake Baron." Rock hated the title and the image it conveyed. In later years, he spoke bitterly about what it had been like to be sold like a piece of meat. He particularly detested posing with his shirt off. And yet it was years before he was able to muster up the nerve to tell the studio executives he'd had enough. When finally he did, he was amazed to find it worked—they never asked him to do it again. "So stupid," he muttered, recalling that time, near the end of his life; whether he referred to the studio's demands or his own hesitation at confronting them is unclear, however.

In *Written on the Wind* Stack played a drunken, neurotic millionaire who finally kills himself; Rock was his best friend, who valiantly fights off advances from Stack's oversexed sister, Dorothy Malone. "As usual, I am so pure I am impossible," Rock said.

Rock and Stack became casual friends. "We went down to Palm Springs to the racquet club, went water-skiing. Phyllis was a nice gal. When you know people, you don't worry about how they got married; you just know them as people."

Two years later, the two again worked under Sirk's direction to make *The Tarnished Angels*, a picture that, as Stack said wryly, enjoyed a great deal of popularity in Europe. "Sirk was ahead of his time," he said. "He had an oblique way of looking at things." This time Stack saw another, completely different example of Rock's generosity.

"We were on location south of San Diego somewhere, in a small airfield. My wife was about to give birth and I was nowhere near a phone. Suddenly one guy looks up and says, 'Jesus, there's an idiot coming at us'—and this stupid plane is coming right at us."

Stack looked up as the plane flew by, with a banner flying behind it, the words large and unmistakable: IT'S A GIRL!

"Rock had managed to call in to the hospital. He had two banners, one for a boy, one for a girl. He had gotten this old plane, which almost crashed taking off, with the banner dragging behind it. Who in hell would have ever thought of doing that? He was a good friend, but I doubt I would have done that. It wasn't a publicity stunt. My God, he almost got killed.

"Not too many things in your life touch you that way," said Stack. "He gave me my one big shot—and then, he did this when my baby was born."

Twenty-one years later, Stack's daughter, Elizabeth, who had grown up on the story, asked her father if he thought she could invite Rock to a party she was giving. He said to go ahead, and she did. "He was the only movie star there, and he was dancing up a storm. That's the kind of guy he was."

Dorothy Malone also starred in both movies with Rock and Stack. She remembered Rock helping her with one scene. "I loved Sirk as a director, but there was one day he just couldn't get through to me." Rock came over, put his arm around her, and explained what Sirk was trying to tell her. He was quiet and patient, and was able to make her understand what Sirk wanted.

More than once, Malone saw Rock's protective side. "He was very gallant," she said. On location for *The Tarnished Angels*, she remembered, she was once hassled by a drunk in a bar in San Diego. "He was being very obnoxious. Suddenly he stood bolt upright—because Rock had looped his arm around his shoulder and said, 'I think you better be heading on home now.'" Rock had been completely calm about it—but had managed to make his point. He had a quiet strength, like Gary Cooper, she felt.

"He was very much of a loner," she said about Rock. "I think he was sad in a way. He was a tender type. He was tender toward me. I just loved the way he would hang his arm over my shoulder—just like a stole.

"We had a camaraderie that I didn't have with many people. It's like when you're going through so much tension and then you look over and see a certain face in the crowd and you know everything's going to be all right. And Rock gave me that sense of security whenever I worked with him."

In 1956 Rock was loaned out to MGM to star in *Something of Value*, along with Sidney Poitier, under the direction of Richard Brooks. The film was based on the Robert Ruark novel about Mau Mau uprisings in Africa and told the tale of two men—one white, one black—who had been childhood friends, but were now on opposite sides of the conflict. Rock flew to Nairobi to meet Brooks, who had already been there for several weeks, scouting locations. Brooks had also run into a problem. The hotel manager had told him that Poitier, when he arrived, would not be able to stay at the hotel.

"I told Rock when he came—I said, 'I have a problem about Sidney staying here at the hotel.' Rock said, 'Well, then, we have a problem—not just you. And whatever you want to do, move or whatever, is all right with me,'" said Brooks.

Brooks and the manager continued to negotiate over the next several days. Perhaps Mr. Poitier would be content with a separate bungalow on the hotel grounds, more sumptuous even than the hotel rooms? "No," said Brooks, "I want him right in the hotel."

"But a black man can't stay here, there'll be a riot," whined the manager.

"Then neither can I," said Brooks.

"This man," said the manager finally, "he is that important?" Brooks said he was. "How much does he make in a movie like this?"

"For three months' work, about thirty thousand dollars," said the director.

"American dollars?" asked the manager.

"American dollars," said Brooks.

The manager left. This time he came back fairly soon. "All your problems are over," he announced grandly. "Mr. Poitier can stay in the hotel, and on your floor."

"Fine," said Brooks. "What changed your mind?"

"It is not me, it is the owners," said the manager. "They have decided anyone who makes thirty thousand dollars for three months' work is not black."

The story, said Brooks, convulsed Rock.

Brooks, Rock, and Poitier got along well during the filming. At night they played poker for pennies, and Rock and Poitier discussed America's racial situation at length. The most important thing for black people in America was education, they both felt.

They ran into further segregation problems several times during the making of the movie. "We'd be on location and break for lunch—and the nearest hotel would say we could all come in except for one. Rock would say, 'Well, why don't we have a picnic instead?' He was always there. Nothing was said, but of course Sidney knew what was going on," Brooks said.

Poitier's character is killed at the end of the film, leaving a child behind. "Rock suggested that we end the movie with him carrying the child out of the jungle—and we did."

Something of Value did not fare too well. "It was banned all over the world," said Brooks. "At that time, Italy was fighting to keep Libya, France to keep Morocco. Everyone was afraid of the thrust of the story." The idea that the Mau Mau, or any other native group, might have a right to govern their own country was a chilling notion in many places.

Although none of Rock's post-*Giant* roles had brought him the praise and attention Bick Benedict did, he was at least working with good scripts and directors; it was a far cry from *Taza, Son of Cochise.* He was also getting a chance to see something of the world. Not long after making *Something of Value,* he went on location in Rome to do A *Farewell to Arms.*

By this time it was becoming obvious that there were rifts in the Hudson marriage. Rock and Phyllis had been spending less and less time together. On his way to Rome, he stopped for a few nights in Chicago to stay with Jim and Gloria Matteoni. Rock told the Matteonis that Phyllis planned to meet him and accompany him to Europe.

However, the night before she was scheduled to arrive, she called. Rock told the Matteonis she had a bad cold and had been advised not to fly. The next day he received another call from Phyllis. This time he told his friends that her medication had caused an allergic reaction, and Phyllis had decided to postpone the trip altogether. Rock flew on to Rome alone, leaving the Matteonis to wonder about the relationship.

Rock loved Rome, and Italy, and he was excited about filming the Ernest Hemingway novel. Unfortunately, the experience was horrible for the most part. Later Rock explained why it had been easy for him to cry in the movie, when he had to: he, along with almost everyone else connected with the film, had been miserable during the entire production.

A Farewell to Arms was produced by David O. Selznick, who from the beginning was less interested in being true to Hemingway's vision than in providing a suitable vehicle for his beautiful wife, Jennifer Jones. His interest lay solely in building up the love story between Jones and Rock, which he felt would be box-office dynamite. As far as he was concerned, the rest of the book could be tossed. This pitted him directly against director John Huston, who instantly began cutting out portions of the script that had not been in the novel, to Selznick's indignation. "Nobody complained when I changed Margaret Mitchell's book," he protested angrily.

In fact, Huston and Selznick fought about everything concerning the movie—even the cut of Rock's hair. Huston wanted it to be in the style of World War I; Selznick thought that might ruin Rock's sex appeal.

Selznick had always been known in the trade as an incorrigible, indefatigable memo writer. His notes to Huston became more and more dictatorial, and Huston, fed up, finally quit on the spot. Selznick then hired director Charles Vidor but continued to keep his hand in, up to the elbow.

Once, during a love scene with Jennifer Jones, Rock happened to glance toward the camera, and saw Selznick whispering in Vidor's ear. "David!" he said. "Sorry, sorry," said the producer. Selznick, in fact, seemed obsessed with the movie—Rock once saw him, obviously deep in thought, actually walk into a wall.

Vidor, whom Selznick had hired mainly because he expected the director to be subservient, began to fire off a few memos of his own. Selznick even managed to infuriate his long-suffering production manager, Art Fellows. During one particular shoot, Fellows lost his temper and socked the aging producer in the eye. Unfortunately, Selznick was wearing glasses, which were crushed. He was rushed to a hospital for immediate attention, while Fellows hurriedly packed his bags and caught a flight to America.

The one bright spot in the movie for Rock was his relationship with actress Elaine Stritch, who had been hired by Selznick after he saw her play the lead in *Bus Stop* in New York. Stritch was exactly the sort of woman Rock preferred to hang out with—flip, tough, funny. "I made him laugh, and that was it," said Stritch. "My façade was very flip, very Rosalind Russell; that's what he liked.

"Naturally, a guy like that, who did not have any serious relationships with women, would go for someone who was fun. He didn't want to go out with somebody who was flirting with him all night, which I didn't know how to do. So I was perfect."

Stritch and Rock went out nearly every night. The young actress found herself spending her entire salary on clothes, "just so I could look as good as he did!" It was a romantic, dizzying combination—Rome, Rock, the movie. "Coming down the steps of the Grand Hotel and meeting Rock Hudson in a navy blue suit and a white shirt for dinner was about as much as a young girl could stand."

Rock made it clear, however, that his feelings were more buddylike than romantic. "He impressed me as someone who was having fun with me, but I'm falling in love and he's laughing," said Stritch a bit ruefully. It was a month before he even kissed her good night, and things did not progress further.

"I'm a good Catholic girl. I grew up very slowly in the sex department . . . but even I began to wonder." It wasn't that she wanted a genuine affair, really. "It would be very hard to have an affair as a Catholic in Rome. The Pope is very close." But she wouldn't have minded the option of refusing.

"It was an enigma for a young girl, because I didn't quite understand what was going on . . . but I didn't figure it out. I was too busy laughing, and buying clothes." Thinking back, she feels she may have subconsciously understood. "Then, though, I was only consciously aware that boy, he was good-looking, and I had a wonderful time. It was a real fling."

She was aware, of course, that Rock was married; that was "the bogus explanation" for why their fling went no further. Not until many years later did she "begin to get the message."

The months in Rome, however, remain a beautiful memory. "I played a secondary part in the movie, but as far as my experience in Rome, I was the leading lady. I felt like I was with a man when I was out with Rock Hudson, a lot more than some of the butch guys I've been out with. He made me feel very feminine, and he made me feel like a woman." Stritch and Rock were to stay in touch for the rest of his life.

Rock's next movie was *Twilight for the Gods*, to be filmed in Hawaii. It was a typical Universal potboiler, but Rock had no problem with it—after the two loan-outs (to MGM for *Something of Value* and to 20th Century–Fox for *A Farewell to Arms*), he felt he owed his studio something. Besides, at least he'd be working with familiar, journeymen moviemakers—he'd had enough of the Selznick genius type to last him quite a while.

The movie also marked a twilight for the Hudsons. Phyllis did visit Hawaii while Rock was on location there, at least briefly, but the marriage was obviously on its last legs. George Robotham, Rock's stunt man, recalled walking past the hotel with Rock and hearing Phyllis call him sharply from their room. Meekly, Rock left his friend and went back to his wife. Later Robotham told Jimmy Dobson about the incident; both men were shocked at this glimpse of the relationship. Rock had acted like a small boy caught sneaking out by his mother. The lesson was not lost on his friends: both of them realized the marriage was not fated to last.

Twilight for the Gods was written by Ernest K. Gann, the author of the very successful *The High and the Mighty*, in a studio attempt to repackage the same theme for the same results.

Joseph Pevney, for one, was leery. The plane in *The High and the Mighty* had a point of no return. How could a boat have a point of no return? "But I couldn't convince them of that," he said.

Universal had bought the property for Rock as a showcase, but Pevney thought it was exactly the wrong vehicle for him. The whole point was that the character had no future. He had nothing but an old tramp steamboat. Rock on the screen radiated youth, health, and energy. Who would believe this man had no future?

Someone like Humphrey Bogart could have filled the role perfectly. "Put a four-days' growth of beard on him, he's a ne'er-do-well. Put a four days' growth on Rock, and he was a romantic hero."

In fact, the point was moot. Though Pevney begged, the studio refused to let Rock appear on the screen with a four-days' growth. The best the director could get out of them was a reluctant agreement to allow their star to sport a one-day's growth, which was hardly noticeable. Rock, as an early makeup man had noted, was simply not very hairy.

"They just wanted Rock Hudson. They didn't give a damn what movie he was in. So long as they were selling Rock, they didn't care," said Pevney.

Production went smoothly, and everyone seemed to enjoy making the film. Rock, who'd always been a swimmer, now discovered he loved everything about boating.

At one point during the film, the director looked down from a cliff and saw Rock, along with several other members of the cast, swimming far below in a blue Hawaiian cove. He called and waved at them—and then suddenly noticed a manta ray—"it must've been thirty feet across, wing tip to wing tip, enormous thing"—swimming in, headed right toward his leading man.

"I screamed, 'Rock, get the hell out of the water.' Everyone laughed at me, said it wouldn't bother him. But I could just see Rock getting devoured by a manta ray and the picture is sunk, they send everyone home. Finally they cleared the beach."

The movie over, Rock returned to the mainland and

almost immediately broke off with Phyllis for good. He checked into the Beverly Hills Hotel on October 17, 1957—a fact that was reported by gossip columnist Sheilah Graham.

Phyllis Gates was awarded a reported cash settlement of $130,000 in the divorce that followed about a year later. She testified in court that her husband had once hit her and at times was "very sullen" and refused to speak for days. In addition, she revealed that Rock seldom took her out socially because he didn't like to wear a tie.

Eventually Rock moved to a place in Newport Beach. Phyllis stayed in the home he had bought, where she lives today. Never remarried, she leads a private life as an interior decorator. Rock paid alimony for many years.

"Rock's marriage was part of the whole mythmaking machinery that invented him," Armistead Maupin said. "There are plenty of gay stars who choose to get married and keep up a front, particularly when they are stars of Rock's caliber. But Rock didn't. He simply didn't have the patience for that kind of playacting. He felt that what he at least deserved after so many years of hard work in the business was to lead the life he chose to lead."

Rock rarely referred to his marriage in later years. "Not a great success," he said of it once. "Except the divorce, that is. In a sense it was a defeat, coming from a divorced family. I said it would never happen to me and it did. I felt somewhat of an outcast for a long time afterward."

"We were young, it was unfortunate, I lived through it. I think the only reason for marriage in today's world is having children," he said another time.

In Newport Beach, Rock became friends with a group of avid boaters—Tyrone Power and his third wife, Debbie; actress Claire Trevor and her husband, Milton Bren; and actor Kurt Kasznar among them. The Powers and the Brens took him out on their boats, fanning the sailing fever Rock had caught during his work on *Twilight for the Gods*. Finally he broke down and bought one of his own—a forty-foot ketch Rig Newporter exactly like Tyrone Power's ketch, *The Black Swan*.

"I'd been telling Ty and Debbie of a terrible movie I'd made with Piper Laurie" (probably *The Golden Blade*). "She was called Khairuzan, which means 'good fortune' in Arabian. Debbie suggested I use that name for my own ketch," he said.

Shortly after, the Powers invited him to dinner and a movie screening in their home. The movie they had picked was the same clunker Rock had mentioned to them.

Rock was very fond of Tyrone Power, whom he had viewed with awe in the days when he was a young contract player at the studio. "I don't know anybody who knew Ty who didn't love him. I don't just mean like him—love him. With all that magnetism, there was no self-centeredness and no conceit. Ty had great warmth. You knew he was a nice man, and that you could trust him. You knew if you told him a confidence that you wouldn't have to preface it by saying you didn't want it repeated.

"His only failing was his desire to please everybody. He never gave vent to anger." In many ways, Rock could have been talking about himself.

Recent years have brought rumors of Power's bisexuality, and with them, more recently, rumors that he and Rock may have had an affair. Power's last wife, Debbie, vigorously denied the possibility. It was a social relationship only, she said; Rock kept his private life to himself.

Power died quite suddenly of a heart attack in 1958, leaving his wife pregnant with his only son. Debbie Power reported that Rock was a great help to her in the following months, taking her out, showing up at the hospital several times after she gave birth to Tyrone Power IV. "Every time he came, the nurses made excuses to come into my room, just to see him." Rock, she said, was wonderful with the baby—"except that every time he picked him up, the baby would throw up on him."

The friendship was reported in the press as a new romance, but it wasn't. "It was a friendship, that's all," said Power. "He would try to encourage me to go out, so I wouldn't be depressed. It was a hard time for me."

Rock also became close to Claire Trevor and her husband. His friendship with Trevor was to last for life.

Trevor was an artist and a cultured woman, and through her, Rock began to learn something about the fine arts. A large portrait of Rock by Trevor—her surrealistic interpretation of his personality, he said—hung in the living room of his Newport home.

Claire's husband, Milton Bren, who owned a production company, helped to teach Rock how to sail and supervised his choice of boat.

In Newport, Rock also met Mary Anita Loos and her husband, Richard Sale. Loos was the niece of Anita Loos, author of *Gentlemen Prefer Blondes*, and a writer herself. Sale was a screenwriter and a director of light movies. He and Loos did eighteen movies together. When Mary Loos wrote the script for *Gentlemen Marry Brunettes*, the couple tried to get Rock to star in it, but he was busy with other projects.

"We knew Rock was homosexual," said Mary Loos. "It didn't seem to make any difference. It was just his personal preference."

Rock took his sailing seriously. He wasn't the type to moor up a yacht just for cocktail parties.

"We always used to sail over to the isthmus or to White's Cove and moor and fool around and visit," recalled Mary Loos. "Occasionally we'd sail around the bay to Cat Harbor, which Rock did too."

His new, single life pleased him greatly. "I have just had the best summer of my life, in Newport Beach with my boat and my house," he told Louella Parsons in October 1958. "I enjoy being alone. I am going to keep my house and my boat and live at Newport Beach all the year round." For the first time in nearly a decade, Rock was taking some time away from work to relax. The marriage had been an immense strain. "I'm certainly not planning another one for a few years," he told Parsons. "I like my freedom too much."

Rock's homosexual life escalated after the divorce. Friends recalled he had numerous lovers, some of whom were aspiring actors working at low-paying jobs, such as waiting tables in restaurants where Rock met them. Rock would often date two or three men at a time.

"He loved the intrigue of it," claimed an intimate of the time. "He was like a little boy—he loved games of all kinds."

During this period, Rock began to cruise gay bars openly. Gossip columnist Joyce Haber recalled that when she came to California around this time to work for *Time*, she did a piece on the Los Angeles and San Francisco gay scene and discovered that Rock was an habitué of the bars.

One gay friend remembers how Rock fell for an assistant cameraman at Universal. The cameraman was straight, but that did not deter Rock. He also did not mind waiting for his conquests. That was part of the game, too.

"The cameraman was muscular, but small—not like the big guys Rock usually picked out. He put out a campaign to get that boy that you wouldn't believe. And eventually he got him.

"They were lovers for several years. But the cameraman would never move in with Rock. That was one of the smartest things he ever did. It kept Rock interested."

Rock never cared much whether his lovers were nominally straight or gay.

"I can't tell you the number of supposedly straight guys who would go to bed with him," his friend recalled.

"The last time I saw Rock on a set in Europe he had four members of the crew in his hotel room with him," his friend recalled. "He called me into the room, and he had four of the best-looking studs you've ever seen. And Rock had been to bed with every one of them. And they were all just waiting around to see who was going to go to bed with him that night."

It was a happy, relaxed time for Rock—with the shackles of marriage dissolved, he was free to lead his own life any way he wanted, within the bounds of discretion. And the public was about to see a brand-new Rock Hudson on the screen—one they had never before visualized. Rock was about to make a jump into comedy.

The leap was not taken without qualms. Given the synopsis of what would eventually become *Pillow Talk*, Rock's reaction was quick and negative. "I said I really couldn't do the film," he recalled later. "It seemed to me dreadful." His opinion changed when he saw the script. The dialogue was polished and snappy. Rock began to be interested.

Followed by *Lover Come Back* and *Send Me No Flowers*, *Pillow Talk* was the first of three successful romantic comedies that linked Rock, Doris Day, and Tony Randall. The teaming was blissfully serendipitous. Garson Kanin, in his book *Together Again: The Story of the Great Hollywood Teams*, ranked Rock and Doris right up there with Spencer Tracy and Katharine Hepburn. The comedies, he wrote with high enthusiasm, were "intelligently crafted, sophisticatedly conceived and brilliantly produced. . . . Neither he nor she ever achieved again the charm or personality or interplay or magnetism they created when they played so beautifully together."

The comedies were a great hit with the public, and *Pillow Talk* was the biggest smash of all.

Producer Ross Hunter claimed most of the credit for tapping Rock for the role of the roué who shares a party-line feud with Doris Day, then woos and wins her in the guise of a visiting Texan. "I never could see him on a horse," he cracked. "He's just too big for those poor horses. Rock is certainly one of the screen's most handsome men and blessed with lots of charm. He belongs in a drawing room, not a cornfield."

"He did have serious misgivings at first, because he had never attempted comedy before," said Michael Gordon, who directed *Pillow Talk*. "He felt one had to be a comedian to play comedy." Gordon was able to convince him that the best way to play a genuine comedy was to do it with complete seriousness. "No matter how absurd the situations may appear to the viewer, to the people involved, it's a matter of life and death. Comedy is no laughing matter."

With that in mind, along with Gordon's assurance that he didn't expect Rock to have "all of the so-called schtick comedians are supposed to have at their command," Rock agreed to take on the part. Even in their preliminary conversations, Gordon had recognized Rock's sense of humor, and felt he would be good in the role.

None of the three leads had ever worked together before, but they hit it off instantly. "We all seemed to be crazy about each other on the set," said Tony Randall. Rock and Doris, whom he named "Eunice," for reasons that are unclear, developed an ongoing bit in which they would regale each other with stories of the summer houses they were building in obscure towns. "They knew the names of all these terrible little towns, and they would claim they were going to build summer houses there, and visit each other. He'd say, 'Oh, the view from L——— is astounding,' naming someplace no one had ever been to, just dreary beyond belief. They kept that going for months," said Randall.

Over the course of making three movies together, the camaraderie between the three grew, although they rarely socialized away from the set. Doris Day was married to Marty Melcher then, an overbearing type who, it was revealed after his death, was busy systematically using up all her money; Randall spent as little time in Los Angeles as he could, taking the plane back to New York as soon as he finished a job. Randall remembered well the three of them watching the rushes of one romantic scene in *Lover Come Back* in which Doris and Rock are in bathing suits, on the beach. "This is a scene you'll never see. There was one take, where he leaned over—and one ball came out of his trunks. And then went back in. We said, 'Hey, play that again.' We were just shrieking and screaming. It nearly got into the picture. It happened so quickly—out and in." The projectionist was forced to replay the footage several times before the hysteria died down.

Randall knew that Rock had never acted in a comedy before. "He wasn't bursting with confidence. Ever. He didn't have the greatest confidence in his own ability. I always felt the reason was he'd become a star too fast and got so many bad notices. I think he really believed he wasn't such a great actor. And probably in the beginning it was true. But he had become damn good. Damn good. You saw how good he was in *Pillow Talk*. He was so funny."

Generally, most scenes in a movie are shot in four or five takes at the most. But at least once on any picture, there will be one scene that requires take after take—ten, twenty, even more. "When that happened, Rock lost his confidence completely," said Randall. "He'd get worse and keep blowing."

Rock had told his co-actors that early in his career, when he was scared to death and had no idea what he was doing, he would stand there—and his upper lip would begin to curl. He would try to keep it from happening, but he couldn't. Now whenever Rock began to blow a scene, Randall would carefully watch his lip for signs of curling. When it happened, he'd crack up. "I don't think it helped him much," he said.

Others had noticed Rock's lips before. When he smiled, one corner of his mouth would turn down, as if in sadness. A complex reaction from the man many dismissed as just a big, good-hearted lug. No happiness without a downward tug, a small mark of sorrow.

"It also had that irony of comedy-tragedy, and he was adept at playing both things, of course," said Jimmy Dobson. "He had no control of his smile. When I'd bring it up, he would say, 'You're full of shit.' He knew it existed. There was no way to lose it."

Randall and Rock spent hours chatting during the movies they made together. Randall, whose sense of the absurd is famous, fully appreciated Rock's humor. One story Rock told still rendered Randall hysterical over twenty-five years later.

Rock (he told Randall) had spent a long day on the set plagued by stomach problems of a familiar sort. The day drew to a close and he jumped into his car, windows closed—and let go. Randall put it delicately: "Apparently it was an enormous release of gas. A thirty-seconder, he called it." Rock then drove his car across the studio grounds to where the rushes were being shown and opened the door.

It wasn't until then that he saw the girl who was in the backseat, crouching low. Just a starlet who had a yearning desire to meet her hero. "I'll never do that again," she told him with complete sincerity.

Few stars could tell such a story on themselves. "He was anything but a self-server," said Randall.

Randall and Rock also appreciated odd situations when they occurred. At one point both actors were preparing for a car shoot—not in an actual car, of course. Both had overcoats on, and the coats and the lights and the closed set made it unbearably hot; they were sweating intensely. Rock held his hands in front of him: one was dry, one sopping wet. "It's the most peculiar thing," he said. "My left hand doesn't sweat."

At this point a crew member leaned into the cardboard car and confided, "I always sweat under my eyes when I eat salad."

"Rock fell out of the set, just doubled up," said Randall. "Such an odd thing to say."

Pillow Talk broke box-office records across the country. "It was the biggest money-maker they'd ever had, except for *The Glen Miller Story*," said Randall. "I think it grossed something like twelve million dollars domestically. That would be like a hundred million dollars today."

Seen now, the film is still charming, though dated. "I have two daughters, both feminists," said Michael Gordon. "I have certain misgivings about it. It stemmed out of a certain male-chauvinist view. An amusing picture, though, no question." It was definitely of its period, 1959, long before the waves of Women's Liberation hit the shore—and yet Doris Day has a successful, respectable job as an interior decorator and seems to have a mind of her own. *Pillow Talk* is a simple, romantic comedy, which may be what dates it most of all.

"It was a happy set," Gordon remembered. "The film had one of the things very characteristic of all of Ross Hunter's productions: a certain sense of elegance and style. It was something of a stamp, his particular hallmark. The sort of taste characteristic of all his work."

Gordon was offered the chance to direct the next Doris Day–Rock Hudson comedy, *Lover Come Back*, but turned it down. "It seemed so similar, I thought people would think they're just repeating themselves." People did, and loved it all the more. "The reception was very good, to my chagrin. I didn't want to repeat myself, but that was . . . an irrelevant consideration."

CHAPTER THREE
Friends

For the most part, critics liked *Pillow Talk*. Rock was not Cary Grant, they were quick to point out, but nonetheless, he seemed capable of displaying a distinct comedic touch. Few of them hid their amazement that Rock, Universal's "Beefcake Baron," not only had a sense of humor, but could use it to poke sly fun at his own image. Everyone knew Rock had played a Texan in *Giant*, and here he was playing it again, but for laughs.

What the critics liked, the audiences loved, and Universal responded to their approval with knee-jerk consistency. The success of *Magnificent Obsession* had resulted in a long string of romantic-hero roles for Rock throughout the fifties. *Pillow Talk*'s acclaim meant that for much of the sixties he did nothing but comedy. For a while, Rock enjoyed it. As time went on and the comedies got worse, he began to find this form of lightweight typecasting as much of a hindrance as the earlier mold had been. Unfortunately, his new image was to have even greater staying power. Long after he had left Universal and moved into television, this was the image that would stick.

"It's difficult," Robert Stack reflected, "to live in the image of what the studio wants, what you think the world wants you to be. You learn quickly, too, that even though you might want to do something different as an actor, you may not be able to. Clint Eastwood likes to sing, for instance. He made *Paint Your Wagon*. But no one wanted to see him paint his wagon; they wanted to see him make my day. No one wants to see Stallone do *Rhinestone*; they want to see him go out and beat the bejesus out of all the people in Hanoi. I don't make any money smiling—I've got to be there with that machine gun. You learn that."

Rock did enjoy his roles in the first two Doris Day comedies, though. "They were both playable roles," he said. "The advertising man in *Lover Come Back*, like the composer in *Pillow Talk*, was a ne'er-do-well. And playing a ne'er-do-well is terrific. You automatically like a ne'er-do-well, don't you? I guess it's because it's what we all wish we were, but don't have the guts to be."

He drew the line at the third, though. "Right from the start I hated that script," he said of *Send Me No Flowers*. "I just didn't believe in that man for one minute." The leading character is a devout hypochondriac who becomes convinced he is going to die. Rock found the jokes about bad health and death in terrible taste.

"Making fun of death is difficult and dangerous," he said. At one point in the movie, Rock buys a cemetery plot for himself, his wife, and her next husband; he found the scene "completely distasteful."

"My kind of laugh comes from the Marx Brothers. Or Wheeler and Woolsey. And Harold Lloyd."

Rock was still living in Newport Beach when *Pillow Talk* was released. Despite the sudden rise in his stock as an actor, he swore that he would never go back to the all-work-no-play syndrome of his early years in the industry.

"Whatever happens, I'll never give up my boat. In this business of ulcers and heart attacks, all that I need is a boat. I can be nervous and upset and beside myself with anxiety and go out on the boat and nothing else matters but the wind and the water. It's great," he said in 1960. Within two years he had sold it. He was too busy to make any use of it. For the rest of his life he missed it, but something was happening that meant more to him than any boat. For the first time in his career, Rock Hudson was beginning to make real money.

In 1960, not long after *Pillow Talk*'s release, Rock, along with Henry Willson, formed his own production company, eventually known as Gibraltar Productions. Now he could own a part of the movies he worked in, and thus be able to make a real profit. Until this point in his career, no matter how well he had been paid, his earnings consisted of salary only.

Rock made no pretense of how he felt about money; he had spent too much time in his childhood without it. "I love it—all I can get," he said. "I've always had to work as a kid, like for thirty-five cents an hour, doing odd jobs. Money is something you need to get along with, that's for sure. If you have it, great. If you haven't, you should figure out a way to get it." A lot of people liked to say it wasn't important to them, he added, but how many of those people were poor?

Often people would notice an odd discrepancy in Rock's dealings with money. Tales of his generosity are legion. When a producer he barely knew, a neighbor, had a fire in his house, Rock insisted the man use his own house until he could rebuild. The man, Alan Shane, of Warner Brothers, stayed there for six months. When Tony Randall, a good friend of Shane, tried to thank him, Rock shrugged it off. "Wouldn't you do it?" he asked.

With his own friends, his generosity could reach extravagant proportions. When a fire destroyed Jimmy Dobson's house, Rock bought him a stove, washer and dryer, and dishwasher, and gave him a fountain he had found in Rome. An old friend of Rock, Emily Torchia, a publicist, heard from him shortly after her mother died. Rock, who was in Europe, insisted on sending Torchia a ticket to Paris so he could console her in person. His presents to friends were always thoughtful and handpicked. "I used to tell him, 'Your mother must have raised you right,'" said Pete Saldutti, his costume designer.

Yet despite this generosity, Rock could often display tightness in small, unexpected ways. A friend who had served the star gourmet dinners for over a year looked forward to the day when Rock took him out to return the favor. To his dismay, they dined at a cheap Mexican restaurant. In the late seventies, working with him on a made-for-TV series, director Lou Antonio tried to prod

Rock into buying drinks for the crew at least once during the production; it was the expected thing, he told him. Rock preferred to skip it. "He tended to be tight about little things," Antonio said.

It was a split in his personality that was reflected in other ways as well. Causes, for instance, held little interest for Rock. He was all but apolitical, declaring once that even his mother didn't know whether he was a Democrat or Republican. The plight of various groups, en masse, moved him very little. He could even at times display a callousness shocking to friends who had come of age in the consciousness-raising sixties. Yet personal hardship—the problems of people he knew—invariably affected him deeply. When Dobson's house burned down, he actually cried. "He knew how much it meant to me," said his friend. When a young woman neighbor who lived near him in Newport died suddenly, leaving her children orphaned, Rock went to a great deal of trouble trying to find out if there was any possibility he could adopt them. (There wasn't—adoptions by single men were frowned on twenty years ago.) Casual about his own physical well-being, he had a deep empathy for people and animals in pain. One friend reported that Rock warned him not to set any rat traps around his house. "I did it, and one day I found a bird caught in a trap," Rock said. "I released it, but then I saw it had a broken leg." The bird flew away, so there was nothing he could do. "But I know the bird could never land." And his eyes filled with tears.

In the early sixties, with his new production company, Rock finally began to make money in earnest. His next two movies—*Come September*, a comedy with Gina Lollobrigida, and *Lover Come Back*—were made by Universal in cooperation with his production company. From *Lover Come Back* alone, he received a reported million-dollar share of the profits. With part of his new largesse, he bought the sprawling Spanish mansion high in Beverly Hills that he would then live in for the rest of his life. It was so big, rambling, and private that friends instantly dubbed it the "Castle." The name stuck. Rather than selling the house on the beach, he gave it to his mother and her husband, Joe Olsen.

Rock had a deep attachment to the new house in the hills. It was to be his hobby and haven, the place where he was happiest. A magnificent, secluded two-story Mexican hacienda, it came replete with balconies, fireplaces, patio, and swimming pool. Eventually Rock had a small movie theater built on the grounds, so he could screen movies. There was plenty of room for friends, visitors, and dogs to roam. Rock had never been allowed to have a dog as a young boy. After moving to the Castle, he rarely had fewer than three or four—nearly always mutts. "They were his babies," said Gloria Matteoni.

Rock's Castle was the ultimate movie star's house, closed in by white walls and accessible only by a pair of electrically controlled black iron gates. The grounds were bright and cheerful, covered with exotic plantings. Rock soon became an avid gardener. "It's the only time I have to really do any thinking," he said once. "When you're working, all you're doing is learning lines. So I evaluate my friends and wonder if they mean as much to me as I think. Do I like them or don't I?"

The house had a huge courtyard that flowed out to a spectacular swimming pool. It was a perfect setup for the kind of informal entertaining Rock loved to do. In the late seventies, Rock became a patron of an artist who sculpted whimsical statues—black, somewhat abstract—of nude young boys. He bought several of the figures and set them up in the courtyard. In one corner a stone youth was frozen in the act of throwing a smaller boy into the pool. Another statue was attached to the wall of the estate, peering out at the world. Visitors to the house were often taken aback by the statuary, which was undoubtedly the point.

The interior of the Castle was cool, dark, comfortable, and very masculine. It was the sort of place, his makeup artist and friend Mark Reedall said, where you could feel at home in jeans or a sports jacket. The furniture was massive and of dark wood. On the walls hung Mexican shields, swords, tapestries, even an African spear—all legacies of his various trips to different parts of the world. There were a number of books in the library, too, although Rock was the first to admit he was no reader.

The house had two living rooms, one decorated Spanish-style, with Claire Trevor's large surrealistic study prominently featured. The main living room held a black mahogany grand piano. Chairs sat on zebra skins.

Rock's bedroom upstairs was enormous, sixty by seventy feet. He slept in a giant-sized custom-made four-poster bed. Paintings of old ships and faded photos of the boat he had given up hung on the walls. French chairs upholstered in black leather were placed around the room. The shower of his private bathroom had windows; the floor of the room was set with Mexican tiles. In his dressing room was a sculpture of a four-foot-tall ninety-eight-pound lady blacksmith, picked up in one of his antiquing forays.

"You can only look and describe," Rock once warned a reporter. "You will never shoot pictures inside." The Castle was his private sanctum and he guarded it zealously. He continued to add to and improve it for the rest of his life. In the end, one of his last requests was that he be allowed to leave the hospital to spend his final days in the place he loved best.

It was sometime during this very lucrative period of his life that Rock chose to make a major change: he broke off with Henry Willson. No one knows the exact reason for the break; quite possibly it was caused by an accumulation of problems. Willson, according to some reports, had become increasingly greedy over the years and had not always played fair with his most important client.

Rock never displayed the slightest interest in handling his own business affairs. As much as he enjoyed having money, Rock, like many performers, preferred to leave the financial paperwork to others. Over the years several men acted for him in this capacity—Willson, Tom Clark, Mark Miller among them. Unfortunately, the more successful one is, the more risky it is to delegate responsibility in this area.

"There was a time when Rock was the biggest star at Universal. They wanted to renew his contract, and he didn't want it renewed. But Henry renewed it without his permission. He talked Rock into it," said Jimmy Dobson. "Rock could be easily manipulated—and I think Henry definitely did manipulate him. It's my personal opinion that in this case he got paid additional money under the table. Henry was responsible for Rock's career, but later on he did just go money-crazy and was thinking of the money rather than Rock's good. Rock was too busy trying to improve himself as a performer to be worried about details like this, and this is one of the reasons why he was so easily manipulated." The situation, said Dobson, was not precisely analogous to the Elvis Presley–Tom Parker relationship, but neither was it too far removed.

There had been many earlier indications that Rock was growing irritated with Willson—he had spoken to Pevney about his concerns ten years before. The problems had been smoothed over each time, and the relationship continued. As late as 1958 Rock told an interviewer that he still had dinner with Willson several times a week and spoke with him on the phone every day.

There is nothing unusual in a star dropping an agent; it is more unusual to stay with the same one for so many years. But whatever the truth is about Willson and Rock's relationship, it was a friendship as well as a business partnership, and the ending was a bitter one.

"Henry was destroyed that Rock had turned his back on him," said one fan-magazine editor. "During Rock's lean years Henry had loaned and advanced him money. Henry was upset because Rock not only dropped him as an agent but rejected him as a friend. He was ill for a long time and didn't have any money. He knew Rock could have helped him, but he didn't."

After severing relations, Rock never spoke to Willson again. The agent drifted out of sight, into alcoholism, and died, impoverished, at the Motion Picture Home. Few people attended his funeral, and Rock was not one of them.

"What is it ends with friends?" wrote poet William Ernest Henley of his own friendship with Robert Louis Stevenson. Rock, say those who knew him, was the most loyal friend a person could have; his friendship was good for life. And yet, with two of the most important people in his life—Henry Willson and, much later, Tom Clark—he eventually severed the relationship permanently in a remarkably cold, unforgiving way. While the relationships were very different, they had some similarities. Both relationships were long-term, lasting twelve to fifteen years. In both, there were business as well as personal ties. And in both cases, although Willson was older than Rock and Clark was not, the men functioned in many ways—indeed, Rock required them to function—as father figures.

In 1965 Rock Hudson made a decision that had a lasting effect on his professional life: he took on a movie role that was the most difficult, exhausting, and challenging he had ever played. In the years since *Pillow Talk*, Rock had made ten films, most of them romantic comedies. This was his most important attempt to throw off the bonds of his industry-created image and to forge a new career for himself as an actor.

Rock had every reason to hold great hopes for the project. He was to be under the guidance of one of the best directors he had ever worked with, John Frankenheimer, and involved with probably the finest cast of actors he was ever to have around him, most of them with solid New York (as opposed to Hollywood) reputations: John Randolph, Salome Jens, Will Geer, and Jeff Corey among them. The screenplay was written by a rising young playwright, Lewis John Carlino; the cameraman was the almost mythically revered James Wong Howe, who would be taking particular care since the film would be his swan song. Rock opened himself up in a way he never had before; he delivered what many would later say was the most memorable performance of his career. Never again did he come so close to achieving true stature on the screen.

The film was *Seconds*, and it was a total box-office failure.

Rock rarely spoke about *Seconds*. He continued to work steadily, making a dozen more movies over the next twenty years, starring in a popular long-running television series, and appearing in three stage musicals; but with the failure of *Seconds*, something went out of his life—the hope that he would ever be taken seriously as a dramatic actor on the movie screen.

Salome Jens, who starred opposite him in the movie, sensed the loss years later when she ran into him on the set of "McMillan and Wife." She described their reunion:

"When he saw me, he gave me this huge wonderful hug—and I saw in that moment that there was a dream that was lost somewhere. There was something—I'm not trying to be romantic about this—something he had sold out. Something he had missed. A chance he had lost."

Today, those who worked on *Seconds* offer various reasons for its dismal failure at the box office, but the root of the problem was undoubtedly the film's unremittingly bleak view of life. Twenty years ago viewers were just not ready for a Hollywood movie that offered a stark portrayal of alienation, horror, and grim hopelessness. And the shock of seeing the popular Rock Hudson, whose *Pillow Talk* era was only a few years behind him, starring in such a film must have been more than they could take. "I have a theory," said Frankenheimer. "Those people who would go see Rock Hudson movies didn't want to see that one, and people who wanted to see that kind of movie didn't want to see a Rock Hudson movie."

The movie, based on David Ely's science-fiction novel of the same name, dealt with a corporation in the business of giving those who could afford it a second chance at life. A banker, played by John Randolph—middle-aged, married, mired in grim routine—is given a chance, via plastic surgery, to begin anew, in another town, with another face (Rock Hudson's).

Of course, it doesn't work. The alienation remains the same; the man's feelings of failure and his inability to deal with life are only intensified behind his new face. Tension mounts, and finally during a party at his new beachfront house, he becomes increasingly drunk and reckless. His identity blurs; he rants wildly of his former life. Suddenly he is surrounded by the other guests—all remade by the company, all launched on their second lives, he now realizes. He escapes to make a visit to his wife, posing as a friend of her husband. She paints a grim picture of their marriage: "The silences between us grew longer and longer." There is no past, no present, no future. Leaving her, he is caught and brought back to the company—where he is ultimately disposed of.

Even today, with the popularity of science-fiction films, such a movie might have trouble at the box office. This was no *E.T.* or *Halloween III*—it was science fiction that cut close to the bone. The writer had based it on reality—the fact that yearly, according to statistics of that time, eighty thousand middle-aged men left their homes and families, never to reappear.

Carlino took a friend to see *Seconds*. "About halfway through the film, I looked over and he was gone. I found him pacing up and down in the lobby. He said, 'Please, don't do me any favors. This is my life. I don't need to come to the movies to see this.'" In that moment, Carlino realized that "the film was not very pleasant to see."

If it was uncomfortable for others, for Rock Hudson, a man who had been manufactured by the industry, a homosexual packaged and sold to the world as a heterosexual, it must have held even deeper pain. To Frankenheimer the parallels between Rock and his character in the movie were almost too obvious to mention. "We discussed everything, but we didn't have to talk about that. I knew about it, he knew about it, you never like to talk about obvious things. He obviously identified a great deal with the part. He said so."

Rock was not Frankenheimer's first choice for the film. According to John Randolph, the rights to the movie were originally owned by Kirk Douglas, who saw a sure Oscar nomination if he were to play both parts. When Douglas was unable to do it because of prior commitments, Paramount took over.

Frankenheimer and his producer partner, Ed Lewis, felt there was only one man in the profession who could handle both the "before" and "after" roles—Laurence Olivier. They flew to England and were able to convince the actor to take the part, but when they came back home, Paramount refused to give him the job. They wanted a bigger box-office draw.

At this point, John Foreman, the producer, then an agent and friend of both Frankenheimer and Rock, suggested to the director that the star might be interested.

"I didn't think the idea was very good," Frankenheimer admitted. "Except Rock at that time was the biggest star in the United States." He met with Rock, who was indeed interested in the role. Rock said he knew he could never play the "before" role, only the "after." Frankenheimer had never thought of casting the part with two actors, but after discussing it with Ed Lewis, decided it could be done. At least this way Paramount would have the sort of leading man they were looking for.

Frankenheimer wanted to be very careful about the "before" role. He had several priorities: he wanted a good actor, the best he could get; he wanted a man whose face was unknown to the general public; and he wanted a man whose face looked enough like Rock's so that the public would at least tentatively accept the premise that plastic surgery could turn one into the other. He was able to get everything he wanted in one actor, fifty-year-old John Randolph.

Twenty years later Randolph's memory is very clear on the subject of *Seconds*, and with good reason. It was to be his first movie in a very long time. A "cheerfully hostile witness" before the House Un-American Activities Committee, he had refused to sign loyalty papers. Consequently, Randolph had been blacklisted from Hollywood for nearly fifteen years. Once a frequent player in movies and early television, he had been forced to move his family to New York. There he was at least able to ply his craft on Broadway. It had been a long, agonizing time.

Randolph had known Frankenheimer for years and respected him. "He had always said to me, 'We young directors hate the blacklisting. One day, you'll work, John.'" But Randolph had come close to losing hope. Every time he was called for a job, suddenly, mysteriously, it would vanish.

This time was to be different. Frankenheimer called Randolph to what the actor thought would be an audition in a New York hotel. It wasn't. When Randolph came into the suite, he saw Frankenheimer sitting with several Paramount executives. The director introduced him, grinning expansively. "I think John would be wonderful in this part," he said enthusiastically. "He knows the agony of the man, because he had to go through the kind of crap you people put him through during the blacklisting."

Randolph grimaced. There went another job, he thought. But he was wrong.

"They just smiled. Because John had done *The Manchurian Candidate,* and he had done *Seven Days in May,* and they were making money. And it was my first indication of Hollywood: if the guy makes money, everything's fine, no matter what he does."

Randolph was aware of just how important the job was to him; it was his big chance back in, after fifteen years out in the cold. "I worked for less money than certainly any other actor in the entire picture, but my agent said, 'Jesus, it's a step in. We don't care about the money.'"

Two other actors hired for the film, Will Geer and Jeff Corey, had also been off the scene. Frankenheimer was determined to get the best talent possible, and as a successful fair-haired boy of the moment, he was allowed to.

It had not been Randolph's acting talent alone that had won him the role, he later found out. Even more important was something he hadn't even known he possessed—a facial resemblance to Rock Hudson. Frankenheimer had enlisted the help of a plastic surgeon to make his choice, giving him a number of pictures of actors to choose from. "He said my eyes were the important thing. That my eyes were like Rock's, the same color. He also said we had basically the same almost oval faces. He showed John what he would do on my face to conform to Rock's face."

Once Randolph had been hired, Frankenheimer took him aside. "Look," he said. "You are the actor. Rock is very good, but I don't know very much about him. I know he did one good serious role in *Giant.* But the aspects of this role are quite demanding. I want you to study him. Certain mannerisms creep into people that no plastic surgery can hide. Study him and make notes."

Randolph realized that Frankenheimer needed him to become as much like Rock as he could in the first half of the picture, so the two portrayals could blend into one.

So he studied Rock—the way he sat, the way he wrote, the way he smoked. Randolph had recently managed to stop smoking, but had to take it up again. He learned to hold a cigarette in his left hand, between the middle and ring fingers, the way Rock did.

He also had to learn how to stand and sit as a very tall man—although Randolph was six feet, Rock was four inches taller. At first, the director and cameraman experimented with lifts in his shoes. Finally, they decided to surround Randolph with smaller-than-average people in his sequences, so his height would appear more like Rock's. Randolph learned to lean on a mantel the way Rock did, to lower himself carefully into chairs. Most chairs are not made for tall men, he noticed.

Randolph watched Rock carefully during the rehearsal period. Rock was not around during the first four weeks of shooting the film. It had been decided that neither should be on the set while the other was working; it would be too confusing. But Randolph later discovered that Rock was watching the rushes every day and making notes on his— Randolph's—performance. Randolph was impressed. "It was not just a one-way street. He was observing me, too. He was approaching it seriously." The man wanted to be an actor, not just a movie star.

Rock told Randolph how important the role in *Seconds* was to him. He had tried to do a serious job in *Giant*, but no one had given him an important dramatic role as a result. He knew he could handle comedy, but it wasn't enough—after a while he was just marking time, doing the same thing over and over.

"I'm going to have to grow," he told Randolph. "This is my attempt to change the image. So I can move forward."

Salome Jens, who played the young woman Hudson meets in his new life, was a respected New York actress. She had known John Frankenheimer from New York but had never met Rock. She was one of six who tested for the role.

During rehearsal—a luxury on a movie set, and one

that Frankenheimer demanded for this movie—Jens got to know Rock. It became clear why this role was so important to him.

"My impression was that he was very dissatisfied with the roles he was being offered. This was an opportunity for him to act, act in a way no one had ever seen him.

"Had the film been successful, I think people would have seen that he had really grown through the years and really knew something about what was going on in that film. It was probably one of the finest acting jobs he has ever done. He was really clear that he wanted to grow and challenge himself. He hoped there would be a new kind of recognition of his talents . . . a newer understanding of what he was capable of being cast in. So it was unfortunate . . . it was a film before its time. It was not a successful film, and as a consequence, both his career and my career got put on a back burner for a bit."

Rock does not even appear in the movie for the first forty-five minutes—and yet the role demanded more of him than had any other in his career. Certainly no other role had ever been as tough on him emotionally.

One memorable portion of the film was the wine-festival scene, in which hundreds of celebrants join together in a bacchanalian rite, naked, stomping grapes in a giant vat. The sequence was shot at an annual festival, which Carlino's research had discovered in the mountains of Santa Barbara. The point, for the purpose of the movie, was to show the liberation of the new man, who is pulled into the vat by Jens and the others.

"I think he had a very bad time, when he was thrown into that tub," said Carlino. "The word I got was that he had freaked out. The people there weren't actors—they actually did this festival every year, as part of their celebration, and they weren't about to tailor this thing to the director's needs. They did it as they did it.

"They pulled Rock into this thing—he struggled—at one point they pushed him underneath the grapes, and he really panicked. Things just got out of hand. Part of the panic you see in that film is very real."

The scene as shot called for nudity—full frontal nudity—from the actors, although these shots were later edited out before the film was released. Salome Jens was not keen on doing a nude scene but finally agreed, telling Frankenheimer he had one shot and that was it.

Jens remembered the grape-stomping well. "The other people at the festival weren't actors, and therefore didn't know what to do, and it was dull as dishwater what they were doing. But Rock was absolutely there for me. He just said, 'Whatever you want, girl, you've got it.' It was great and it worked. In that instance, I think John has us to thank for it."

Randolph felt that the choice to edit out the nudity had a particularly bad effect on the film's reception when it was shown at the Cannes Film Festival later that year. "It was supposed to show the liberation of the new man. It was complete and total and uninhibited, and that's the way it should have been. When they edited it, you just saw them jumping in and barely caught a glimpse of bare skin—and it looked childish to the French. They laughed at it, and that took away from the second part of the film."

Whether or not the wine-vat scene caused Rock any traumatic moments, it is certain that another scene did— the final scene, one of the most chilling in the movie. Rock, struggling desperately on a gurney, is wheeled into surgery for "the final stage"—which he realizes means his death.

"His struggles on that table were very, very real," said Carlino. "Very real dread. Of course there were parallels with his own life—because the banker was a projected image of his culture, as Rock was. I think a lot of what John touched in him was part of his own frustration."

Rock's makeup man, Mark Reedall, present on the set the day Rock filmed that sequence, remembered it well. In his struggles, Rock, fighting with all his strength, actually managed to snap the straps of the gurney—a very difficult thing to do under ordinary circumstances.

But the scene that cut closest to the bone for Rock was unquestionably the drunk scene, in which Rock, as the new man, falls apart. It is a harrowing scene—a man crying out for the right to his own identity. Even Rock, who despised introspection and self-analysis, had to realize when doing the scene how dangerously close he was coming to acknowledging the deepest problems of his own life. Rock broke down completely doing this scene.

Frankenheimer was determined that the scene be as realistic as possible. He wanted Rock exhausted—and he wanted Rock actually drunk. What he got was more than he bargained for.

In trying to do the scene drunk, Rock began to lose control. The character's unbearable pain became his own; the veneer between make-believe and reality cracked completely. He broke down totally, unable to continue. The filming had to stop.

"A lot of really traumatic feelings began to surface at that time," said Jens, who was there and was furious with Frankenheimer for having helped bring on the breakdown. "I'm sure it was also because of what came up in the film and what he was dealing with as an actor. I was aware there was in him a great deal of pain. . . . There was a part of Rock that was very private, a part that was very sad, that he felt incomplete about.

"And when that thing became unloosed, he broke down completely—he could not stop," said Jens. "Whatever got released, it was an avalanche."

Frankenheimer realized the filming could not continue. He gave the signal to stop shooting. He knelt beside Rock, who was sobbing on the floor, put his arms around him, and held him, trying to soothe him, but the actor could not regain control. The rest of the cast and crew finally left. The director spent the rest of the night on the floor with the star, holding him and rocking him for hours, trying to comfort him, while Rock sobbed out his fear and pain. Frankenheimer held the grown man in his arms, the way a father holds a fearful little boy—the way no father had ever held Rock.

Frankenheimer today does not want to discuss that night, except to confirm that it did occur. On the relationship between acted and real emotions, he was terse. "What's real and what isn't with an actor? I don't know. Acting is reality in imaginary circumstances."

"He [Frankenheimer] was rather amazed at what had happened to Rock," said Jens. "But . . . what you realized was that Rock was a human being. And that he had a lot of pain. It's not easy being a star. You pay an enormous price for success. When you're a star, you've got more to lose. It's scarier."

It had been a mistake to try the scene with Rock truly drunk, Jens felt. The scene as it was finally shot the next day, with Rock sober, is unquestionably one of the best he ever did in his life.

Jens was aware of some of the causes of Rock's breakdown that night. "Rock had . . . an inability to have the confidence that he could be who he was with other people. Having to cover his homosexuality all the time must have been very hard on him. The industry people knew, yes, but the ordinary people didn't.

"Lies are the one thing we can't handle. And he was lying. And it drove him nuts. He was an alcoholic, too, and couldn't stop. He was one then. I'm one myself, with five years on the program, so I know something about it. He was always controlling, as I was. Neither of us ever got fired from a job, or landed in the gutter. But Rock could not stop after one drink, and that was the way he handled his pain."

And yet, said Jens, "I think it was a happy life, even so. He did lots of wonderful things. He was a person that brought joy and happiness with him. . . . I think it was something he was able to create, wherever he went.

"He loved to work—in some ways, work saved his life."

In the industry, "we all knew about his homosexuality, and loved him. It was so wonderful to have a friend that went beyond sex! And I must say, those love scenes really worked for me. I never had any sense that he wasn't loving me. He loved women—there was never any anti-woman feeling in him."

What she remembered most about working with Rock is "his incredible generosity. He was truly a star, in the sense that he was never threatened by anyone else."

Shooting *Seconds* was not all *Sturm und Drang*. Very few movies can be completed without spawning at least one after-dinner anecdote, and *Seconds* was no exception. Frankenheimer remembered it.

Rock was never the sort of star to pull his weight. He seldom asked for favors. When he did, naturally the inclination was to grant them. Pete Saldutti, Rock's costume-designer buddy, had asked Rock if he could find a small part for his girl friend in the film. Rock took the request to Frankenheimer. There was a tiny part for a stewardess in an airline scene, involving eight words—"Pillow, Mr. Wilson?" and "You all right, Mr. Wilson?" Would Frankenheimer mind very much if Saldutti's girl friend did it? It seemed a minor request, and the director agreed readily.

Cameraman James Wong Howe, a perfectionist, had insisted the short scene be shot on an actual plane in flight. Arrangements had been made for cast and crew to take a short flight. "It was only a very simple scene. We figured we'd go up around San Francisco, turn around, and come back," said Frankenheimer.

But the girl froze. "She absolutely panicked. She never could get the line out. We made four trips, from L.A. to Seattle, back to San Diego, back to Seattle—we were in the air all day. We practically had to land for fuel. It took hours. Rock was dying because it was his idea. Unbelievable—the hardest thing in the movie. We finally had to loop it" (replace the dialogue).

John Randolph has another memory of the movie, a sour one, but important too for what it tells about the world Rock Hudson lived in all his life.

Randolph had done the first four weeks of shooting, and his mood was more ebullient than it had been in years. He insisted that his wife join him in Los Angeles to meet the people with whom he had been working. "I told her how wonderful everyone was. I had my own trailer, my own dressing room with my goddamn name on it. Everything was exciting."

When Sarah Randolph came to the set, her husband was eager to introduce her to the director, the cameraman, and crew. To his surprise and embarrassment, every one of them was brusque, even rude, brushing the couple off. "I don't think they're as nice as you said, John," his wife told him. "I think they're phonies." Randolph returned to New York somewhat chastened.

Five weeks later he flew to Los Angeles again, for final shooting, and Frankenheimer called him into his room for a private chat. "He said, 'I want to talk to you before you hear it from anyone else.' And my heart fell. I thought, Here it goes, the same old blacklisting shit. After all this."

But what Frankenheimer had to tell him was something even Randolph could never have imagined, with all his experience. The day Randolph had brought his wife to the set, director, cast, and crew had been very busy—they were screen-testing Rock for Randolph's role in the movie. Someone, said the director, had obviously realized there'd be an Academy Award in it for Rock if he could do both the "before" and "after" roles.

"It had cost millions to do the shoot with me," said Randolph. "And yet they were ready to go back and do the whole thing over again. Frankenheimer said that on the day I had brought my wife to the set, they were making up Rock to look like me—so that's why they had all been so nervous, seeing me."

As it turned out, Rock couldn't do Randolph's part, and so the whole idea was dropped.

"I can understand it as a mature person, but I can tell you this: if it had happened, I would have blown up Hollywood."

Randolph's shock was still reverberating over twenty years later. To have returned to Hollywood after fifteen years of blacklisting and to run into yet another conspiracy was almost more than he could bear. Yet he knew this was part of the mentality of the industry.

Rock, by now, understood the double role's potential. As generous as he was, he had been willing this once to put his own ambition ahead of another person's needs—or at least allow the industry to do it for him. He felt so strongly that the role in Seconds was his last chance to succeed as a dramatic actor that he was willing for once to step on someone else.

"I hated it," said Randolph. "And yet the movie was a hell of an experience."

Years later, Randolph ran into Rock, visiting a friend in his apartment house in Los Angeles, where the Randolphs now live. A day later, the doorman brought the couple a small bunch of red roses—Mr. Hudson, he said, had wanted them to have it. They were from his garden.

"He was a truly fine actor who was trying to use himself in every way he possibly could to grow and develop. If that movie had made money . . ." Randolph sighed.

In some ways, the most extraordinary part of the film was watching Frankenheimer and James Wong Howe work their technical magic. "This young man [Frankenheimer] and this old man, who'd been an Academy Award winner many times, worked together to develop different techniques that nobody in the industry had ever used before."

They insisted on shooting the film in black-and-white, at a time when no pictures were made that way. They built in cameras to achieve different shots; they used various grains of film for different effects. In the airplane sequence, Rock was filmed briefly in the rest room—the real airplane rest room. The cameraman could hardly fit in there with him, and had to use a hand-held camera. And yet the feeling conveyed by the scene—the cramped bathroom, the desperate man—could never have been achieved in a studio.

"I surely believe that Rock must have been proud of this film," said Jens. "I know that whenever we met after that, our relationship was as if it was perfect—he remembered the experience perfectly. We knew we had shared something, something we'd really cared about, something worthwhile. We felt so sure. We didn't worry about how the public would react, we didn't question it at all, at the time. We knew there were all extraordinary people involved, that it was being done with integrity. It was a privilege, a wonderful privilege." Even given the fact that the film was a failure could not take away from the experience of doing it.

None of the work, talent, and immense care and dedication that went into the making of *Seconds* was rewarded—initially. The film, as they say, dropped dead at the box office. And yet with the years, *Seconds'* reputation has grown.

"The only film I know," said Frankenheimer ruefully, "that has gone from failure to classic—without ever being a success."

Years after the film's release, Randolph attended a party for the Royal Shakespeare Company. He was astonished to find that everyone in the company recognized him at once.

"Apparently there's a cult, a society that shows *Seconds* once a year over there," he said. "It's become a cult film all over the world."

Sometimes talent, care, and good work do win out, at least in the long run. And there is one final irony to the *Seconds* story.

The movie, when released, had a bad effect on nearly everyone's career—with one exception. John Randolph, who chose to live through fifteen years of blacklisting rather than have Hollywood dictate to him the way he should behave and who came perilously close to being dumped from the first film job he'd been given in all that time, was never out of work again. His most recent role, at age seventy, was that of a Mafioso in *Prizzi's Honor*.

For Randolph, then an unknown actor, *Seconds* was a success; for Rock Hudson, the star, who had opened himself up more fully and revealingly before the camera than he ever would again, it was a failure. For Rock, the lesson of *Seconds* seemed to be that Hollywood had done its job too well—the public would never accept him as the serious actor he longed to become. He had taken a chance, courageously, and lost. It was nearly ten years before he would take another—and then it was in a very different arena.

At the core of Rock's personality was a boy who never grew any older, no matter how many years went by. He retained many of the needs, the appetites, and the vulnerabilities of the child he was in Winnetka for his entire life. Psychiatrists say we all carry around unfinished business from our childhood—the worse the childhood, the darker the shadow cast on the rest of our life. Rock's childhood was poor by any standards. It included a father who abandoned him at age four, an age when he was old enough to experience terrible pain at the desertion; a stepfather who abused him emotionally and physically; a mother too overwhelmed by her own problems and economic necessities to create a safe haven for him. Of course, it was not all gloomy. There were friends, music, a lively bunch of cousins. But these bright spots were not enough. For the most part, Rock's childhood was a bleak, deprived place. The yearning to correct it, to create the security, to find the unconditional love, to go back one more time and do it right had to be terribly strong. In fact, it affected the rest of his years.

Childhood is the one place no one can truly return to—that is both the blessing and the curse of growing up. But the need to return can be so great that it stunts an entire life. In some very important ways, this is what happened to Rock.

To the very end of his life, he lacked confidence in his ability and his attractiveness to others. It did not matter that he was accepted in his profession as a major star, that his fan mail poured in for years at the rate of thousands of letters a week. It was not enough to convince him; nothing would have been. No one can go back in time to comfort a deprived child.

Most of us develop a thick shield against vulnerability over the years. Rock never did. A few years before his death, he astounded a director by asking him, with childlike simplicity, "Are you going to hurt me?" He was a major star, a worldwide celebrity, a tall, graying, handsome man in his late fifties. And behind the eyes, those brown eyes that had mesmerized women around the globe, was a fearful little boy.

There were other traits, too, that marked Rock as boy, not man. His heavy drinking and smoking, for instance, were habits that he continued to indulge in all his life, despite the heart problem that made them extremely dangerous. He hung on to them stubbornly, in the face of all good sense. Right up to the end he seemed to have a young boy's notion of his own immortality—not a man's. A man, particularly a man in his fifties, knows he will die. A boy, never.

There is no question that this childlike aspect of Rock's nature was related to his sexuality to some degree. No one knows what "causes" someone to become homosexual, or even if there is a cause. It is true Rock had what in another day would have been considered the perfect early atmosphere for fostering homosexuality: cruel stepfather, domineering mother. And yet most reputable psychiatrists today would laugh at such an explanation. The truth is that no one knows.

There are undoubtedly aspects of the homosexual lifestyle that would appeal greatly to a perennial boy. Homosexuality is no longer considered an immature choice, as it once was; the percentage of homosexuals who are mature, adult, completely integrated members of society is undoubtedly as high as the percentage of heterosexuals. Yet there is no denying that certain patterns of behavior that flourish in the gay community—the promiscuity, the lack of commitment, the unbridled sexuality—resemble nothing so much as protracted adolescence. One does not expect an adolescent to form a lifetime commitment to anyone; one does not expect an adolescent to forge an emotional-sexual attachment that has very much lasting power. One expects an adolescent to act on a passing fancy and to have plenty of them to act on. No one expects an adolescent to marry, raise children, and take on the responsibilities of an adult. These are the hell-raising years.

In many ways, Rock's sexual life-style remained adolescent to the end. From a number of reports it seems likely that Rock was not a particularly sexual man; many actors are not. It was the pursuit, more than the capture, that intrigued him—the playful prelude, the long-drawn-out flirtation. Rock had many fleeting encounters with men over the years—one-night stands that were no more emotionally involving to him than a Scotch-and-soda was. He also had a number of more serious attachments to men that can be defined in only one way: they were crushes, just like the kind every teen-ager has. Often these crushes would not even be consummated; perhaps he never wanted them to be. Consummation would have destroyed the magic. It seems quite possible that one of his most widely rumored relationships with a younger television actor fell into this category.

Many of the crushes—and a number of the brief

encounters as well—eventually developed into friendships. Rock had a true talent for friendship, even if he lacked the knack for deeper, long-term emotional commitment. Matthew West, a friend from New Zealand, said he often saw various men hanging around the Castle—invariably good-looking, virile, straight types. He specifically remembers a doctor. When he asked who they were, Mark Miller, Rock's secretary, would label them casually as last year's, or one from two years ago. "Never anyone current," said West. He felt strongly that while Rock was a wonderful, loyal friend, he was not a person you wanted to be emotionally involved with. Rock was emotionally a boy.

Rock's relationships with women also had an adolescent cast to them. All his life, women responded to Rock. There were his looks, of course, but even more, there was the vulnerability behind the eyes—the irresistible combination of big virile man and lost child.

And Rock loved women. Many of his closest friends, his most treasured companions, were women. There were perhaps no other people in the world he loved as much as Nancy Walker, Claire Trevor, and Carol Burnett. But for the most part it was a love made up of admiration, even adoration—a young adolescent's yearning. Or perhaps a small child's.

Producer-director-writer Sylvia Fine, wife of Danny Kaye, defined it. "It was a young, fresh quality, a youthful quality, an innocent quality that stayed with him all his life. He was very affectionate with women, physically affectionate with no hint of any sexual feelings. It was like an adolescent.

"There are an awful lot of homosexual men who do not like women, and it's quite clear, and they make no physical contact with them whatever." Rock, however, was never like this. He was very demonstrative and loving with his women friends. His first impulse when greeting a woman he knew was to grab her up in his arms in a giant hug, often sweeping her off her feet, with the enthusiasm of an overgrown teen-age son. It was lovely and warm—"but at the same time, it was very clearly not sexual at all," said Fine.

But the love was always there; any hostility or anger

that Rock may have felt for his mother as a small child, for her harried neglect of his needs, for her marriage to an abusive man, was gone—or buried so deep it never surfaced. Unless it surfaced in his choice of sexual partners; for that, Rock turned to men.

Completely? Certainly in the last twenty years of his life it was true. Yet was it always?

Tony Randall said that for years he never thought Rock was gay. He had heard the rumors but discounted them completely. When Randall first met him, Rock had been surrounded by beautiful starlets most of the time—"there were always two or three gorgeous creatures around"—and he had seemed to revel in it.

"He told me he liked girls," said Randall, simply. "He said he liked to take out the young starlets, because, he said, you know you're going to get laid, and they don't expect you to marry them or see them again."

Another time, sitting around waiting to be called to the set, Rock turned to Randall and made a curious comment.

"He said homosexuality is based entirely on fear of women. He said, that's the only problem with all the faggots. Maybe he didn't use that word, but it was some vernacular."

It was not until many years later that Randall realized that Rock must have been talking about himself.

Early in Rock's career the fan magazines ran themselves ragged reporting his various dates and supposed relationships with women. He was dating, he was falling for, he was madly in love—at various times—with Piper Laurie, Vera-Ellen, Debbie Power, Betty Abbott, Marilyn Maxwell, and, of course, the woman he married, Phyllis Gates. Was any of it true?

Possibly. Jimmy Dobson is positive Rock had affairs with a number of women over the years, including several actresses. Even Marc Christian, one of Rock's last lovers, believes Rock had a real relationship, sexual and emotional, with Phyllis Gates—before they were married. Christian claims that Rock told him it had fallen apart with marriage.

Piper Laurie, Elaine Stritch, Debbie Power—all of whom were reported to be romantically involved with Rock at one time or another—today admit cheerfully the relationship was one of friendship only. Phyllis Gates is not talking.

The rumor with the most staying power was the one linking Rock with Marilyn Maxwell, a minor film star out of the "gorgeous blonde" mold. "Marilyn Maxwell made the statement that even though she couldn't get Rock to marry her, she still wanted his child," said Lori Nelson. "I do recall that she really wanted to have his child." But Nelson admits, "I was young and naïve then." Still, it was plain that Rock adored Maxwell, as he did so many women. One Christmas he presented her with an elaborate evening outfit, which even included a coat. Was there anything more to this relationship than friendship? There may well have been. Maxwell, who died in her forties of a heart attack—in fact, it was Rock who discovered her body—was married three times. Beautiful and voluptuous, she was manifestly not the sort of woman one thought about in buddy terms. Even her third husband, Jerry Davis, reported feeling a bit uneasy at the amount of time she spent with Rock (by then, supposedly, their relationship had turned to friendship). Everyone in the industry "knew" Rock was gay. Davis knew he'd be laughed at if he complained too much, and yet . . .

Rock, he said, was omnipresent during his marriage to Maxwell in the fifties. Davis, then a writer, would return home nearly every day to find "this handsome six-foot-whatever man who was absolutely in tune with my wife. I felt a little like Woody Allen—'Hi, honey, I'm home.'" But Maxwell headed off any complaints. "She would get quite defensive. 'Are you paranoid? Do you actually think this man has any interest in me?'" Basically, Davis accepted the relationship as a "remarkable friendship," nothing more.

It seems likely that Rock experimented earlier in his life with heterosexuality. He was, after all, a movie star—women were throwing themselves at him constantly. A comment he made to Stanley Shapiro, screenwriter for a number of comedies in which Rock starred, is revealing.

Shapiro reported that Rock told him he had immense difficulty in bed with women. "They see me up on the screen, they expect a movie-star performance." He said their expectations were an enormous burden to him; how could he possibly live up to them?

Whatever the pattern of his sexual life, whether it was solely homosexual or at one time bisexual, his emotional life remained that of a boy who never grew up.

Where Rock did form lasting attachments was with his friends. He had a small group with whom he hung out, drank, shopped, partied, and played intricate, insane practical jokes. There are problems that come with being a boy who never grows up—an inability to take hold of the reins of life, to move ahead, to realize one's potential fully—but no one is denying that such people can be the most delightful, enjoyable companions on the face of the earth. Rock as a friend—not the movie star, not the remote private person—was such a person. To his close friends, he was always deeply generous, completely loyal, and invariably a pleasure to be around.

As a teen-ager in Winnetka, Rock had had his special pals—Jim Matteoni and Pat McGuire. The Triumvirate, they called themselves, and for many years they were inseparable. There was nothing sexual about the relationship. Both Matteoni and McGuire were straight, and it seems unlikely that the gay side of Rock's nature ever surfaced back then. He came of age, after all, in the forties, in a conservative Midwest town. "Gay bars?" said Matteoni. "We didn't even have strip joints."

Growing up, Rock had buddies, as any teen-ager does, and it was a type of male friendship he was exceedingly comfortable with his whole life. Easygoing as he was, he was basically a very private person—he did not make close friends easily. Once he had made them, though, they remained his friends forever.

In Hollywood, Rock developed similar bonds, but not with fellow actors. There were many he liked (and a few he detested), undoubtedly some he was involved with sexually and/or romantically over the years. But for buddies—Matteoni-McGuire–type buddies—men he could feel completely comfortable with, he looked toward the film crews.

Mark Reedall and Pete Saldutti became Rock's closest pals in the industry. Reedall was a makeup man, Saldutti a costume designer who rose to be the head of costume design at Universal before he quit to free-lance. Rock met both men sometime during the fifties. For the rest of his life, whatever set he was on, anywhere in the world, he did his best to bring them too. Over the years, both men worked with Rock on at least thirty different films.

Though Reedall and Saldutti, who are straight, knew Rock was gay from the beginning, it made no difference—it certainly had nothing to do with their friendship. Rock kept that part of his life far away from the set. Both men shared certain qualities that endeared them to Rock. They were fun-loving, hard-drinking, down-to-earth guys, warm-hearted, loyal, loving friends.

There were others, too, almost as close to him— dialogue coach Jimmy Dobson and George Robotham, his stunt double. On the set, these men were Rock's family. They teased him, nagged him, made sure he got to the set on time no matter how horrendous the hour. They were his buffers against the outside world, both on the set and off.

There were so many in Hollywood who wanted some-thing from him—his autograph, his smile, his presence, his body, his signature, his money, his name. His buddies only wanted his friendship—and that they had, till the end of his days.

What was it that clicked between Rock, Pete, and Mark? Probably just a matter of "personalities that really got along," Pete said. "Rock felt comfortable with Mark and me. Basically he was a very shy person. He was friendly, but not overly friendly. He certainly didn't like strangers.

"I guess," he added thoughtfully, "we just enjoyed each other's silly personalities. We used to laugh over nothing. People thought we were crazy. We'd just look at each other and go into hysterics. I remember Doris Day calling us the Three Musketeers."

Rock and his pals did more than just hang out, play cards, and swap stories. They also participated in an amazing number of practical jokes. Over the years each found himself on both the passing and the receiving end numerous times, but Mark and Pete are in agreement on one point: Rock was most often the butt.

Frick and Frack, Rock called Mark and Pete—interchangeably. "When he'd see us on the set, he'd just say, 'Uh oh, there's trouble,'" said Pete. And he was generally right.

"Mark is the master of the double double cross," said Pete. "He could con Rock like I've never seen anybody. And Rock was aware, and he was on guard." But it never helped. "It was amazing, he could always trap him. He nailed Leroy so many times." (Both men generally called Rock by his given name, or, alternatively, Leroy. They knew, as Pete said, that he was "never really nuts about 'Rock Hudson.'")

Mark, according to Pete, had Rock's number. "I could never trap him, I'm not that sharp. He'd set us both up, nail us both." It didn't matter how many times he'd done it before, either. Like Charlie Brown, eternally trusting that this time Lucy would not remove the football at the last minute, Rock continued to be fooled, again and again.

They were minor things, mostly—just enough to keep Rock constantly off guard. Mark remembered when Rock was recovering from a car accident that broke a few bones and he was asked to throw out the baseball for the opening game of the World Series in San Francisco. "He said, 'You know, since the accident, I don't really have much strength in my left hand.' And his driver, a burly guy, Bernie Hellerstein, said, 'Hey, I'll throw it out for you.' Just kidding. And that was the end of it."

Only Mark had spotted an opening, the kind for which he was constantly on the lookout. A few minutes later he cornered the driver alone and gave him instructions: Bernie was to leave, then return a few hours later and tell Rock he had cleared it with the studio and had alerted his family that he would be the one to throw the ball out.

"A couple of hours later he went back in the trailer and said, 'It's great, the studio's going to send me up there and everything.'" Rock's face fell. "Bernie, I was only kidding," he said. Bernie was deflated. "Oh," he said, and left.

"I waited till it was all over, then I went in," Mark said. "Rock told me all about it. He felt awful. Rock wouldn't hurt anyone for all the tea in China." Mark let Rock get it all out of his system. "How could he have believed me?" he moaned, feeling worse and worse. "I was just kidding!"

"Yeah, I know," Mark finally said sympathetically. "I put him up to it."

"Rock just looked at me—and said, 'Fuck you, fuck you, fuck you.' And then we both laughed till we cried."

Both Mark and Pete remember another incident clearly—"God, there were so many, we played so many jokes on each other," said Pete. This one was memorable because it was Rock's idea—and, as usual, he was neatly one-upped by Mark.

On the set of one of the Doris Day comedies, Mark was handling makeup, Pete costumes. One afternoon, shortly before they were through for the day, Rock cornered Mark with a gleam in his eye. "Know what I'm going to do?" he said gleefully. "I'm going to hide all the clothes I'm wearing tonight, after we finish. I'll just take them off and put them in the refrigerator. It'll drive Pete crazy tomorrow trying to find them. You just make sure you keep him out of my dressing room while I do it." As costumer, Pete was responsible for readying the star's wardrobe.

Mark was encouraging. "Good idea," he said, and rushed off to find Pete.

"Of course, Mark double-crossed Leroy. He told me to hide in the closet, which I did," said Pete. To this day, Pete remembers Rock rushing into his dressing room, racing around, frantically tearing off his clothes, trying to stuff them all into the refrigerator before Pete showed up. "He ended up at the closet door only in his shorts. When he opened that door, his hair must have gone straight up. It was the last place in the world he expected to find me." Rock screamed, then took off after Mark, who'd managed to do it again.

Only once does Mark remember Rock ever managing to scotch a prank in progress. It was when the three were working on the film *Man's Favorite Sport* in 1963, with director Howard Hawks.

Rock's car had broken down, so Hawks offered to lend

him one of his. Rock was reluctant—everyone knew that Hawks took immaculate care of his cars. He tried to beg off, but the director insisted, and Rock finally agreed.

The Sunshine Boys were more than ready. "The minute we heard, Pete and I ran outside to Hawks's car," said Mark. Working in concert, with hardly a word spoken, the two men unscrewed the hubcap and started to pile bolts inside so that the car would make a terrible noise the minute it started to roll.

They were just finishing up, replacing the hubcap, when they sensed someone behind them. Slowly Mark turned around. Rock was standing several feet back, staring impassively, watching them.

"He didn't say a word. I reached in, started taking out all the bolts, put the hubcap on, and he got in the car and left. There wasn't one word said." The one-upper had gotten his comeuppance for once.

Not all the practical jokes were planned. The three men had such a rapport, such a perfectly shared sense of the absurd, they were poised to take advantage of any situation that occurred.

Pete remembers one incident with special relish. The film was *Strange Bedfellows*, released in 1965. He was lounging around in the back of stage 12 at Universal, when he thought he heard someone on the set yell that they needed Rock's coat for the take.

In fact, Rock was in his room, giving a taped interview to several magazine reporters, but Pete didn't know that. He ran to the dressing room, jumped up the four steps to Rock's door, and, still holding on to the railing, swung into the room.

Or at any rate, that was what he planned to do. What actually happened was that he caught his foot on the step, tripped, and sailed into the room, landing with a mighty crash, sending tape recorders, coffeepots, mugs, glasses, ashtrays, cigarettes, and various other impedimenta flying all over the place.

For a long moment after the explosion there was total silence. Pete lay on the floor amid the wreckage, staring up at the group. Then Rock eyed his friend coolly, unblinking. "Oh," he said quietly. "May I introduce Peter Saldutti?"

Later that night, Rock and Pete replayed the scene endlessly. "What the hell were you doing?" Rock demanded. "Did you see their expressions?" And they would both collapse again in hysterics.

"He was so calm, he did it so well," said Pete, still impressed years later. "Just—'May I introduce . . . ?' The timing was perfect."

Rock had a definite touch for the put-on. For many years a favorite activity of his was to show up at places like Disneyland and Grauman's Chinese Theater accompanied by a friend or two. There he'd watch carefully for tourists snapping pictures. At the exact moment the picture was being taken, he would stick his head into camera range—then take off into the crowd. It tickled him to think of sightseers back home examining their vacation photos and going crazy trying to figure out if the man in the background really was Rock Hudson.

Mark, of course, was a master of improvisation. He, Rock, George Robotham, and Jimmy Dobson were coming out of a bar one night when a drunk stepped up and started harassing Rock.

Dobson, who is small, reached up, grabbed the guy, and shook him, saying, "You leave him alone." The drunk stared down at him, amazed, and was about to make his move when Mark spoke up.

"You better listen to him—he's a black-belt judo man," he said sternly. "We call him the 'Chopper.'" The drunk hightailed it, terrified, while everyone else cracked up.

If those particular pranks were purely spur-of-the-moment, there were others that required hours of planning. One, in fact, took place over several months—and as far as Pete is concerned, it is still hanging fire.

This time Pete was the butt, at least originally. Mark, Pete, and Rock were on location in Florida, filming *Blindfold*, in 1964. Pete had gone out to dinner with the cameraman, had a few drinks, and came back to the hotel.

"I walked into my room. Or rather, I attempted to walk into my room. I couldn't open the door. There was a baby crib wedged against the door. I thought, Oh God, I'm in the wrong room. I must've drunk more than I realized.

"I checked the key, the door number, but everything corresponded. So I pushed my way in. I managed to push past the crib, then I tripped on a chair. They had rearranged all my furniture, loosened all the light bulbs. I tried to find my way to the john, but tripped over things three or four times."

By this point, Pete recognized his pals' work. But the worst was yet to come. Once in the bathroom, he flipped on a cigarette lighter to see—and screamed at the top of his lungs. Out of the toilet rose a gigantic growth, which looked like nothing so much as a being from another planet. Certainly it was unlike anything ever seen on this earth in a toilet before.

"What they had done, those miserable guys, they had gone out to dinner and decided to play a joke on me. In Florida they have these road markers in the middle of the highway—sort of a half-moon top, made of concrete, connected to a steel rod. They'd dug one out, and took turns carrying it for miles—they really had to have tremendous motivation. The thing must've weighed fifty pounds." Once at the Holiday Inn, Mark and Rock had carted their prize up to the second floor, to its resting place in Pete's toilet.

As soon as Pete stopped screaming, he could hear laughter, very familiar laughter. Outside, on the balcony, Mark and Rock were doubled up against the wall in hysterics, "having a few more drinks, which they needed like a hole in the head."

Both men now came in, still laughing, eager to show Pete the extent of their work: besides rearranging furniture and loosening bulbs, they had also packed his bags, destroyed his bathroom with a can of shaving cream, and in general run amok. The joke had worked beautifully, and they were ready to call it a night.

But Pete was looking toward the future. "I thought, I'm going to get back." So when the crew packed up and left Florida, he had the alien-marker shipped back along with the rest of the equipment. Very quietly. Once home, he stowed it in his garage, where it rested for a long time. "I was waiting for the most opportune time," he said.

It finally arrived months later—the night of the Academy Awards. Rock was annoyed when Pete showed up at the Castle that day. He was putting on his tuxedo, waiting for the limousine that was to take him to the Awards dinner; he was escorting Claudia Cardinale. "What the hell are you doing here? I'm busy," he snapped at his friend.

Pete was reassuring. "I'm not even here to see you, I'm here to see your housekeeper," he said. Rock glared at him suspiciously, but the limo was at the door, and he had to leave.

Pete was as good as his word. He had come to confer with Rock's housekeeper, Joy. He needed her help to get the Florida road marker into Rock's bedroom. She was pleased to help; even Rock's gardener joined in. With three of them working at it, they were able to expand the project—they attached hair to the concrete half-moon and drew a face on it. Satisfied, they stuck it in Rock's bed, tucking it carefully under the covers.

"I told the housekeeper, 'I'm sure he'll be home late, and I'm sure he'll have had a few drinks, at the parties, but could you do me a favor? Just listen, okay? Because I sure would like to get a reaction,'" said Pete.

The next day, Joy filed her report. Rock had come home late, and she had heard him going up to his room. She heard him get ready to go to sleep, in the dark, and then finally climb into his bed. She heard him settle down—and then she heard the loudest, longest scream of her life. Rock had found the marker.

Pete felt the satisfaction of a job well done. Rock never mentioned it to him—not a word. But a week later, one of his staff members said something. "Don't think for a minute you've heard the last of that," he told Pete. "He's going to wait years, until you forget all about it, and then . . ."

A couple of years ago, Pete went into Rock's garage to get him a screwdriver and saw the marker lying in a corner, covered with canvas. "I thought, Oh boy, he's still waiting for the rematch. Everywhere I go, I keep an eye out for that thing—even now. I know if he had lived longer, it would have shown up again."

All of Rock's buddies shared a strong protective feeling

toward the actor. Whenever they'd go out to dinner with him, they automatically kept an eye out, scanning the territory. They knew Rock valued his privacy—which many people feel no celebrity has any right to in the first place.

"He was so nice," said Pete. "If people just approached him, said, 'Excuse me, when you have the time, I would love your autograph.' But some of the approaches . . ."

One time in a New York restaurant an aggressive woman fan actually grabbed Rock's arm just as he was bringing a spoonful of hot soup up to his mouth. At times like these, Pete, Mark, or George Robotham would try to step in and mediate. Fast.

"I'd say, 'Give me the paper, I'll get the autograph for you, but we're having a private dinner here,'" said Pete. It wasn't that they expected Rock to blow up or throw a punch, but he could be sarcastic on occasion; they didn't want him to do anything to hurt his image. Working in concert, his friends managed to keep most of the truly obnoxious types at bay.

Not all of these were members of the public, either. George Robotham clearly remembers a run-in he had with a restaurant manager in Los Angeles.

Pete, Mark, George, and Rock had decided to try out the restaurant one night. Normally a manager is thrilled to see a star come in the door—it's good for business. Often they'll even send a round of drinks to the table, just as a goodwill gesture.

This time was different. Not only were there no drinks, but when George got up to go to the rest room, the manager pulled him aside, very annoyed. "Jesus," he said. "What are you doing bringing that big faggot in here for?"

George had a visceral reaction. "It just triggered something in me," he admitted. He reached out and grabbed the manager with his big fist, roughly, and pulled the man's face close. "Listen, mister," he said in a dangerous undertone. "I'm not too sure you're not a fag. I've never seen you diddle a girl; how do I know?"

The manager, very nervous now—George is a big, muscular man, and his fury was barely under control—backed down at once.

"There just was something about him that made you care about the guy," George said, remembering the scene. "You didn't want to see him hurt, not by anyone."

All of them—Mark, Pete, George, and Jimmy—spent time up at the Castle. "We'd go up to his house, have a few drinks, laugh—he was so much fun," said Pete. "I'm sure his life was a lot more complicated than he let on, but . . . we're all seeking out happiness in different avenues."

And Rock went to their homes. "He'd go to parties at my house, and once my friends realized he was a human being, forget his name was Rock Hudson, he would blend right in—play the games."

On the set, no matter what movie it was, Rock liked to have music around. Mark and Pete would set up speakers outside his trailer, put on a record, something like *Camelot*, and wait for their friend to arrive. The minute they spotted him, they'd drop the needle.

"It was a great atmosphere. I never realized what a difference music could make to a crew," said Pete.

When he and Rock worked together on a picture, they had a routine. Early on, before any of the shooting, they'd go out shopping together to find the clothes Rock needed for the role. Many of the clothes Pete would design specially for him, but there were also extra things—sweaters, shoes, slacks—that they could pick up from the stores.

It was always great fun, up to a point. By midafternoon, Rock would get thoroughly sick of traipsing through store after store and be ready to quit. "He'd say, 'I'm tired of this stuff, let's do it tomorrow.' And I'd say, 'Come on, you're not the only actor on the picture.' And he'd say, 'We're going home now.' And I'd say, 'Oh ho, the big movie star, listen to this.'" It was that sort of relationship.

Whenever Rock had really had it with the shopping, he would do something that he knew drove Pete crazy. Rock had a trick he could do—he'd stare straight ahead, his face utterly blank, as if his brain had suddenly stopped functioning. He'd look at such times as if he had just woken up after a serious head injury that had left his faculties alarmingly altered. "What issss it?" he would slur, staring at a shirt as if he had never seen one before in his life, swaying slightly.

"Come on, damn it," Pete would say, infuriated. "Quit clowning around. We got to get this stuff done, this is serious."

"Yesss, I know, it's ssserious, Peter, yesss," he would answer in a slurred monotone, still in the same fogged-in state. And Pete would generally know it was time to pack in the outing and go home.

In the last weeks of Rock's life, Pete managed to visit him at the hospital several times. Both he and Mark felt strongly that the best thing they could do was to try to cheer him up a little—give him one last laugh, if they could. There were plenty of mourners around. But as Mark put it, there was going to be lots of time to mourn later on. Now the man was still alive.

It wasn't easy: their friend lay on the bed, his body completely ravaged, his face unrecognizable except for those great, expressive eyes. But they tried. Jimmy Dobson showed up with a bunch of balloons. Mark even did a few bits with the doctor. Once, when they were preparing to give Rock a shot, Mark stared at the syringe, straight-faced, and said, "Come on, is that the biggest one you've got? You've got to have something bigger than that." The doctor stared at Mark as if he had gone insane, but Rock shook his head and even managed a smile, so Mark knew he had caught the joke.

Pete realized he didn't have Mark's talent for the put-on, but he wanted to do something. So in the hospital, the last time he visited—with George and Mark—Pete finally threw Rock's old line back at him, the one that had always infuriated Pete so. Staring down at his friend, doing his best to imitate Rock's slur, Pete said, "What issss it?"

"He just looked over at me with those eyes, and I said, 'Ahh, you dumb bastard.' He didn't speak, but I know he understood."

Rock's private life—the gay part—never intruded on his friendships with his pals. "It never surfaced, and it never had to surface. He respected our way of life, we respected his; it had nothing to do with our friendship," said Pete. "He guarded his private life. He had friends he loved that he would do anything for—and thank God I was one of them."

Every year, Rock would go out to shop for Christmas presents for his friends. Each of them has a different story to tell of his generosity. Once when Mark was on location with him in Italy and his family was visiting, Rock arranged to have an English-speaking driver take his three kids to Rome for three days and paid for the whole excursion. "He did so many nice things for people. I'm sure no one will ever know," said Mark.

If they were walking down the street, Rock would nudge Pete if a good-looking girl walked by and he had missed it. Just a favor for a friend. Yet none of the men would ever have teased Rock about his gayness. "He wasn't the sort of man you'd do that with. It would have been bad taste. A very gentle, private man," said Pete.

Many times Pete would go to Rock for advice on one girl-friend problem or another. He always listened. "He'd say, 'Okay, now give me some more details . . . let's try to figure this one out.' He was that kind of friend—someone you could lean on."

All the friends, but particularly Pete and Mark, still like to get together and reminisce about Rock, the crazy things they did together. Looking back, "you never think about the long hours, the directors you didn't care for—just the fun," said Mark.

People have to realize, said Pete, that gays are human beings. There has to be mutual respect. "If Rock taught me anything, he taught me that.

"I lost a close, dear friend, who I think of constantly. So many times I'd love to get on the phone, say, 'Hey, I've got a problem, Rock, what do you think I should do?' It's a loss."

Doris Day sang a song on the episode of her cable show, "Doris Day's Best Friends," that she did with Rock in July, the one not aired until after his death. It is simple and moving. "My buddy, my buddy, your buddy misses you." They do—all of them.

By the mid-1960s Rock's homosexuality had become an open secret in the close-knit Hollywood community.

Friends and associates accepted his sexual preference without question.

One of Rock's closest friends, Sylvia Fine, recalls being at numerous social gatherings at the Castle when "almost everybody was homosexual except me and maybe one other lady. I would go to dinners and it would turn out that eight of the twelve people were homosexuals."

Leonard Stern, another close friend who became executive producer of Rock's hit TV series "McMillan and Wife" in the 1970s, recalled that Rock's mother was often present at the gatherings.

While there was never a suggestion of Rock's homosexuality on the set, Stern and other friends said that it manifested itself when Rock was at home, relaxed and among friends.

"If you entered Rock's private world and you were a friend and you went to his home, you might see an indication [of his homosexuality], but you would have to know what to look for in advance—such as a certain group of friends being there," Stern said.

Producer-director Bob Finkel, who also worked with Rock on the "McMillan" series, said, "Rock exuded such masculinity and led such a private life that one never thought about his homosexuality when they looked at him or dealt with him—even though it was common knowledge in this community that he was gay."

Among friends, and with a few drinks in him, Rock would sometimes act campy—imitating a famous actress, for instance, or playing a pansy role with good-natured jest. He would have his straight and gay friends rolling on the floor with laughter.

"He would do it right there with everybody—it was never closeted," recalled Matthew West. "He was a real comic, but I never saw him do anything that would be awkward or embarrassing."

Years later, one of Rock's last lovers, Marc Christian, said, "He was one of the manliest men I ever knew. Even in private there wasn't an ounce of effeminacy in him whatsoever. None of his masculinity was ever put on. If anything can be said in Rock's favor about his image, it's that what you saw on the screen is basically what he was in private."

While millions of female fans swooned over him as the ideal heartthrob, Rock had a small circle of celebrity female friends who were aware of his sexual preference but still found him attractively masculine. They included such women as Carol Burnett, Elizabeth Taylor, Dinah Shore, Claire Trevor, and Marilyn Maxwell.

"I never thought of Rock as gay," said Susan Stafford, a former hostess on TV's "Wheel of Fortune" and a close friend of the actor. "Because when Rock would pick me up and kiss me and hold me, I'd get chills. You don't say to yourself, 'I'm not supposed to get chills because this guy's gay.'"

Aside from blind items in gossip columns by Joyce Haber, there was never a published report about Rock's sexual proclivities. "The press departments at the studios buried more scandals than dogs bury bones," noted Sylvia Fine.

Veteran casting director Gus Schirmer believed Rock's homosexuality escaped scrutiny and exposure because "people liked him so much personally that nobody wanted to air anything about it." As a result, the general public had no inkling he was gay until a crazy rumor spread across the country that Rock had married actor Jim Nabors.

Despite the fact that there was no truth to the rumor, it remained in the public's consciousness and thereafter Rock was considered homosexual by many people—although the rumor did not have a negative impact on his career.

As is the case with such rumors, people can't really pinpoint when and how they first heard it. Some in the industry recall hearing the story on a radio or TV newscast (which seems doubtful) and others seem to think they saw it in a gossip column (which is more probable)—but no such item has been documented. The other question is when the rumor first started; some say as early as 1965, others swear they first heard it in 1971. Two facts are clear: everyone seems to have heard the story, and the impact of the hoax was devastating to Nabors at the time.

The rumor is believed to have started when two Los

Angeles homosexuals jokingly sent out party invitations announcing the engagement of Rock and Nabors. Several copies of the invitation were anonymously sent to gossip columnists and other copies circulated among industry gays. From there, the rumor shot across the country by word-of-mouth.

Rock and Nabors had been good friends for years— they'd often dine and take trips together. Their mutual friend Carol Burnett would invite them on her TV variety show together—and that fact was known to the two pranksters who created the invitations. They did it for a laugh, since they knew that Rock and Nabors were not involved romantically and, furthermore, no one could ever imagine as lovers Rock, the heartthrob, and Nabors, the twangy, bumbling Gomer Pyle of TV fame. Before too long, their "marriage" was the talk of every beauty shop from Beverly Hills to Birmingham.

"The first time I ever heard a story that Rock might be gay was when I heard the Jim Nabors rumor," said Jim Matteoni. "I frankly dismissed it. I never asked Roy about those rumors. I didn't believe them."

Among friends, Rock expressed his displeasure with the story but was advised to grin and bear it, which he did. "But the rumors made it impossible for them to be seen together, which is very sad," said Armistead Maupin, a friend of Rock.

On the other hand, Nabors took the prank hard. "He said it was a vicious lie and that it was going to cost him his job at CBS," recalled Dorothy Malone, who had dinner with Nabors in Dallas at the height of the rumor. "Jim was so mad, so angry, he was ready to chew nails. He said, 'There's no way to disprove it. For God's sake, will you marry me and get me out of this mess I'm in?' I guess he was kidding about marrying me but I know he was really hurt by the rumor."

Whether the rumor had anything to do with it or not, CBS canceled "The Jim Nabors Hour" in 1971 and he never had his own TV show again. Nabors all but disappeared from the national entertainment scene, moving to Hawaii, where he tended a macadamia-nut farm in Maui between occasional singing engagements. In early 1986 he still declined to talk about the rumor and was preparing a made-for-TV movie called "Return to Mayberry," a one-shot revival of "The Andy Griffith Show," which had made him a star.

There was a zany footnote to the rumor. In 1982 the *Harvard Lampoon*'s parody of *Newsweek* announced that Hudson and Nabors were divorced.

After *Seconds*, Rock made five films, all relatively forgettable. Then, in 1968, Rock became embroiled in another fiasco, which in many ways was reminiscent of his experience over a decade earlier with the ill-fated *A Farewell to Arms*. Once again he was working overseas, under the supervision of a headstrong director, Blake Edwards, who had cast him opposite his actress wife, Julia Andrews. Edwards had dedicated himself to the job of stripping away Andrews's Mary Poppins/Maria von Trapp image, which he did in part by stripping Andrews herself and putting her in a shower with Rock. Unfortunately, the result of all this effort, *Darling Lili*, a World War I spoof with music, charmed no one. It was a costly, resounding flop, the *Heaven's Gate* of its time, practically bringing Paramount studios to its knees and sowing dissension and bad feeling all around—between executive and director, director and star, actor and actor. Edwards himself was so traumatized by the experience that he needed to make another picture, *SOB*, just to deal with his reaction to it.

The script for *Darling Lili* was written by Edwards and William Peter Blatty; it revolved around a British music-hall singer (Andrews) who seduces soldiers into betraying military secrets to the Germans. She is redeemed after falling in love with Hudson, but for the public it was too late. Mary Poppins sleeping around and trafficking with the enemy? The movie sank like a stone.

Problems multiplied during the making of *Darling Lili*, many of them in the act-of-God category (even the fates seemed put off by the idea of America's favorite nanny jumping in and out of beds). Filming in Paris was interrupted by riots; filming in Ireland was held up for weeks because of weather—first, lack of sun, then lack of clouds. Various Paramount executives began dropping in on location to see what was holding up the works. In the end, Paramount production chief Robert Evans described the film as "the most flagrant misappropriation and waste of funds I've seen in my entire career. . . . [Edwards] was writing a love letter to his lady and Paramount paid for it."

No one on the set was feeling particularly gracious as week followed dismal week. "A very, very unhappy set," said Jimmy Dobson. In addition, ill feeling was fanned by several gossip columns written by Joyce Haber.

Rock's old friend from Universal, Dick Morris, visited him on the Darling Lili set in Ireland, and found Rock living unhappily in a Dublin hotel. Edwards and Andrews had rented a castle on the outskirts of the city, where they ruled like royalty, or so Rock thought. Rock felt like the Black Prince, banished from their court.

"They even ran the daily rushes out at the castle," said Morris. "They were completely isolating Rock."

Morris and Rock had a wonderful weekend in Dublin, though, which cheered Rock up immensely, if only temporarily. They went out for a bit of typical Irish entertainment—to the sing bars. At these boisterous places people who want to sing can send up a card to the band. When their name is called, they get up in front of the band—and all the drinking Irish—and belt out their song.

Naturally Rock wanted to sing.

"I don't know if they knew who Rock was," said Morris. "I think he probably used the name Roy Fitzgerald. But he certainly was a great big good-looking Irishman."

Rock was momentarily able to forget his troubles on the set with Edwards and Andrews. He himself later told gruesome tales about his experience working on Darling Lili. He told one friend that Andrews had proclaimed haughtily, "I'm the only queen on this set." And Edwards, he told another, had pushed him aside during a love scene and snarled, "Get back, faggot—I'll show you how to do it."

Both Edwards and Andrews deny the stories vehemently, and it seems likely that Rock, who always enjoyed a good tale, at the very least embellished them a bit. "I never saw him anything but even-tempered," said Andrews. "The supposed rift between us is a complete mystery to me. The working relationship was tremendous." Told of her supposed "I'm the only queen" comment, Andrews chuckled. "Oh, come on, can you see me doing that? That's ridiculous. That would really cement a relationship, wouldn't it?"

About Haber's columns, Andrews said, "My recollection is we all giggled about them. She just for some reason seemed to have it in for Blake and me, and I guess Rock got included in that."

Edwards remembers one Haber column implying that he, Rock, and Andrews were having a *ménage à trois* and all frequenting San Francisco leather bars together. "I wanted to kill this woman. I was furious and I went to Rock and said, 'Can you imagine this bitch writing this kind of stuff?' And he was so wonderfully cool. He looked at me and said, 'I wonder how she found out about it.' I thought he handled it brilliantly."

Told about the "faggot" story, Edwards seemed shocked. "Oh, my God. Come on. First of all, the man's too big," he pointed out reasonably. "I wouldn't have tried anything like that even if I—I mean, that's absurd. It's totally untrue."

Haber acknowledged using the kissing scene and gay-bar items in her column. She used initials to identify Hudson, Andrews, and Edwards. The letters "V.V."—for "visually virile"—were used to disguise Hudson's name, Haber recalled.

The day after she ran the gay-bar item, Haber got a cable saying, SAW YOUR COLUMN OF YESTERDAY. SUGGEST YOU SEE MY LAWYER. YOU WILL HEAR MORE. ROCK HUDSON.

The cable must have been someone's idea of a practical joke because no legal action was ever taken, even though the threat upset Haber. In fact, a few months later, Rock sent Haber a Christmas plant. Tom Clark assured Haber that Rock never sent the cable. About a year later, Haber wrote a positive column about Rock that made no reference to his life-style or to incidents on the set of *Darling Lili*.

Both Edwards and Andrews say they remember no dissension on the set. Andrews, in fact, clearly recalls one very nice thing. "I'd been up to his house a few times, and he had the most beautiful orchid tree in his garden. I admired it tremendously, and when the film was finished, he sent me an orchid tree of my own. It was a tremendous thrill for me. I planted it and it's thriving. I think, in fact I'm fairly sure, I wrote him a very loving note saying, 'My God, how wonderful of you, I'll treasure it always.'"

Despite these rosy recollections, it seems probable that the three did not get along terribly well. "He wasn't happy at all over there," said George Robotham, who worked on the film for five months. "It was spring but it rained like hell all the time." Having dinner with Rock one night, Robotham finally asked him what was wrong.

"They just have the strangest attitude," said Rock of the director and his wife. "There's no congeniality there. She's the reason he's making the picture."

Edwards, said Robotham, rewrote the ending of *Darling Lili* to put more emphasis on Andrews. "There were a lot of things. It was a cold atmosphere between [Rock, Edwards, and Andrews]." However, the stunt man did not believe the two anecdotes were true.

Both Edwards and Andrews say that after *Darling Lili* was completed, stories began coming back through the grapevine about Rock's resentment. "I heard from other people that he was upset with us, that I showed preferential treatment," said Edwards. "At one point I even tried to run it down." Edwards called Flo Allen, who was then Rock's agent, to ask about the stories.

"I was very very concerned about it, and I said to Flo, 'Will you go ask him? I really would like to know because maybe there's something I'm unaware of.'" According to Edwards, Allen's answer was vague and unsatisfying, and he was never able to get a real explanation. "If he felt that way, I don't know what it was based on. It's possible that we were doing something that I was unaware of that rubbed him the wrong way. It's always puzzled me, because I never had one cross word with Rock."

Andrews too was upset, she said. "We did try to find

out about it, but nothing substantial came back. It was fairly hurtful. I had assumed we'd had a wonderful time. I can only assume somebody put a bad flea in his ear and he took it and ran with it. He was professional, fun to work with. Never sour or sulky. It's very odd indeed."

Edwards had specifically wanted Rock for the part. "We were looking for that kind of matinee-idol person. He was the first choice." In general, however, his appreciation of Rock's talent was minimal.

"Not a great actor at all," he said. "He had a nice kind of style about him but he really wasn't very deep. His biggest problem was that he was limited. He couldn't really expand that. He knew his lines well and he gave you as much of Rock as you could ever get. He had a charm about him and a nice quality when he did comedy, and he was able to be dramatic enough, but if you expected him to search around and expand, it didn't happen. He was predictable." However, he insists he got what he wanted. "I wasn't looking for anything more than that. I wanted Rock Hudson."

Whatever did or didn't happen on the set of *Darling Lili*, one thing is clear: it was a place Rock was happy to leave at the end of the week. Early in the filming, he met Matthew West through a publicist named Harry Mines, who was working on the film. West, a New Zealander living in London, was a publicist who had worked for Judy Garland and Peter Sellers.

"Mines—who Rock used to call the oldest living publicist—called one day and said they were in Dublin and were coming over to London for the weekend, what was going on? So I arranged a party," said West.

He and Rock became good friends, exploring London together. "He'd been there briefly, but always sheltered in limousines, staying in hotels. So I was able to walk him around and show him my London, the London I knew he'd enjoy." Rock and West caught double-decker buses, walked around King's Row, stopped into pubs. "Nobody said anything to him. He was left alone, and he loved that." Rock dressed conservatively, wore glasses, and had his hair fairly long; he blended in perfectly and no one gave him a second glance.

West rented a country house, called the "Deer Tower," some forty miles south of London in Sussex. Rock spent many weekends there, helping him putter around the garden. "My life was being in the country with my dogs and my house, and he was comfortable with it," said West. West would invite other friends down; Judith Herd, another New Zealander and publicist, would often come to cook. Rock never spoke to West about the making of the movie. "All I know is he was always thankful to get the hell out of there Friday night. I know that. He would call and be on the first plane he could get out of Dublin. I think what he enjoyed was not even thinking about it until he had to get back to work."

West was on hand the day Rock paid his last alimony check to Phyllis Gates. "He said he wanted to go out and have a few drinks and get silly, because he'd paid his last alimony check." The two men went to see Danny LaRue, a well-known female impersonator who had a nightclub in Hanover Square. "We got a table there, drinks, and had a great night. That's how he celebrated it. He was just glad it was over."

The two men—both tall, easygoing, gentle-giant types—remained friends. Whenever West went through Los Angeles on his way back to visit New Zealand, he'd see Rock. Eventually he moved to Los Angeles and worked in real estate. Rock let him stay at the Castle while he was getting settled. West would often house-sit while Rock was away.

"He used to not want to be Rock Hudson," West said. "He wanted to be Roy Fitzgerald, with his dogs and his garden." He remembered one day, Rock's birthday, when Carol Burnett was planning a big celebration bash at her Malibu house. "He loved Carol Burnett, but the fuss was what he didn't really enjoy. I remember saying, 'It's your birthday, what do you want to do today?' And he said, 'I know what I'd like to do: let's pull down that old brick wall in the back of the garden and stack the bricks and dig out all the muck.' In other words—work. Skip going out to lunch and all that. 'Let's get that done today and in a few days maybe build a wall.' He enjoyed stuff like that so much and wasn't always able to do it, because everybody wanted him to be Rock Hudson."

The two men shared a hang-out, pals' sort of friendship—what West calls a "kick it around" kind of relationship. "I never had an emotional thing with Rock, but I loved him as a friend," West said. "I would hate to have fallen in love with him. I'm sure there were broken hearts, people who would have loved to be closer, gone on with the relationship . . . but because of this shroud he put around himself as a protection. . . . He was a Scorpio, and Scorpio people are inclined to break hearts. They're good-looking, inclined to hurt people falling in love with them."

What they did enjoy was telling stories, the sillier the better. "He'd tell some trashy story—he loved to tell them, usually pretty disgusting—and I'd add to it and he'd add to it. It was all fun."

Tom Clark, the man who was to become Rock's closest friend for most of his last fifteen years, grew up in Oklahoma City, the son of a respected businessman. His father, Harold Clark, Sr., ran an insurance agency for thirty-two years and was a popular member of the community, a Mason who loved hunting and fishing. Born in 1930, Tom Clark grew up in a stable, middle-class environment, quite unlike Rock's, but he too knew tragedy at an early age. His mother died of cancer when he was fifteen. Tom's father remarried quickly; his wife, Mary, had a son, Harold, Jr., within a year.

Tom Clark felt himself drawn to the world of theater just as Rock had been. "He was the first and only one in the family that had an interest in show business," recalled his stepmother, Mary Clark, now seventy-four. "I would say theater was always in his blood."

During his years at Central High School, Clark acted in a number of school plays, even playing the lead in the senior-class play. His class yearbook of 1947 shows a blond young man with a sweet smile, surrounded by teen-age girls. Maybelle Conger, drama coach at Central High, remembers him well.

"He could have gone to the top. He had extraordinary talent, and I knew then he could have been an actor. I wanted him to go on with his theatrical work."

Conger, a warm, motherly woman who was completely dedicated to her students, was responsible for starting more than one theatrical career. One Conger graduate, Don Chastain, played the lead in the Broadway hit 42nd Street. Two others, the Antonio brothers, Jimmy and Lou, became respected directors. Jimmy received an Oscar for directing Something for Joey, while Lou directed several episodes of "McMillan and Wife" and an NBC miniseries called "The Star Maker"—both projects starring Rock Hudson. Lou Antonio never knew Clark in high school, but after they met in later years, they were careful always to greet each other with greatly exaggerated Oklahoma accents.

As alluring as the theater was to Clark, he was still his father's son. At the University of Oklahoma, he majored in business administration, not drama. After graduation in 1951, Clark moved to Houston, where he worked at a series of sales jobs. None of them held much excitement for him, however. When he heard through friends of an opening in the publicity department at MGM in Hollywood, he jumped at the chance.

Clark took to Hollywood instantly. He loved the glitter, the fantasy, and, most of all, the stars. Friends paint a picture of a friendly, down-to-earth guy with a good business head who was nonetheless a consummate fan— and who remained one. Years later, long after Tom Clark had moved into the Castle, Matthew West recalled a night when Lana Turner came to his house for dinner. "Rock was glad to see his old buddy, of course," said West. "But he said, 'Let's not tell Tom, we'll make it a surprise. Tom will die when he walks in and sees her.'" Rock knew Clark would be knocked out, and he was. Stars did not lose their luster for Clark.

"He was a fan—not just of Rock, he was a fan of the business, of everybody. Stars, he loved the stars," said West.

At MGM, Clark began to learn the publicity end of the business. In the late sixties, he took a public relations job with Rupert Allan, who handled Rock Hudson, among other stars. Soon Rock became Clark's personal account, his bridge partner, and, with time, his closest friend. Clark was steady, unpretentious, and good company—"a good ole boy," George Robotham tagged him. Sometime in the early seventies, Clark moved into Rock's house.

"He just felt comfortable with Tom," West said. "I'm sure Rock was sick and tired of all the running around, all the carrying on, and suddenly realized he was sitting right opposite his best friend."

Leonard Stern, one of the creators of the "McMillan" series and a longtime friend of Rock, believed one of the roots of the friendship was Rock's need for some consistency in his life. "I don't think Rock liked to be alone."

Rock became Tom Clark's personal star, the one he would revolve around for the next fifteen years. He devoted himself to taking care of Rock—arranging his business matters, his social life, hundreds of necessary details. If Rock wanted a party, it was Clark who would plan it and issue invitations. If he went on a trip, Clark would attend to the reservations, the limousines, and the schedules. Rock's friends in and out of the industry came to accept Clark as a constant. If Rock was invited out to a dinner or a party, it became expected that Tom Clark would be there too.

"Tom truly handled Rock's affairs," said Jon Epstein, producer of "McMillan and Wife." "Rock could never deal with that sort of thing. Rock would make a dinner date, and if Tom didn't write it down, Rock could just as easily not show up. Not because he was cavalier about it, but because he just wasn't organized."

Clark's devotion was complete, and his presence constant—too constant, some of Rock's friends felt. Resentment was inevitable. Clark, said some, was too possessive.

Jimmy Dobson said, "I think he wanted to be Rock. Tom would always say things like, 'Well, after we gave our performance . . .' or 'After we did the show . . .' Of course, Tom never did the shows, Rock did, but Tom always put it that way."

Actress Elaine Stritch, who got to know Clark when he and Rock saw her and her husband in England during the seventies, had another view. "At first I wasn't quite sure of Tom, but then I got to know him. I think he was genuinely very, very attached to Rock and really loved him."

Rock became a loved and accepted member of Clark's family. He sent Mary Clark poinsettias at Christmas and flowers on other holidays. Clark's father and stepmother visited at the Castle a number of times.

"We loved to play bridge, all four of us," said Mrs. Clark. "We had lots of good bridge games together. Rock would have dinner for us or we'd go out together. It was like a family visit."

Clark and Rock also made several trips together to Oklahoma City. When Clark's father died in 1979, Rock went to the funeral with his friend. He brought the widow a small gift—five pounds of Jelly Bellies he had found at a local mall.

"I called him a buffer for Rock. Whatever needed to be done at the time, Tom would handle it," said Mrs. Clark. "He was sort of like a middleman."

Leslie Easterbrook, an actress who worked with Rock when he toured in On the 20th Century in 1979, was impressed with Clark's diligence. "Tom would say, 'It's time to go home.' Or, 'Do you really want to go tonight?' You went to Tom first if you wanted Rock to do something. Rock wasn't as good taking care of himself as Tom was. Rock was a bit of a party boy, he liked having fun; he liked to drink, and if he wasn't monitored, he'd drink a little too much." Easterbrook found Clark "very decent, very caring. He had the best interests of the man at heart."

In the late seventies and into the eighties, one of the favorite haunts of Rock and Tom was the Rangoon Racquet Club in Beverly Hills.

Jay Richards was the maître d' during those years. "When they were coming over, Tom used to give me a call. I knew what they liked to eat."

Rock was always a simple man to satisfy in the way of food. What he preferred at the Rangoon was a New York steak, fresh vegetables, especially spinach, and a small green salad. The main ingredient of Rock's meal in those days, though, was gin.

Tom would sip a few Scotches, while Rock would invariably down between half and three-quarters of a bottle of Tanqueray gin, consumed in the form of double martinis on the rocks.

Rock and Tom would come to the Rangoon as often as twice a week. Sometimes others would join them, often young men from the show-biz world. The Rangoon was an expensive place, and their table's bill was usually two or three hundred dollars. Rock was a lavish tipper as well.

"Rock used to get blind drunk every time he came in," recalls Richards. "I don't know whether it was a release for him or what, coming in there and always getting drunk."

Generally Rock's party came at eight and left around eleven-thirty or midnight. By that time Rock would be blotto.

Despite the fact that Rock would be getting tanked, his table was generally a pleasant one. Actually, Rock would be rather quiet, and Tom and the others would do most of the talking and laughing, Richards observed.

As much as he drank, Rock never passed out. His capacity for alcohol appeared without limits. Nor was he ever asked to leave the Rangoon. On the contrary, management was always happy to see him. Management rightly regarded the Hudson table as an attraction. Many customers were happily entertained at the spectacle of an aging matinee idol getting quietly plastered.

"Sometimes he would be so drunk he couldn't stand," said Richards. "Rock would hold on to our shoulders. Tom always drove. He was very conscious of Rock always getting drunk. I guess that's why he never used to get into that state himself."

Clark had appointed himself Rock's caretaker, and that was the role he played for many years. Later, there would be a serious break in their friendship. When Tom learned that Rock was dying, he returned to care for him until the very end.

CHAPTER FOUR
TV Star

Rock was one of the few major movie stars to make a successful transition to television, when he became the star of a new comedy-detective series, "McMillan and Wife." The move saved his career as it was beginning to fade.

The type of films that had brought him acclaim—the light comedies with Doris Day, for example—were no longer box-office. Rock had recently made a string of duds—*The Hornet's Nest*, *A Fine Pair*, and *Pretty Maids All in a Row*, among others. Adding to the problem was the severe weakening of the motion-picture economy. People were spending more time at home watching television.

Rock's first TV appearance was on an episode of "I Love Lucy" that aired April 25, 1955. His first serious attempt to break into television came four years later. Unfortunately, it was such a dismal failure that CBS pulled the plug before the critics had a chance to get their claws into it.

In October of 1959, the year *Pillow Talk* was released and Rock was big box-office, he was signed to be one of the hosts of a "variety extravaganza" series called "The Big Party." Sponsored by Revlon, the 9:30 to 11:00 P.M. show was to alternate with the respected "Playhouse 90" on Thursdays.

The show's set was a living room with a party going on in the background. Making his TV debut in a tux, Rock was so nervous that viewers could actually see him shaking. The show also featured a rare TV appearance by Tallulah Bankhead, who, like Rock, looked as if she was about to have a nervous breakdown. The show had one of the shortest runs in TV history: it premiered on October 8, 1959, and had its wake on New Year's Eve of that year.

The experience made Rock afraid of pursuing further TV offers other than sporadic guest appearances.

In 1967 Rock was invited to be one of the celebrity hosts of "The Kraft Music Hall" on NBC. That season the producers decided to make each week's show deal with a different theme. Rock's program focused on "The Hollywood Musicals." It went well. Rock seemed perfectly at ease.

In 1970 producer-writer Leonard Stern had an idea for a TV series modeled on the sophisticated and glib private-eye Nick Charles and his wife, Nora, the characters in the popular 1940s *Thin Man* movies. An old friend from the early Universal days, Stern developed the concept for an updated *Thin Man* with Rock in mind for the lead.

"Rock was the last remaining leading man who was in a suitable TV age bracket and who was well acquainted with charm and mischief and could combine them in a dramatic role," said Stern. "Rock had done those Doris Day movies, where he combined sophistication and manliness."

The result was "Once Upon a Dead Man," the pilot for what became a long-lasting "McMillan and Wife" series. Stern had talked up the script to a friend who passed the word to Flo Allen, Rock's agent. She responded favorably and advised Rock to do the two-hour "Movie of the Week" pilot—but not to commit to the series, at least not immediately.

The show brought Rock back to Universal, which co-produced the series. The salary was right, too. The first year Rock got fifty thousand dollars per episode, a fee that more than doubled by the time the series ended.

Stern was determined to get Rock for the show. His reasoning, a bit zany even by Hollywood standards, was this: "In the old movies all the actors—Raft, Cagney, Grant—wore hats and they wore them in their own style. Then suddenly the hats disappeared and all the actors were five-foot-three, intense, and ethnic. So I decided that if 'McMillan' was to be done, I'd have to bring back the hat or get Rock."

But Rock had qualms. Even though his movie career had slowed down, he was afraid to commit himself to a series that might totally destroy him. He was aware of how television ratings could wreck a career overnight. Rock was never a big television fan—he called it "illustrated radio." He only watched football and old movies. In addition, he was nervous about moving from the big screen to the small one. Rock was comfortable on movie sets; he knew little about television.

Rock realized that the woman who played his wife would have to be a perfect match for him, a Nora to his Nick. A search was started immediately for a leading lady. The finalists were three young actresses: Jill Clayburgh, Diane Keaton, and Susan Saint James. Rock would make the final decision based on which actress he felt most comfortable with.

"Rock and I would go to dinner with these ladies and talk to them because we wanted to find the right rapport," said Stern. "He was most comfortable with Susan. A lot had to do with her personality, because she was shy. She put him at ease. She had a sense of humor, she was fun, and she seemed to be the right age. It turned out to be an admirable choice because there was a magic and a chemistry."

Jimmy Dobson, who was Rock's dialogue coach on the series, remembered, "Rock said he gained seven pounds at the dinner with Susan and told Leonard, 'Hire her!'" Anyone he could eat with, he felt comfortable with. Later there were conflicts on the set between Saint James and Rock that the audience would never know about.

Rock played cool, sophisticated San Francisco Police Commissioner Stewart McMillan and Saint James his sexy, scatterbrained wife, Sally, who would often help him solve cases. A hulking actor named John Schuck was cast to play bumbling Sgt. Charles Enright; comedienne Nancy Walker played the McMillans' sarcastic housekeeper, Mildred.

"McMillan" was to be one of the three rotating

elements in the "NBC Mystery Movie," which included "McCloud," starring Dennis Weaver, and "Columbo," starring Peter Falk. Of the three, "Columbo" was by far the best-written and had the most popular character. Despite pedestrian story lines, "McMillan" had a certain charm and the show surprised critics by running six years, only to reappear later in syndication.

Rock was a stickler for the sort of detail that would establish and help define the character of Commissioner McMillan. There would be a scene, for example, in which the commissioner and Sergeant Enright would each have to make a telephone call. Both men only had a quarter (at the time phone calls were still a dime). In delineating the characters, Rock decided that the commissioner should drop the quarter in the slot for expediency, whereas the good sergeant would look around for change, not wanting to waste fifteen cents.

Rock also decided that the commissioner should have an inherent dignity about him and should show a paternal side in his relationship with his younger wife. He was vulnerable in certain areas and avuncular in others.

Rock's reading of the character was right on the money: the television audience loved "McMillan." Rock was able to project the same easy charm and sexiness that had made him a movie idol. As a star in the movies, Rock's fans had been mostly women, but as TV's McMillan—the strong, silent police commissioner—he started attracting a large male following. At the height of the show's popularity, Rock was receiving three thousand fan letters a week—nothing like the deluge he had gotten during the fifties, but a strong indication of his popularity with TV audiences.

One of the reasons Rock was enthusiastic about the show during the first few seasons was that he had some control over it. "I'm not stamped Studio Property anymore," he told an interviewer. "I have the right of story approval, script approval, casting approval, director, everything down to music and special effects. Sometimes I get dizzy just thinking of how independent I am. Finally."

But working in television was different from making movies, as Rock had already begun to realize.

"There's a tremendous difference [between TV and movies]," he said. "Nobody told me. I had to find out for myself. In television you can't forget for a second that the result of what you're doing will only come out of a little box. So you've got to punch up your work, play your scenes bigger than life. On 'McMillan' I can't underplay, as I would in a movie, or my character would get lost in the shuffle. I'm an old dog learning new tricks. I haven't been excited by work for a long, long time as I am now, trying to lick television. I think I've learned enough to be a director or a producer. Maybe I'll have a turning point after all."

After the first three years of "McMillan," the scripts started getting tired. A new producer, Jon Epstein, was brought in. He had been producing "Owen Marshall, Counselor at Law," another popular series. Epstein was not happy with taking on "McMillan" in midstream but saw it as an opportunity to get into long-form television (ninety-minute and two-hour programs).

During the first week, Epstein screened all the previous shows and found them "pretty awful. The quality wasn't there. They dealt with bizarre subjects, nothing to do with Rock. I never considered 'McMillan' an award-winning show. It wasn't 'Lou Grant' or 'Hill Street Blues.'"

Epstein was impressed with Rock's acting ability. "The kind of performance that he gave of being cool, casual, and offhanded is very hard to do. Very few actors in television know how to do it well. Everyone thought he wasn't acting, and that's the hardest kind of acting to do. He realized there was no meat to the material and yet he made it come alive."

By the time Epstein came aboard, Rock was no longer talking about his excitement with the world of television. In fact, he was all but fed up with the show. "Bored to bloody tears" was the way one of the show's directors, Bob Finkel, put it.

"I don't like doing the series at all," Rock complained to one of the tabloids. "I'm pleased people like it, but I wish the shows were better. I only do it for the money. The whole series is done in too much of a rush. There is no time for any kind of artistic endeavor or professional satisfaction, so all that's left is the money."

On work days, Jimmy Dobson would have to wake him up at home and drive him to the studio, usually hung over. When not involved in a scene, Rock would spend hours in his trailer with one of his co-stars, usually Nancy Walker, telling off-color jokes.

To kill time, he even took up needlepoint. Many times a visitor would enter the trailer to find Rock, Dobson, and Walker sipping Scotch or laughing at a dirty joke over their needlework.

Rock became close friends with Walker during the series. In February 1974 Rock had a minor operation on his toe and had to recuperate at home. His friend Matthew West was staying at the Castle at the same time because he had torn the cartilage in his leg. Walker came to the house every day to visit Rock, West recalled.

"We both had our toes and feet up in the air and Nancy would visit and entertain Rock. She's a very bright woman, with a great mind, and Rock loved that in her. He admired women with intelligence. I remember sitting there listening to her quick wit and Rock's laughter," West said.

"Sometimes when Rock would watch the show on a Sunday night and be distressed by it, he would come in on Monday having drunk too much," recalled director Lou Antonio. "He'd be a little bloaty, a little sweaty. I almost couldn't shoot a close-up until after lunch—his breath. I'd say, 'Rock, go gargle!' and he'd say, 'I did.' And I'd say, 'Chew gum!' and he'd say, 'I did.' I'd say, 'Eat a mint!' And he'd say, 'I've got five of them in my mouth.' The man was fantastic."

Rock found the hours long and tedious; he couldn't wait until the end of the day to leave the studio and party. Rock's alcohol consumption soared, as did his nicotine intake.

"I'd really get ripped," he admitted. "I was tired at the end of the day and it didn't seem I was drinking that much, but I was. I was smoking too much, four or five packs a day. I rarely got to bed before two A.M. and was up before six. I drove myself to the edge and began to feel it."

Friends claimed the pressures of the show caused him

to become more promiscuous. During this period in his life he'd often go out to hit the gay bars.

Frustrated playing the police commissioner of San Francisco, Rock sought escape from the show by making weekend trips to that city and its open gay community. There he and friends such as media consultant Ken Maley and writer Armistead Maupin would visit popular gay discos such as the Trocadero Transfer and the I-Beam.

"I'm going to be honest," said Epstein. "I don't think he was terribly prepared [for the show] because he was having a wonderful time in life. I don't think he looked at the script the night before. He didn't study his material. He would learn his lines while we were lighting the set. But he never slowed us down. He was always there.

"Even though he may have been a bad boy from seven at night until two in the morning, when he rolled out of the sack, he was a perfect professional."

Rock's stunt double, George Robotham, remembered walking into Rock's trailer early in the morning and finding him very depressed. "He didn't like the scripts. 'The words are unsayable,' he would tell me. He was very professional and he liked everything to be right."

As Rock grew disenchanted with the show, his relationship with Susan Saint James also became strained, almost to the breaking point.

"He detested Susan," said director Finkel bluntly. "One of the reasons is that she taxed him, and that's why I think he didn't like her. She would come to a scene with such enthusiasm and such preproduction work—and this was a shock to Rock because now he had to change what was planned. He would have to go to work.

"Rock could get by with just playing a scene as it was originally planned, but Susan tried to bring some creativity to the set and Rock couldn't deal with it. He just liked to do his little number and go right back to the trailer."

Finkel also believed that Rock became bothered by the lovey-dovey relationship of the characters that he and Saint James played. There were very few episodes in which Mac and Sally didn't smooch and allude to their hot sex life. The connubial bed was a major prop on the set.

"This probably rubbed against the other life he was leading," said Finkel. "I detected in him that he was irritated about her in general. He just didn't like her. She was a kind of a hippie in those days and he may not have liked that."

But Rock never spoke out against Saint James. Antonio remembered the day that Saint James decided not to show up on the set because of a contract negotiation. It was the first day of shooting a new season. There were a hundred people waiting on the set, including Rock. Rock never said a word.

"Susan was not the best-behaved girl during those years," said Epstein. "She was in constant conflict with management. If she was bothered by something, she might appear late on the set. Rock knew what was going on, but there were never any games from him—like 'I'll wait until Susan comes on the set.' When he was called, he went."

Saint James's husband at the time worked as a makeup man on the show. He and Rock did not get along. "That was part of her deal. Rock was impatient with that sort of thing, so that caused friction," said Epstein.

"Her husband wouldn't even speak to Rock," said Dobson. "In the beginning Rock and the guest stars, Susan, and I would go to his trailer–dressing room to rehearse lines. For the first year Susan would do this, but after she got married, it didn't happen as often. She was affected by her marriage. Rock couldn't have liked it too much because it was affecting the show."

Despite tensions on the set, Rock became upset by any public displays of anger. "He had a fear of having any kind of altercation," recalled Finkel. The director remembered one very hot day when he chewed out the cameraman for not having the proper equipment on the location. "Rock was shattered by this explosion that I had," Finkel said. "As a matter of fact, he went to Jon Epstein and expressed his unhappiness at my display."

Rock loved to get laughs out of the cast and crew. In one episode he had to jump in a lake that was located on the studio back lot. It was a miserable day and the water was cold. Right in the middle of the scene, Rock looked seriously into the camera and said, "I have to make a wee-wee." Everyone yelled, "So go ahead." And they all stood around while he did. He finally gave a thumbs-up sign, got a round of applause from cast and crew, and the scene was reshot.

On location in San Pedro for another episode, stunt double Robotham was supposed to make a dive into the water. But Rock told Robotham he would do it instead. The director, John Astin, nearly went into shock. "Don't worry, Rock's probably a better diver than I am," Robotham told Astin as Rock made the dive successfully.

While he loved water, Rock had a real fear of heights. In fact, he was so afraid that he even refused to watch stunts that involved high places, which would literally make him sick. During one production meeting, a director outlined a scene in which he wanted Rock to get into a crane and be lifted onto the roof of a building. Rock looked pale. Robotham shook his head and spoke up for Rock. "No way," he told the director. "He's too old and too rich."

For one episode, the cast and crew had gone to San Diego to shoot some scenes in an amusement park. One scene called for Rock and Schuck to get on an enormously high Ferris wheel and ride to the top, where it would get stuck. Rock, who had not read the script, was called from his trailer and reported to the director, Bob Finkel. It was Finkel's first "McMillan" episode, and he was unaware of Rock's fear of heights. "What's up?" Rock asked. "I want you and John to get on the Ferris wheel and we'll take you up and then it will get stuck." Rock slowly looked skyward and began to tremble. He looked sick. "I'm not going up in that!" he said. "I don't like to go up high to begin with, but *that* high, no way!"

Finkel, who had been hired to cut production time on the episodes to fourteen days, didn't have time to worry about Rock's acrophobia. "I had planned the shots. I had the camera cranes ready. This was my first show, and it was a difficult one to deliver," said Finkel.

So the director played on Rock's sympathetic nature, which was well known throughout the industry. "I guess I'm going to have to get on the phone and call Jon Epstein and tell him I can't even get my star to do the script. I'll never work on this lot again."

Rock looked up at the Ferris wheel, looked back at Finkel, and finally gave in. "Oh, Jesus, all right, I'll try it," he said, looking deathly ill.

"Any other star would have walked away and said, 'If you need me, I'll be in my trailer,'" said Finkel. "But it bothered him a great deal that I could get into trouble. He was a very decent man."

Saint James got pregnant, so the fact that a little McMillan was on the way had to be brought into the script. It was a baby that never came downstairs. All the baby scenes were off-camera. "Rock didn't want a baby," said Stern. "He did not want any scenes with the baby. He said, 'There's so little that you can do other than say, "Isn't the baby cute?"' He felt we couldn't further the story with the baby."

Saint James's actual baby, however, was all too present on the set. Saint James insisted on nursing her between takes, which annoyed Rock, according to Finkel.

At the end of the 1975–76 season, Nancy Walker and Susan Saint James left the show. Walker went to ABC to star in her own show, and Saint James left in a reported dispute over her contract.

Saint James was written out of the script by having Sally McMillan die in a plane crash. As a widower, the commissioner hired a new housekeeper named Agatha, played by Martha Raye. For the final season, the show was renamed "McMillan."

NBC was hesitant about putting Raye on the show when her name was suggested by Epstein as a replacement for Walker. "They said, 'Nah, you don't want to use her. She's too old. Nobody knows who she is.' They were stupid reasons. Rock thought she would be wonderful and asked me whether I wanted him to get involved and make a call. The next day NBC called and gave me the go-ahead to use Martha. Rock managed to get it done."

"Rock adored Martha," said Finkel. "When she came on the show, it was a whole new Rock. They had been friends before. There are certain women in the business who are darlings of the gay set—Joan Rivers, Martha. I don't know what it is; they are outlandish or something."

So exhausted was Rock with the show that he demanded and got a clause in his contract giving him the right to leave the set at six o'clock every night, whatever might be happening. On Monday nights, he'd rush home to watch "Monday Night Football." "Would you believe we shot a two-hour episode in fourteen days?" he told an interviewer. "That's a ridiculous amount of pressure, drive-you-up-the-wall type pressure."

By this time he was getting $125,000 an episode. "They started making the money so attractive that I couldn't resist," he said, giving his reason for signing a new contract.

Tragedy struck during the last season. Rock was on the set when he got word that the most important woman in his life, his mother, Kay, had died. She was seventy-seven, a victim of Parkinson's disease and a stroke. A small funeral was held in Newport Beach, where she lived in the opulent house he had given her. Actress Claire Trevor was the only celebrity he invited to the service.

"Rock was very stoic about her death," said Dobson, who went with Rock to the service. "He didn't cry and he rarely talked about her again—only if someone brought up the subject."

Rock never even called childhood pal Jim Matteoni to let him know that she had died. It was only during a subsequent visit to Illinois, when Matteoni mentioned that his mother had died, that Rock told him about Kay.

Throughout his career, until her death, Kay and Rock were more like friends than mother and son. He would call her often and visit on weekends, when they would play bridge. Tom Clark often accompanied Rock. Kay was aware that Clark was living at the Castle. She also attended parties at the Castle when many of the guests were homosexuals. It's certain that she knew of Rock's sexual preference, but that knowledge never interfered in their warm relationship. Rock and his mother sometimes took trips together. He often took her shopping in Beverly Hills. Kay was extremely proud of her son. When friends visited, she would regale them with the latest news about Rock's career.

"I made sure she had a good life as well as I could give her," Rock said. "I sent her on trips—she loved to travel. I sent her around the world twice. [Because of her illness] she couldn't cook anymore. She couldn't hold cards anymore. She had a stroke, went unconscious, never recovered. Boy, I hope I go that fast." Rock made this statement in August 1984—two months after he was diagnosed as having AIDS.

His mother's death caused one major change in Rock's life: he never again celebrated Christmas. Rock always loved the holidays. He and his mother would cook a Christmas feast, and dozens of friends would be invited to the Castle to partake, with Rock and Kay hosting the shindig.

The week before Christmas, Rock would become a little boy again, buying elaborate presents in Beverly Hills for his friends and then spending his evenings wrapping them himself in the garage in a tangle of ribbons and gift paper.

There were no more parties after his mother died. His reason for celebrating Christmas was to make his mother happy. "After she died, it just wasn't Christmas to him anymore," Dobson said.

Christmas became a day he would skip. "He always went away," said Sylvia Fine. "When his mother was alive, Christmas was big. When she died, that was the end of it. He went on long boat trips usually."

Rock returned to the "McMillan" set the day after the funeral and carried on as usual. In all, he did forty-two episodes.

"The shows got progressively more difficult to do just because they were familiar and we had lost the husband-wife relationship," said Stern. "We tried to find something to substitute for it but nothing worked."

Rock was thrilled when "McMillan" finally ended. One friend said that as soon as the series was finished, Rock sold his residual rights back to the producers for several million dollars rather than wait until the program went into syndication.

Rock got a physical after the series ended and was told he had high blood pressure for the first time in his life. "My doctor said it was because I was working on 'McMillan,'" he said. "I was under strain, overweight, and getting no exercise. As soon as I finished the series, he had me take brisk walks—not runs—in the hills. Within two weeks my blood pressure was back to normal."

After "McMillan" finished its run, Rock took some time off. He went to New York, where he bought an apartment in the Beresford, on Central Park West, which he shared with Clark.

"He loved the energy of New York," said Matthew West. "He wanted to get the stimulation of living there a while, get away from all the sun in L.A."

In New York, according to friends, Rock got caught up in that city's frenetic gay scene. "He was a hell-raiser," recalled a young man who became a friend of Rock during that time. "He was a lot of fun. Once he had a couple of drinks in him, he didn't care about being seen in the bars or what he was doing."

Rock had a succession of lovers, mostly one-night stands, the friend said.

"He was intrigued by the gay scene in New York. It was so much raunchier than in L.A. Rock never got involved in the kinky stuff, but he was intrigued by the openness of it all in the clubs," a friend said.

In New York, Rock's ambitions to be a more serious actor resurfaced. Rock asked acting teacher Uta Hagen to coach him privately. She wasn't interested in giving private lessons, but she told Rock he could come to one of her classes at H.B. Studio in Greenwich Village.

Rock told Hagen how insecure he was about his acting ability. He said he felt he had succeeded on his looks and with luck—not on his skill. All his life critics and enemies could sting him to the core—and frequently did—with statements about how much of a Hollywood package he was. "Rock Hudson is completely an invention of his agent," carped one typical debunker. "His name, his voice, his personality were all made up for him."

"He felt he was not skillful as a stage actor," said Hagen. "That was probably true, although I don't know. He was very interested in studying. I found him unbelievably

Roy Harold Scherer, Jr., at two, with his aunt Evelyn. (*Pictorial Parade Inc.*)

Three-year-old Roy enjoyed a happy home life. (*Syndication International: Photo Trends*)

Above, left: Roy's high-school graduation photo. His name was changed after he was adopted by his stepfather, Wallace Fitzgerald. (*AP/Wide World Photos*)

Above, right: Aged eighteen, in the U.S. Navy as an aviation mechanic. He was later transferred to laundry duty. He had his teeth capped later. (*Syndication International: Photo Trends*)

A rare photo of Roy with his real father. (*Pictorial Parade Inc.*)

Newly named Rock Hudson, with his mother, Kay Olsen, on location. (*AP/Wide World Photos*)

Henry Willson, the agent who launched Rock Hudson into stardom. (*UPI/Bettman Newsphotos*)

Below: By the late 1950s, Rock Hudson began to see the fruits of his labor. (*AP/Wide World Photos*)

One of Rock's first publicity dates was Vera-Ellen. Fan magazines claimed their breakup made Rock marriage-shy. (*Movie Star News*)

Rock and Piper Laurie both attended Universal's acting classes for contract players. (*AP/Wide World Photos*)

Mamie Van Doren, another Universal contract player. (*Kobal Collection*)

Rock was rumored to have been in love with actress Marilyn Maxwell. (*Photo Trends*)

Dorothy Malone starred with Rock in an early Texas saga, *Written on the Wind*. (*AP/Wide World Photos*)

Jane Wyman presenting Rock with a Golden Globe. The film they co-starred in, *Magnificent Obsession*, made him a movie star. (*AP/Wide World Photos*)

Rock called his part in *Giant* "a marvelous role." On the set, he and co-star Elizabeth Taylor formed a lifelong friendship. (*Kobal Collection*)

James Dean was killed in a car accident before the film's release. (*SYGMA*)

Henry Willson arranged Rock's marriage to Phyllis Gates in 1955. (*AP/Wide World Photos*)

It is probable that the couple cared for each other and worked at their relationship. "Marriage destroyed it," Rock said later. (*John Bryson/ SYGMA*)

"World Film Favorites" Rock and Doris Day. *Pillow Talk* focused on Rock's comic sensibility and became a smash hit. (*AP/Wide World Photos*)

Rock and Tony Randall shared a sense of humor and a penchant for the absurd. (*Movie Star News/Universal Pictures Company, Inc.*)

Rock had a deep attachment to the Castle, the grand, secluded Spanish-style mansion he purchased in the early 1960s. (*Peter Brandt*)

An uncommon photograph: Rock at home. (*SYGMA*)

Above: Rock as seen through the eyes—and lens—of Gina Lollobrigida. (*AP/World Wide Photos*)

Right and above, right: Two of the best of the ruggedly masculine candids that publicists used to secure Rock's heartthrob reputation. (*AP/Wide World Photos*)

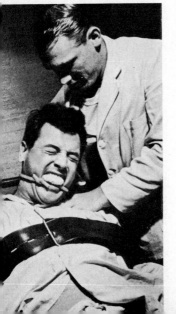

Above: Controversy surrounded the set of *Darling Lili*, starring Rock and Julie Andrews. (*Kobal Collection/Paramount Pictures Corporation*)

Top: Leading men. (*AP/Wide World Photo*)

Left: Rock's performance in *Seconds* was sometimes eerily realistic. (*Kobal Collection*)

In his last movie, *The Ambassador*, Rock took second billing to Robert Mitchum. (*SYGMA*)

Above: "Gambling with his life" was the phrase used to publicize "Las Vegas Strip Wars," filmed in 1984. Rock was beginning to look ill. (*AP/Wide World Photos*)

Right: A love scene on "Dynasty" caused a furor when it was revealed that Rock had AIDS. (*Movie Star News*)

Rock and Tom Clark. (© 1985 Ron Galella)

Marvin Mitchelson and Marc Christian. Christian was catapulted to national fame when he hired Mitchelson to sue Rock's estate for fourteen million dollars. (© 1985 Ron Galella/Smeal-Galella Ltd.)

Rock's appearance stunned the press at the conference announcing Doris Day's new cable television series, "Doris Day's Best Friends." (*AP/Wide World Photos*)

courteous, eager, and modest. I was terribly impressed with him and I would have loved to work with him.

"I don't do private coaching," she told him. "He had asked me to do that and I said no—that he should sit in my class and see if he felt comfortable."

Hagen taught advanced acting. Ninety percent of her students were professionals, but they were not stars. In these classes, students did exercises and scenes. Rock would have had to jump right in and mix it up—just as if he were back at Universal as a young contract player.

"I've found that I've had a lot of stars who came in and just were intimidated by making fools of themselves in front of young colleagues," said Hagen. "It's very tough. I've had people do it, and I've thought they have tremendous guts."

Rock came to about three classes. "He only audited," Hagen recalled. "He only sat in and watched, and talked to me in between. But he never did any work for me at all. He was welcome to. It isn't like I closed him out. I would have been happy to have him.

"I said to him, 'This is going to take a lot of courage. And I don't know if you're up to that. Or if you want it that badly.'"

Rock didn't want it that badly, and returned to the West Coast. "I think the atmosphere frightened him," said Hagen. "It was a class and there were much younger people there. I think that frightened him. It wasn't the right atmosphere."

Rock continued doing long-form TV, starring in four miniseries. The first was the TV adaptation of Arthur Hailey's "Wheels," in 1978, followed by Ray Bradbury's "Martian Chronicles."

By the late seventies, with the "McMillan" series behind him, Rock had come to approach most television and movie projects with a jaundiced air. Any hopes he had once harbored that he could cast off his matinee-idol image and emerge as a respected actor had long since died. But the dream persisted, and the gap between it and reality was what made him smoke more, drink more, and eat more. On the set he remained his usual pleasant, uncomplaining, professional self. He did the job, took the money, and maybe had a little fun joking with his pals along the way; he didn't make the mistake of expecting anything more. As far as great hopes went, Rock had been burned once too often.

When "McMillan" director Lou Antonio came to him in 1980 with a script for a television miniseries, Rock was unenthusiastic. Mediocrity was one thing; out-and-out trash another. Antonio was persuasive. No one, least of all he, was pretending "The Star Maker" was anything more than junk, but they could have a good time doing it anyway, couldn't they?

Antonio himself was up for the project. He had just finished doing a movie of the week about New York's Guardian Angels, who tend the subways. After a month in the bowels of the Bronx, he wanted nothing more than a chance to get back to Los Angeles and do a tits-and-tinsel extravaganza. "And sure enough, up comes this piece of dreck called 'The Star Maker.' The people are pretty and they dress nice and it was about show business and it was total sleaze," he said. Just what the doctor ordered.

It took a little doing to convince Rock. The leading man was a Roger Vadim–type director, who fell in and out of love with his leading ladies. "I wanted Rock because I thought he epitomized a positive side of Hollywood, and this thing was so anti-Hollywood," said Antonio. He also wanted Rock because a number of other stars, including Michael Caine, had turned it down flat.

Finally, the director was able to talk him into it, telling him that he intended to make changes to improve the script. Rock's character had plenty of dramatic scenes to play, and Antonio knew that appealed to him. "He had some sensitive stuff to play, some stuff he had to use himself, his emotions, to get to. I knew that would appeal to him." Suzanne Pleshette, Ed McMahon, Brenda Vaccaro, Melanie Griffith, and Jack Scalia were among the others Antonio persuaded to do the project.

The character, a heavy smoker and drinker, ends up dying of a heart attack, and that did interest Rock. "Rock did a bunch of research on it, because he had to have the attack on-screen." He studied the symptoms carefully so he'd be able to portray them. It was the sort of extra work Rock often did to prepare for any role, just part of his professionalism. Only in this case, there was another dividend: nine months later it saved his life.

"He told me after his bypass that he'd been having these odd feelings in his chest. He didn't feel so hot, a little draggy. And he started thinking back on the research he had done, and he said, 'Son of a gun, maybe.' And he went to his doctor and his doctor said, 'Maybe, my ass—yes,'" said Antonio. Within days, Rock had met with a surgeon and was scheduled for a quintuple bypass, which was performed in November 1981.

The mood on the "Star Maker" set was very cheerful, even silly. No one had any mistaken notions about the caliber of the project, so everyone could relax. Certainly the director had no pretentions. Antonio was careful to save some of the more outrageous outtakes, including one of him mooning the camera. In another, an actor removes a slice of salami from a pile. "What is this?" he says. "Fried horse cock," says Rock, straight-faced.

The camera also recorded an appealing outtake in which Brenda Vaccaro tore off her wig and staged a mini-rebellion against her part. "I hate this character. This is not a real woman. I hate this woman," she emoted, to loud applause from her co-stars. In yet another, Rock was shown giving a long, serious speech about the importance of the camera to a movie star. "It catches it all," he said earnestly. "The slightest emotion." He gestured toward the camera. "You have to respect this . . ." and blanked. "This . . . wiener."

During one very emotional scene at a graveyard, Rock wept deeply. Unfortunately, his nose gushed at the same time. At the end of the shooting, Antonio proudly presented him with a framed picture of the result. "It looked like a big icicle coming out of his nose," the director recalled fondly.

Antonio and the others did get to see one side of Rock's personality that impressed them greatly—his amazingly stoic reaction to personal pain. In one scene, Rock had a fistfight; Antonio had arranged a stack of pillows for him to pummel, for the close-up. "I'd learned from therapy that just pounding it out sometimes releases emotion, and I knew the big fellow carried a lot of really strong feelings in him," the director said.

Antonio told Rock to pound as hard as he could, to "see what would come out." Rock was enthusiastic about the idea, and went at it with a will. Only moments later there was a sickening sound—*craack*. In his fervor, Rock had smashed his hand straight into the camera. Strips of flesh from his broken hand were hanging on the camera.

Rock was rushed to the doctor, and Antonio started planning to shoot around his leading man for the next week. But only two hours later, Rock was back. He had insisted that his doctor, Rex Kennamer, give him a removable cast so he could continue shooting. The doctor had tried to convince him that his hand wouldn't set right if he did that, but Rock had insisted anyway.

Since a hand has so many nerves, a broken one is extremely painful. Rock's hand was so swollen and discolored that makeup had to be applied to it every time he appeared on camera. He made no complaint and continued doing his work.

True to the doctor's prediction, Rock's hand did not set correctly with the removable cast. He was forced to have it rebroken and set again a few weeks later. This time, he told Antonio, the Novocain hadn't taken—his hand had been broken without anesthetic. Yet Rock still insisted on a removable cast, so he could continue to work.

Antonio was overwhelmed. "When you see a guy like that, who's got every excuse in the world to lounge around, and he comes right back to work—it inspires the whole set. It certainly brought tears to a lot of eyes. He would never baby himself, ever, ever." As he had done before, Rock was able somehow to put the pain aside, compartmentalize it, almost as if it were happening to someone else, and get on with the show. His courage and stoicism amazed everyone; it was heroic yet oddly puzzling. People wondered how anyone could manage to ignore that kind of pain and disability. It was a question many of them would be asking again four years later.

"The Star Maker" aired on NBC in May 1981, breaking no records and enhancing no one's career, as expected. For Rock, it had just been another journeyman job, forgotten the moment it was over.

After "The Star Maker," Rock starred in another NBC miniseries, "World War III," in which he played a beleaguered president on a fatal collision course with the Soviets.

Before production started, Rock was anxious to meet the director, David Greene, to discuss the script. Greene had been brought in to direct the series at the last minute, after the original director, Boris Sagal, died tragically when he walked into the tail rotor of a helicopter while shooting footage on the slopes of Mount Hood.

Rock called Greene a week before production started and the two met for lunch at La Cere, a show-business restaurant in the San Fernando Valley.

"I found him very shy and anxious," said Greene, an Englishman. "Suddenly, apropos of nothing, in the middle of lunch Rock said to me, 'You're not going to shout at me in front of other people, are you?' I said, 'Is that why you wanted to have lunch with me?' And he said, 'Well, I'm afraid of directors I don't know.' He was anxious not to be hurt and embarrassed by a director. It seemed to me that he had that kind of experience with some previous director. He showed me his vulnerability."

Greene was surprised that Rock was still so sensitive after having spent so many years in the business. The director was able to reassure Rock that there would be no such problems, and the two men developed a close relationship during the production.

"I always thought of Rock as a very lightweight actor because of some of the films he'd done, like *Pillow Talk*. I wondered how good he was going to be as the president of the United States in a serious movie," Greene said.

Before shooting started, Rock called Greene at home virtually every night with ideas about how a president would behave under different circumstances. "He was very insightful and right in every case," the director said. "I made these changes in the script and he changed my mind about his suitability for the part."

In one scene Rock impressed the crew, co-stars, and director when he was able to show the emotions of a world leader about to order bombers to Russia. Rock actually broke down and cried on the set—real tears. "Rock's agonizing in making that decision was very sincerely felt by him," said Greene. "It wasn't just acted on the surface. He became that character."

In another scene, Rock had everyone on the set in hysterics. Greene wanted to make the president as realistic as possible. He thought it would be appropriate to show him in the bathroom washing up and singing a bit of opera. Rock told Greene that he knew "Celeste Aida" from the opera Aida. Rock went into the bathroom with the camera rolling and started to sing, but in fact all he knew were the two words celeste aida, which he repeated over and over, slightly out of tune. Still laughing about that scene, Greene said, "I felt it was suitable for a president not to really know it, so we used it and it worked."

After "McMillan," Rock swore he'd never do another TV series, but in 1981 he signed for a new NBC detective show, "The Devlin Connection." "I like to work," he gave as the reason, which was the truth. Rock's production company, Mammouth Films Inc., co-produced the show.

With some embarrassment, he told an interviewer, "You know, in the fifties, I looked down on television. I thought it was beneath me. I was a star. After ["McMillan"] I said I'd never do another TV show. But I think as you grow older, you learn to keep your mouth shut more because you never know how badly you're going to embarrass yourself later."

Rock played a character named Brian Devlin, a suave and sophisticated former CIA agent who somehow became managing director of a cultural center in Los Angeles. A twenty-eight-year-old son he never knew he had shows up on the scene and the two start solving crimes together.

The son was played by Jack Scalia, thirty-two, a handsome model turned actor from New York who had also appeared in "The Star Maker." Scalia was Rock's protégé, handpicked by him for the part.

The first four episodes were taped during October and early November 1981, just before Rock's fifty-sixth birthday. During production Rock started experiencing chest pains and shortness of breath. He was smoking three packs of cigarettes a day, drinking heavily, and not exercising and was under a lot of stress from the show.

"Then finally one night, in the middle of the night, I had terrible pains and I thought, Oh, no. This ain't indigestion," he said. "I also had a dead feeling in my arm and thought, Oh, God, not me. I immediately went to the hospital, to emergency, and they did all these tests. The doctors discovered these blocked arteries. I just thought, This is ridiculous. This happens to other people, not me."

Rock's doctor, Rex Kennamer, told him that he would need bypass surgery, and an operation was scheduled for a few days later at Cedars-Sinai Medical Center.

Fortunately, the six-hour quintuple-bypass operation was successful. "The heart surgery was my second chance at life," Rock said. "You have to think about your health."

Rock had a quick recovery and went on a twenty-four-day Caribbean cruise, returning to "The Devlin Connection" set in January 1982. "He still smoked," said "Devlin" director Christian Nyby III. "I was amazed. I think he felt guilty about it. Every once in a while he'd say, 'I shouldn't be doing this.' But then he would light up."

"The bypass really knocked the wind out of his sails," said Matthew West. "I don't think he was ever really the same. He lost weight, his gauntness showed. His bypass was not a simple one. He'd show me his legs where they took the blood vessels out, and all that ghastly business."

"Devlin" finally premiered on NBC in October 1982. The reviews were terrible. *TV Guide* said the stories lacked "crispness and clarity." *Variety*, somewhat kinder, said the show had "room for improvement." Another critic put it this way: "There is absolutely nothing unique or different about 'The Devlin Connection.'"

"I think perhaps the chemistry between Rock and Scalia wasn't really there. That was probably the primary problem," said Nyby. "Jack was a nice person, but he really was unschooled. At times it would work between them, but the audience didn't buy it. And the story line got a little preposterous for the audience to accept."

Not unexpectedly, "Devlin" didn't return in 1983. "It was an unsuccessful series, which I never should have done," Rock admitted later. "That series undid me."

Rock's irritation with "McMillan" and the assembly-line world of television did have one positive effect: it led him to take a step into a new world, one that both terrified and intrigued him. In many ways it was the bravest thing he had ever done professionally. After twenty-five years of films and television, Rock Hudson went on the stage.

Salome Jens, who had worked with him in *Seconds*, was only one of many in the industry who were impressed. "I think it was phenomenal that he did that. And did it well. Very courageous. He was really clear that he wanted to grow, and challenge himself. He was willing to work and put himself on the line. Not many stars are willing to do that. He had a lot of guts."

The stage is a very different world from that of the movie studio. There is no editing to handle the mistakes, no camera angles to mask incompetence. Rock had suffered from stage fright all his life, even when doing movies. He once said that he only bit his nails when he was in a film—then bit them nonstop. The terror had never left him. Now he was close to fifty, a time when many men are slowing down, looking for lesser challenges. He knew he was setting himself up for the possibility of brutal ridicule from the critics. Yet it was a chance he felt he had to take.

During the seventies, Rock worked in three musicals: *I Do! I Do!*, *Camelot*, and *On the 20th Century*. He had always loved musicals and had never had the chance to do one before. Universal Studios had stayed away from them. "To me, this is what entertainment really is," he once said.

It wasn't easy for him. He was terrified, shaken, wracked by insecurity. But he loved every minute of it.

Doing the musicals gave him some of the happiest moments he had ever had in his professional life.

"I don't know how I ever got the nerve to step on a stage," Rock admitted. "Much less a musical stage. I had made a couple of appearances on Carol Burnett's TV show and fooled around a little singing and dancing with her. But that's all it was, just clowning around. She's the one who talked me into doing I Do! I Do!"

"I joined his fan club years ago," said Carol Burnett later. "When I wanted an actor for a live production of I Do! I Do! who could learn the whole show and its nineteen songs in three weeks, I thought of Rock. He'd never done a play and never sung on stage, and singing on stage is naked, but he called me back in two minutes and said he'd do it.

"At the premiere, I never saw anybody so frightened in my life, but in five minutes he was into it. He's no Fred Astaire, but he just clumped around and enjoyed it. He was such a joy to work with. It was one of the greatest experiences I've had on stage."

The play previewed in San Bernardino before coming east in 1974. It was Rock's first time on stage, and he had to sing the opening lyrics of the show.

"Because the stage was small, they had to push the curtain to let me sit down. So I actually felt the curtain go up," Rock said. "My heart jumped into my throat and I knew I was not going to be able to sing. Happily, the audience burst into applause. It lasted a minute or so, and it gave me time to push my heart back where it belongs. From then on it was easy."

At the actual opening, in Connecticut, Rock was "scared shitless. I thought the critics would murder me." Instead, one wrote, "Rock Hudson is having the time of his life on stage—and it's catching."

"After that I was hooked."

Rock had had a yen to star in a musical for years; as far back as 1965 he had told Sheilah Graham he was interested. He had been encouraged, he said, by the success of performers such as Rex Harrison and Robert Preston, who were not actually singers. But when he did it, he was determined to sing every note in the score. He had begun taking singing lessons with Herb Green, just to prepare himself. Later, he studied with David Craig, the husband of Nancy Walker and a highly respected coach who had helped many stars step into musical comedy roles—Raquel Welch, Jean Simmons, and Alexis Smith among them. His ultimate wish was to appear in a Broadway musical instead of on tour, but this was never to happen.

After the American run of *I Do!* was over, Rock starred in a London version, with Juliet Prowse, in 1976. The London critics were nastier. "He wasn't as bad as I'd hoped he'd be," said one, infuriating Rock.

By this time, Rock had had enough of a taste to know he wanted more. In 1977 he toured with *Camelot*, playing, among other places, the Westbury Music Fair in New York. In 1979 he went on the road with *On the 20th Century*.

Rock was comfortable with show people—actors, singers, dancers, and crew. The friendliness, the jokes, the team spirit, the entire atmosphere was more like what he had experienced during his studio years than what he'd found when working in TV. Making musicals was light-years away from the fast-paced, grind-'em-out world of television. Here, there was time for fun.

"He was such a beacon for everybody," said Leslie Easterbrook, who understudied female lead Judy Kaye in *On the 20th Century*. "He was always telling me how nervous he was afterwards, but he never displayed it. He was like—the beacon on the head of the ship."

In *I Do!* Rock had had his pal Carol Burnett to lean on; in *Camelot* Stockton Briggle, the director, was a good friend. In *On the 20th Century* he was under the direction of Hal Prince, who was not a friend and who had a tendency to crack the whip.

"Hal was very difficult and hard on him," said Easterbrook. "He treated him like any other actor. He'd say, 'Come on, do it this way. Hey, I'm not getting it.' Hal's not a particularly easy person to work with, and he was giving Rock very harsh instructions."

Easterbrook was amazed at Rock's reaction to Prince. "I thought, Why is he taking this? He never showed any kind of anger or pouting, things that actors, especially stars, will do when a director really takes them to task. My main reaction was, 'Boy, he's a real actor. He really wanted to learn, to work hard."

Rock got along well with the whole cast. "He never made any distinction between principals and chorus, stars and bit players. It didn't make a damn bit of difference," said Easterbrook. Both Rock and Tom Clark, who was with him throughout the show, spent after-hours with the cast while on tour. Easterbrook had never met Rock before the show and was initially nervous. After all, this was a star. But Rock went out of his way to put her at ease.

"He was a bit of a father confessor. I had problems, missing my husband." Easterbrook had married just before leaving on the tour. "Rock would always ask how we were doing." As usual, Rock volunteered nothing about his own life or problems. "I got the feeling he'd love to really talk. But he wasn't giving on his end, he didn't let you become involved in his life. It was a haunting thing. I think it was hard for him to really let go."

Touring for many months in a close-knit setting, Easterbrook became aware of a striking characteristic of Rock's life-style—his lack of discipline. In the theater, especially the musical theater, heavy drinking and smoking are uncommon. Dancers particularly look on their body as their most important instrument, and treat it as such. "He had great discipline as an actor, but not in his personal life. He liked to eat and drink and smoke, and it was very difficult for him to curtail any of those activities on his own," said Easterbrook. "That was the child in him."

At one point, even Rock realized that his heavy smoking was hurting his voice; if he could quit, he thought, maybe the singing would come easier. In Chicago, he and several other cast members went to a hypnotist. It worked like a charm for a couple of weeks. After that, Rock started sneaking smokes again, soon working his way back up to his two-to-three-pack-a-day habit. When Easterbrook worked with him during "The Devlin Connection," the first thing ock did was ask her for cigarettes. "When I said I didn't smoke, he said, 'Then what good are you?'" Rock had just recovered from heart surgery. Easterbrook couldn't help being a little shocked.

Generally Rock was able to mask his nervousness, but Easterbrook remembered one time when his façade failed him. In Los Angeles, Judy Kaye became sick, and had to leave the theater midplay. Rock offered to announce to the audience at intermission that Easterbrook would take her place in the second act. But as he stepped out in front of the curtain, he froze.

"Judy Kaye has had to leave, due to illness," he said. "She will be replaced by Leslie . . . Leslie . . ." Rock had forgotten Easterbrook's last name.

The understudy was also a good six inches taller than Kaye. When she came on stage in the second act—wearing the star's outfit—the entire audience burst out laughing. Both Rock and Easterbrook forgot their lines, and joined in. "It was fun, but it was a horrible feeling. Rock was sweating. Sweat was running down his face," said Easterbrook.

For Rock, being on stage meant terror and elation. But he was working at something new, flexing himself, doing something he could be proud of.

PART II

CHAPTER FIVE
Changes

In the fall of 1982, a new man—young, sexy, and vital—came into Rock's life. Marc Christian MacGinnis was six feet, blond, blue-eyed, moustached, and well built—the ultimate Southern California surfer boy. He had a winning smile and a quick, biting wit. He sported nicely faded jeans, open-collared sport shirts, and white tennis shoes—a perfect "hunk." Christian, by his own admission, was bisexual. At the time he met Rock, he was living with an older woman named Liberty, with whom, he claimed, he had shared an intimate relationship. Christian and Liberty had been friends since he was twenty.

Clean-cut, athletic, and masculine, Marc Christian was the kind of young man to whom Rock had always been attracted. Then twenty-nine, twenty-eight years Rock's junior, Christian wasn't just another pretty face on Santa Monica Boulevard. He was bright and articulate, interested in politics, knew theater and film, and claimed he was a musicologist working on a project dealing with the history of pop music.

Just as Roy Fitzgerald secretly dreamed of becoming a movie star in Winnetka, Christian grew up in the conservative Orange County, California, community of Villa Park in the late 1960s with visions of becoming a rock musician or an actor. Only after he moved to Los Angeles did he acknowledge his sexual proclivities to his parents. Christian claimed his parents were accepting.

161

In 1982, when author Gore Vidal was seeking the Democratic nomination for U.S. senator in California, Christian and Liberty met Vidal at a university lecture. Liberty claimed they became friends. As a result, Christian became a driver and advance man for Vidal, shuttling him around as he spoke at political gatherings in Southern California that year.

One of those meetings was on Ventura Boulevard in the San Fernando Valley community of Sherman Oaks, just over the Hollywood Hills from Rock's place in Beverly Hills. Rock met Christian at this meeting. They shook hands firmly. Rock asked Christian if he was involved in the campaign, telling the young man that he himself was apolitical but had come to the party with a friend. They had a drink. Rock chain-smoked. They small-talked.

Somehow the conversation turned to music. "Rock told me he was a jazz buff," Christian recalled. "He liked a lot of the jazz records from the thirties and forties. I told him I was working on a project on the history of music, so I dealt with a lot of the types of records he liked."

Christian's project was a chronological history of pop music, starting with Edison's invention of the phonograph. The project involved tracking down records, transferring them to tape, compiling biographies of the artists, and documenting when the records became number one. He hoped to sell the project as a documentary for radio.

As the other guests swirled around them, Rock and Christian stayed in a corner together. There was an immediate chemistry between them, and a mutual interest. Rock asked whether it was possible to clean up the quality of old 78s and transfer them to tape. "I said yes. And he told me about his enormous record collection. He asked me if I could transfer some of his records to tape and enhance the sound quality. I said, 'Sure.'" (In fact, Rock owned professional music equipment and was quite knowledgeable about recording techniques himself.) Rock appeared pleased. He asked for Christian's telephone number and said he would get in touch.

Christian didn't think Rock was coming on to him by asking for his number. "I had just met him. I knew that he was gay. Everybody did. But I didn't know whether he had a relationship or what was going on in his life. He was attractive, but I had no inclination at the time."

Three days later Rock called. "I'm getting all my records out of boxes for you," he told Christian enthusiastically. "I'm going away for a few weeks, and when I get back, I'll call you and you can get started."

As promised, Rock telephoned when he got back. "Are you free this afternoon?" he asked. "I'd like to drop by." A short time later the movie star parked his Mercedes 450SL in the driveway of the two-story, yellow frame apartment building on a quiet, palm-lined, blue-collar residential street between Sunset and Santa Monica where Christian shared a small, neatly furnished unit with Liberty. It would have come as a shock to any passersby or residents who might have spotted Hudson getting out of his car that November day in 1982 and walking up the rickety outside steps to Christian's apartment. It certainly was a surprise to Christian.

"I thought it was strange at first that he'd come here— a big movie star like him coming here. Usually they like people to come to them. But actually I thought it was very nice that he wanted to come to where I lived."

Later Christian became convinced that Rock called on him because he wanted to hide the budding relationship from Clark and others in the Castle.

On that first visit, Rock brought some Benny Goodman for Christian to hear—"What's New?" and "A Long, Long Time." Christian played some of his tapes that he had transferred successfully. Rock was impressed. Rock and Christian spent two hours listening to and talking about music. When Liberty came home, Christian proudly introduced Rock to her. A few days later, Rock telephoned to ask Christian to lunch in Santa Monica. He also hired him to work part-time on his record collection for $150 a week.

"Our relationship developed gradually," Christian said. "We had lunch almost every day. We didn't really get to a conversation about us for a long, long time. He seemed intimidated. I think he was intimidated by my mind. 'How do you know so much about so many things?' he asked me. 'You see, I didn't have much of an education.' When he finally did start to tell me how he felt about me, he was very inhibited. He even asked me once, 'Do you think I'm attractive?' It was as if he needed the approval."

Rock began seeing Christian on the sly regularly. He'd drive to the apartment around noon, and they'd go out for a drink or lunch. Afterward, Rock would drop Christian off at his apartment so that he could get back to the Castle by 4:00 P.M. without arousing the suspicions of Clark, his secretary Mark Miller, and the other household help.

After about two months of midday meetings, Christian got fed up and demanded to know why Rock hadn't taken him to his house. According to Christian, Rock told him about his friendship with Tom Clark. Rock claimed the friendship had soured and that the situation at the Castle had become difficult.

After Hudson opened up to Christian about Clark, their relationship became more intimate and intense. Christian claimed they saw each other almost daily from the fall of 1982 to the fall of 1983, when he moved into the house.

Christian claimed that he and Hudson had sex sometime in spring 1983, about six months after their first rendezvous at Christian's apartment. "We'd been out to dinner at the Black Forest [a German restaurant in the Valley, one of Rock's favorites] and he didn't want to go home," Christian recalled. "'I'm just going to stay here in the Valley. I don't want to go back. I'll just get a room.' He asked me if I would stay with him. I said yes. We went to a motel." They had sex that night. Rock was nervous, according to Christian.

"He told me he had only been in love twice in his whole life and that I was the second time. The first time was in 1960 with someone named Lee, a blond-haired guy named Lee. I don't know anything about him. He just said that he was young and blond and my type and that he flipped out over him and that it didn't last very long, maybe six or seven months."

Rock also sneaked Christian into the house for a tour

while Clark was on a trip to New York in April and Miller was out on an errand. The only person in the house was Rock's English butler, James Wright. "James probably thought I was just some guy off the street," Christian recalled.

Rock continued seeing Christian through the summer of 1983—still hiding the relationship from Clark. In September, Rock took Christian on a trip to San Francisco, where they stayed at the Fairmont Hotel and ate at the Blue Boar, a French restaurant in the Pacific Heights—Marina area.

The lovers toured the city and strolled down Castro Street, stopping for drinks at a couple of bars. Rock was happier than he'd been in months. "I was a little worried about going into the bars," said Christian. "Oh, God, I thought, what if somebody recognizes Rock? It could be a problem for him. But nobody did. He got recognized more in L.A."

Rock wasn't worried when he went out in public with Christian. "He kept saying he didn't care what the public thought. He said he wouldn't go out of his way to tell people he was gay. 'If they know, they know,' he'd say. 'If they don't, they don't. Fuck 'em!'" Most of the time they went to gay bars and restaurants anyway. One of Rock's favorites was the Rose Tattoo on Robertson near Santa Monica, in predominantly gay West Hollywood. Rock was especially fond of going to talent night, on Mondays, which featured amateur singers. The place had an intimate atmosphere. Rock was well known there and felt comfortable. No one bothered him.

After returning from San Francisco, Rock confided in his secretary, Mark Miller, that he was seeing a young man, but did not tell him who he was.

Miller, a year younger than Rock, had become his secretary in 1972. Miller had been the manager and companion of George Nader, Rock's actor friend from the Universal days. Accompanied by Miller, Nader had gone to Europe in the early 1960s to make films and do television. When they returned in 1970, Mark Miller needed a job. Rock hired Miller because of his friendship with Nader.

Miller eventually became a central figure in his life and a controlling influence at the Castle during his illness.

With Christian in his life, Rock turned his attention toward his failing career, which was at an all-time low. Flo Allen, his longtime agent at the William Morris Agency, hadn't come up with a decent project that excited Rock in several years. Rock's last feature film had been *The Mirror Crack'd* in 1980; subsequently there had been some forgettable television films. Rock wanted to work, but no big parts were coming his way.

In recent years, Rock had gotten offers that never materialized into pictures, deals from producers that nobody had ever heard of in Spain and Italy. The salaries were in the range of $150,000 and $200,000.

"He liked her as a person," Christian said, "but he didn't like her as an agent anymore." Rock was usually docile in such matters. He always let others control his career. He was never one to complain, even though he might be inwardly seething. But Rock—so anxious to get work—went out of character for once and dropped Flo Allen—just as he was soon to cut his ties to Clark.

In the late summer of 1983 Rock Hudson was clearing all decks for a new life—one that was to last only two more years.

Enter Marty Baum, agent extraordinaire, who solicited Rock's representation when it became common knowledge that he had left Flo Allen and the William Morris Agency. Baum, who works for Creative Artists, one of William Morris's major competitors, held meetings with Rock in August.

"I discussed what I thought our agency could do for him," said Baum. "He discussed the fact that he hadn't made a picture in a long time. He said he was interested in quality projects. He wanted to stay busy. It wasn't a question of economic need. It was a question of being active."

Baum's pitch must have been impressive, because on September 19, 1983, Rock signed with Creative Artists. Marty Baum wasted no time. Three weeks later he called

Rock with good news. "He was in shock when I came up with a five-hundred-thousand-dollar offer, working with Robert Mitchum." The movie, produced by the Cannon Group, was called *The Ambassador*, a thriller about Middle East intrigue in which Hudson was to play a CIA agent.

"Rock was happy to be working with an actor of Mitchum's ability and stature," Baum said. While the money was good and the cast impressive (Ellen Burstyn also was a co-star), the role for which Rock signed was not. Still, though Rock's part was secondary to Mitchum's, it was his first acting job since the ill-fated "Devlin Connection," and he was excited to be going back to work. Rock was scheduled to leave for Israel in November. Baum, already working on the next project, promised Rock more work when he got back.

J. Lee Thompson, *The Ambassador*'s director, went to Israel with the Hudson part still uncast. Thompson received a call one day from Cannon head Menahem Golan. "Menahem telephoned me and said, 'What do you think about Rock Hudson for this part?' I didn't think Hudson would play it. I didn't think the part was really big enough for him. It was a subsidiary part. 'It would be wonderful if you can get him, but I doubt it,' I told Menahem. Other people had been mentioned for the part, but no one of Rock's stature. Naturally I said, 'If you can get him, it would be marvelous.' Menahem said, 'I can fix it right away.' I was delighted and I immediately telephoned Rock. Right from the start he implied we would have to do something with the part, to make it stronger and better. We did our best, which was unfortunately not really good enough."

In the movie, Mitchum plays a foolishly idealistic ambassador who thinks that by bringing young Arabs and Jews together a peaceful solution can be found to the Middle East turmoil—and, of course, the plans go wrong.

"Unfortunately," Thompson said, "in order to get the film made, there was a subsidiary story which I was never at all happy with. It was weak, not important, not really very good. Unfortunately, the subsidiary story, the thriller part, was carried largely by Rock Hudson."

Hudson was to play a CIA agent involved in a faction trying to blackmail the ambassador into resigning. "I very badly wanted to do the political side of the film, and I was hoping the thriller side of it would mesh. I don't think it was a very good match."

In October 1983, just before Rock was scheduled to leave for Israel, Clark moved out of the Castle. Clark and Rock agreed that they should spend some time apart. Clark decided to stay at Rock's Central Park West apartment in Manhattan.

"I was very fond of Tom Clark," Jon Epstein said. "Clark was very much in evidence all through the years that I was doing 'McMillan' and obviously I was aware that suddenly Clark was out of the house."

"When I come back from Israel," Rock told Clark, "I'll stop off in New York and we'll talk about it."

But Rock had no intention of talking it over with Clark, Christian maintained. "Once he was out—he was out. At the time, I was still doing the records for Rock. I said, 'Well, Tom's going to be out of the house and you're going to be leaving for Israel. Can I come up to the house to work? Could you let your secretary know or whatever?' And Rock said, 'Well, just stay there. I'll be gone for two months. There will be nobody there at night except for James. So stay in the house.' So I moved in. When Rock came back, I stayed. Tom didn't come back to L.A. for a year. By the time I'd moved in, he'd heard about me and knew there was a relationship going on."

Even in Christian's own words, Rock's invitation to him to stay in the house appeared to be casual. It was not unusual for Rock to have friends (and occasionally lovers) stay in the house when he was away. After he returned, some remained indefinitely to help around the Castle.

Rock left for Israel alone. It had been a stressful time. He was not in a good emotional state when he arrived in Tel Aviv to begin two months of strenuous shooting, his first work in a long time.

"He was very depressed," recalled Thompson. "He was extremely depressed the whole time he was in Israel. I would imagine it was partly due to the part. I don't think he was feeling too good. He hated Israel. He complained daily about how wretched the food was.

"Whenever I could and whenever he felt like it, we'd spend time together. He'd go to parties but he always left when I did. He didn't really hang around with any of the cast. He was always perfectly charming, but he was not having a happy time. He was alone, didn't have any visitors. He was in a very great depression.

"He still smoked, too, and wasn't supposed to. And he had a bit to drink, quite hard sometimes. He wanted to go home. He'd ask me, 'Can't you get me out of here?' I did what I could.

"There was something very much worrying him. Naturally, I thought it was his career that was on his mind [because] this was not really a star part."

While in Israel, Rock began losing weight. He blamed it on the food, but the weight loss, along with his depression, were probably early symptoms of AIDS.

To make matters worse, Rock had to sit around for one five-week period while Thompson and the crew concentrated on shooting scenes with Ellen Burstyn, who had no scenes with Rock. Consequently, he had virtually nothing to do but sit in his room and brood.

No one on the set considered the possibility that Rock might have been ill. On the other side of the world, a woman who had known him all his life glanced at her local paper and saw an Associated Press photo of him taken on location in Israel. She sensed that something was terribly wrong.

Betty Kimble, Rock's first cousin, two years his senior, had stayed in touch with Rock all his life, seeing him whenever he happened to come through Chicago. When he was in Chicago with the road company of *On the 20th Century*, he had taken her to dinner, and then arranged to get tickets for the twenty-three members of Kimble's family. She said he had been a delight.

She had been in touch with him after his bypass operation in 1981 and knew he had weathered it well. "He told us everything was fine. He said he felt like he did when he was a teen-ager," she said.

But the picture of Rock on the set of *The Ambassador* struck fear in her heart. "I knew he was sick. I thought right then, There's something wrong with him."

Kimble immediately called her sisters, Dorothy Raychek and Helen Folkers. All three women had been close to Rock when he was growing up, sharing parties, activities, school events. The other two women looked at the clipping and agreed with Betty Kimble that Rock was not well.

For the next eighteen months, the three women, concerned about their cousin's health, tried to reach him repeatedly by letter and phone. It proved impossible. They never saw him alive again.

Rock wanted nothing more than to be home in the Castle, particularly on his birthday. At home, there was always a big party with friends filling the house. Instead, he grumbled, "Birthdays are for kids" when the cast and crew presented him with a cake to celebrate his fifty-eighth birthday in Israel.

"There were many evenings," J. Lee Thompson recalled, "when I called his room and asked if he'd like to go out, and he didn't want to. I knew he was sinking into a very big depression. When you're working with someone, you know. He was down, and there didn't seem to be anything I could do."

Christian said he received several letters from Rock sent from Israel. "In all the letters he kept saying how much he missed L.A. and his house and me. He said he was glad to be working because he hadn't done a film in a while, but he said he didn't like the conditions over there, the food. He just wanted to be home. He wrote me three or four letters. They were very romantic and heartfelt."

The letters were later to become evidence in Christian's controversial fourteen-million-dollar lawsuit charging that Rock and others had put his life in jeopardy by not telling him Rock had AIDS. His attorney, Marvin Mitchelson, felt the letters "established a relationship" between Christian and Rock.

While Rock counted the moments until he could leave Israel and return home, his friends in California were adjusting to Marc Christian's arrival, and Tom Clark's departure from the inner circle.

Mark Miller and George Nader gave a party at a home owned by Hudson on Mullholland Drive.

"I was invited to a dinner for eight to be introduced to Marc," said Susan Stafford. "I thought Marc Christian was so sweet. I was told he was the new man in Rock's life. Everybody seemed to know. I was invited to the dinner specifically to meet Rock Hudson's new friend. I felt, If Rock's happy, I'm not supposed to judge. But I sure missed Tom, that's how I felt."

Another guest at the party, Matthew West, said the introduction of Marc Christian came as a surprise to him. "I walked in and I said, 'Is Tom Clark coming?' And Mark Miller said, 'Oh, Matthew, I want to have a quick word with you.' I said, 'What's happening?' And Mark said, 'There've been some changes made.' He smiled and said, 'Tom Clark is in New York and there is now Marc Christian.' I said, 'Who the hell is Marc Christian?' And he said, 'Well, I just want to tell you we don't discuss Tom Clark anymore.'

"Five minutes later, in walks Marc Christian—nice-looking, young, and all that."

Christian said he met most of Rock's friends, and initially they accepted him into the fold. "The night that I met Ross Hunter, he threw his arms around me and said, 'Oh, you're the one we've been waiting for all these years!' I felt like 'mail-order bride' or something," Christian quipped.

In Israel, on location in Nebi Mousa, on the Occupied West Bank, Hudson often sat dejectedly in his dressing-room trailer in the Judean desert smacking flies with a rolled-up newspaper. After a day of shooting in the desert sun, Hudson usually looked tired.

Rock wasn't getting the kind of perks he was used to in the old days, when he was the number one box-office star. "Playing a secondary part, it's not quite the star structure. . . . The dressing room isn't quite as good. I don't mean he ever said that, but I felt it a little," Thompson reflected. "It must have affected him. I don't mean he was treated badly. He wasn't. The cameraman did everything for him. I know Menahem Golan had great respect for him, was delighted that he got into the film, I'm sure he paid him much more than the part warranted. But it's inevitable that when you're playing a secondary part, you don't quite get the star treatment. I minded that this great star was playing a comparatively subsidiary role.

"It was not a very good part. And being the last film he made, it's a little sad. He was excellent in it, looked excellent. But the film didn't extend him enough, that's why it's sad. In retrospect, it was his last film and it wasn't a worthy part."

In fact, the film was so bad that it disappeared after a few previews around the country. It wasn't even shown in Los Angeles. It was a bomb. *The Ambassador* was dragged out of mothballs in February 1986 and scheduled for home-video release and cable television to cash in on the fact that it was Rock's last film.

Rock returned home around Christmas time looking terrible. "He looked tired and he had lost a lot of weight," recalled Susan Stafford. Before leaving for Israel, Rock had been slightly overweight; by the time he returned, he looked twenty pounds lighter.

Rock's depression seemed to fade after being home a few weeks. Exhausted from the shooting in Israel, he needed rest, palatable food, and the comfort of the Castle to get him back into better spirits. But the weight he lost never came back. It was now 1984—the last full year of his life.

Christian was happy to see Rock. They hadn't been together in two months.

"When Rock got back from doing *The Ambassador* was when we really started living with each other," Christian said. "It was the best for the first six or eight months of 1984. He was very happy. Even Mark [Miller] said, 'I haven't seen him smile like that in five years.' He cut down even more on his drinking. He couldn't really quit smoking, but he tried. He was just happy. He just bounced around. We spent a lot of time with each other."

Indeed, friends said Rock and Christian seemed a happy couple. Matthew West, for one, often invited them to parties and dinners at his house. "Rock would bring Marc with him quite a lot. They were fine together. Rock certainly was very fond of him, attracted to him. When they came up here, it all looked fine."

Rock also introduced Christian to his friend Jimmy Dobson. "At first I didn't know that he was living there," Dobson said. "He seemed to be very nice. I liked him very much. I found him to be bright and likable."

Producer Jon Epstein recalled meeting Christian on several occasions at the Castle. Epstein said he "surmised" that Rock and Christian were lovers.

In the spring, Rock met Christian's parents for the first time. "They didn't know the true nature of our relationship," Christian said. "Out of the blue Rock said, 'Let's take your parents out to dinner.' He was apprehensive. He was worried about what their opinion of him would be. I called my mom and told her we were all going out for dinner. When we arrived to pick them up, all the neighbors were out on their front lawns. We drove to Laguna in Rock's Cadillac—Mom, Dad, Rock, and me."

Rock was very generous to Christian's parents. They held their fortieth-wedding-anniversary party at Rock's house, and Christian's sister had her wedding reception at the Castle. When Rock died, Christian, his mother, and his sister attended the service. They even brought along Liberty.

The relationship seemed to be flourishing. And yet Rock continued his nonmonogamous pattern. Shortly after meeting Christian's parents, around Easter 1984, Rock took a trip to Hawaii, telling Christian only that he was staying with friends. Christian said he discovered later that Rock had taken another young man on the trip, someone Rock had met shortly after he found Christian. After Rock's death, Christian asked Mark Miller about the Hawaiian trip. "Oh, he was just another one," Miller said breezily. "Rock wasn't sure that you were going to work out, so he wanted to have someone in the background."

When Rock returned from Hawaii, Christian recalled, their relationship continued as before.

A year earlier, Rock had had a luncheon meeting at the Castle with Jimmy Hawkins, a one-time child star who had appeared on "The Ruggles," "Annie Oakley," "The

Donna Reed Show," and "The Adventures of Ozzie and Harriet," among other shows, and who had become an independent producer for television. The meeting was set up by a mutual friend, Susan Stafford.

Hawkins had a brainstorm: why not bring Rock and Doris Day together again in *Pillow Talk II?* Golden-oldie sequels were doing well—the "Gilligan's Island" crew had been brought together, as had the Brady Bunch, and the "I Dream of Jeannie" gang, to name a few.

Rock told Hawkins he liked the idea. Over lunch, he regaled the producer with funny anecdotes about Doris Day and himself on the set of *Pillow Talk.* "I'd be very interested in doing something," Rock told Hawkins. "I speak for Doris and Doris speaks for me. We would like to do something." Hawkins quoted Rock as saying.

Hawkins told Delbert Mann, who had directed *Lover Come Back,* one of the three Hudson-Day films, about his *Pillow Talk II* idea. Mann was enthusiastic. They got together with Bruce Kane, a writer, and talked out a story line. Now, in the late spring of 1984, Hawkins called Rock and set up another meeting at the house. It was just a week or two before Rock was diagnosed as having AIDS.

Rock sat in the living room as he listened intently to a synopsis of the story:

> It's the present, and Doris and Rock are divorced. Their daughter is getting married to Tony Randall's son. So Rock has to come to the wedding. Getting his dates mixed up, he arrives a week early. Tony, who has always been in love with Doris and finally believes she's going to marry him, suspects Rock is there to woo Doris back. Tony bets Rock a red Maserati that he can't get her back. Rock doesn't want to make a wager, telling Tony, "If you two guys are happy, great." Tony starts getting suspicious when two days go by and Rock still hasn't put the make on Doris. Tony and Rock go out to play golf. They are driving in a golf cart when a pretty girl catches Rock's eye and the cart runs into a tree. Rock falls out of the cart,

hits his head, and gets amnesia. He can't remember who he is. He doesn't recognize Doris. The doctors tell Doris that the only way to help bring back Rock's memory is to take him places and do things that remind him of the past. She takes him to all the places they went when they were courting, and they fall in love again. Tony accuses Rock of faking amnesia. Rock admits it. Tony says he'll tell Doris. Rock says if he does, she'll know she was the prize in a wager between the two of them. The twist, the kicker, is that Doris planned the whole thing. She wanted to be wooed back. She didn't know how he would go about it, but she knew he would. She played along with the scam and Rock never realized it. He's just happy to get Doris back.

"Rock was getting very enthused with the story," Hawkins said. "He started interjecting ideas of his own. At the end he said, 'This is terrific. People have pitched so many ideas for us over the past twenty-five years, but this is a wonderful project. Let's get Doris involved right away.'"

Day asked Hawkins to tape the story and send it to her home in Carmel. According to Hawkins, she wrote back saying she liked the story but wanted a few changes, which were made and approved by Day. The producer pitched the story to an executive at Universal Cable, who also expressed excitement over the project. Hawkins got a letter from Rock saying that if the final script was as good as the synopsis, he'd love to do the film. Hawkins thought he had a winner. But the deal for what could have been a blockbuster movie revival fell apart by year's end. By then Rock was dying.

In the first half of 1984, Rock was still resting after the filming in Israel when Mary Baum called him with another project that sparked real excitement. Producer Allan Carr was planning to replace Gene Barry on Broadway in the wildly successful musical *La Cage aux Folles*. Hundreds of stars had seen the show, many offering to jump in if a role came up. In fact, when word got out that Barry was about to be replaced, even Jackie Gleason called Carr: "If I could get into the dress, I'd play it myself," he told the producer.

But Carr was interested in Rock for the role. Rock was intrigued. He loved the show, which he had seen a year earlier in New York with Clark.

"I was present at the meeting at the house with Alan when he made a big pitch to Rock," said Baum. "Rock intimated he wanted the part. It's interesting to me because, for a guy who was known in the business as being a homosexual, it didn't bother him to consider playing a homosexual on Broadway."

Carr had seen Rock on stage in *Camelot, I Do! I Do!,* and *On the 20th Century,* and was impressed with his stage work. He also was aware that Rock had worked with vocal coach David Craig.

"Rock had terrific stage presence. He was quite funny," observed Carr. "The best was at the Huntington Hartford Theater [in Los Angeles], where he appeared with Carol Burnett in *I Do! I Do!* He was just wonderful, really terrific. He had the same kind of commanding, leading man performance that he had in the movies.

"Everybody gets mixed reviews in their careers. But overall, as you look back, people will say—and not because he's gone—that he was a really wonderful movie-actor star. He brought all the qualities of the Doris Day movies to the stage. He was a big stage presence, what I call a bigger-than-life stage presence, and it shows when you are up against such a talented lady as Carol Burnett."

Rock was enthusiastic at the meeting with Carr and Baum. He told Carr he had seen the show at the Palace in New York and enjoyed it thoroughly. "I'm really seriously considering this and I want to take the score and work on it a little bit," Rock told Carr, who was overjoyed. The plan was for Rock to work with the script and then do an audition for the director.

Carr did notice that Rock was thinner than he had ever seen him. "He wasn't unhealthy-looking. I just thought he had aged somewhat. Having been bulky and big all his life, he did look different. He still looked good enough for the show. Some actors will say, 'I can do six performances a week, not eight.' But Rock never brought that up, so I had no reason to question his health."

Carr left confident that Rock would take the role. He had no suspicion that Rock was seriously ill. The weight loss Carr noticed was only the first, most visible symptom of the disease that was to take his life in less than sixteen months.

As Rock played with the *La Cage* project, Marty Baum found more work for him—a made-for-TV movie called "Las Vegas Strip Wars." The script had already been approved by NBC. The part that Rock eventually signed for had not yet been cast. The agent submitted Rock's name, and the network approved. "We got him a very good fee— two hundred thousand dollars to two hundred and fifty thousand dollars," said Baum. "Rock was again very happy with the money. He was very happy that he was working. He liked the script and he liked the character."

Rock was scheduled to start shooting in Las Vegas in July. That same month, as a result of Baum's efforts, Rock was asked to appear on the world's most popular nighttime soap opera, "Dynasty."

CHAPTER SIX
Denial

Rock had not felt well since returning from Israel. He never regained the weight he lost there, and his condition continued to be run-down. In April, he scratched the back of his neck and discovered a small growth. Worried in general about his health and in particular about the bump on his neck, he went to his doctor in May for an examination. A biopsy was performed on the growth. Blood and other lab tests were done.

On June 8, 1984, Rock was given his death sentence. He was told he had Acquired Immune Deficiency Syndrome (AIDS). The biopsy revealed that the growth, one of a small number found on his body, was Karposi's sarcoma, a rare form of skin cancer. The purplish lesions, along with the results of the blood tests, confirmed the fatal disease.

A monstrous virus, AIDS was mostly striking gay men, and, to a lesser extent, intravenous drug users. Among homosexuals, the virus was transmitted primarily through anal intercourse. Semen carrying the virus entered the bloodstream through tears in the anal wall. The virus could lie dormant for years before symptoms appeared. Eventually, the victim's immune system would be damaged, making him susceptible to all forms of secondary infection. There was no valid treatment or cure for the disease when Rock was diagnosed. Researchers felt there would not be a treatment or a vaccine until the 1990s at the earliest.

According to the lawsuit Christian filed after Rock died

178

in October 1985, only Rock's doctors, Mark Miller, and Rock's business manager, Wallace Sheft, knew Rock had AIDS. There may have been others.

One of them is said to be an actor who had befriended Rock in the last few years of his life. Because of the nature of the following allegations, the actor, a homosexual in his fifties, must remain nameless. Because he possessed a positive attitude toward life, Rock felt very comfortable with him. According to several sources, Rock confided in this man and revealed to him that he had AIDS.

"Rock had to tell someone," said one of the sources. "He couldn't keep it inside. Rock felt secure with _____." Understandably, the actor felt intense compassion for Rock. He saw the depression and anxiety that Rock was hiding from the world. With what must certainly have been a misguided sense of friendship and loyalty, the man began supplying Rock with sexual partners, mostly young men. They had no idea Rock had AIDS. The trysts were held at the man's apartment. "Rock met a lot of boys at _____'s place," said one of the sources.

After Rock died, the man revealed to an acquaintance what he had done. "He was bragging as if he had done a good deed for Rock," an insider asserted. "When I told him that he could have been sending those kids to their deaths, he told me, 'I told them to wear a rubber and they'd be all right.'"

After the news broke that Rock had AIDS, one of the insiders claimed, "There were a lot of nervous boys who had been to bed with Rock, riding up and down the elevators at _____'s apartment building."

Attempts were made to interview the actor to determine the truth of the allegations, but the actor declined, he said, on the advice of an attorney.

For thirteen months, from the time he learned he had AIDS until it was revealed to the world, Rock lied about his health to everybody—friends, fellow actors and actresses, directors, producers, lovers—even to himself. The revelation of his disease and his homosexuality the following summer would shock the world. But until that time, the dying star put on the best performance of his life—acting as if nothing was wrong, despite a visible physical and mental deterioration that first worried and later horrified everyone who saw him.

The question one has to ask finally is: Was it entirely an act? Certainly Rock Hudson had been told he had AIDS in June 1984; undoubtedly he had also been informed that there was no cure, that the prognosis was fatal. But much—indeed, most—of his behavior during the last year of his life suggested that he had simply failed to assimilate these facts.

It is important—and relevant—to remember that Rock Hudson had spent nearly his entire adult life as a movie star. Not just an actor, but a star, a creation of the industry. Is it possible, or even probable, that a man could play the role of a great American screen idol for so many years without having it affect, to some degree, his perception of the world and himself?

Several times in the past Rock had shown an amazingly casual attitude toward his health—laughing off or even ignoring injuries most people would treat seriously. Even his bypass seemed to cause him very little anguish. It was as if he didn't quite believe, even before June 8, 1984, that anything truly bad could happen to him. Rock knew, or at least had been told, that he was about to die. But by all accounts, he was able to push that knowledge far, far away.

Marc Christian observed: "He was an actor. He was in a dream world. Everything was celluloid phoniness. When you're a Rock Hudson, you think nothing's ever going to happen to you. You feel invulnerable. You're never going to get run down by a car. Everything you do is sanctified."

"All of a sudden he was told that his life was over," Marty Baum said sadly. "Here was a man who was fifty-eight, with an estate worth millions, a man in love, a new agent, getting lots of work, and all of a sudden he's told that he's dying. The amazing thing is he kept working, kept functioning, and never allowed anyone to see that depression he must have felt. What this man must have been going through emotionally is beyond belief."

The dying Rock Hudson showed up on location in Las Vegas in July to begin shooting "Las Vegas Strip Wars." He was full of false enthusiasm about the project, telling

George Englund, the writer—director—executive producer, "I couldn't stop reading the script." Rock knew Englund from Universal in the sixties. In the film, which aired in November 1984, Rock played Neil Chaine, a prominent Las Vegas hotel owner who, after being double-crossed by his partners, takes over a floundering hotel across the Strip with the goal of making it the city's top draw. Rock's co-stars were James Earl Jones, Pat Morita, and Sharon Stone.

"From the beginning, Rock had an enthusiastic and vivid interest in the subject," Englund said. "He didn't know much about the hotel business, didn't know much about gambling. He had a lot of questions, intelligent questions, the right kind of questions that you hope an actor would ask to help establish himself in the landscape so he would be confident in it. There were some very emotional scenes for him and he really reached out—he wasn't hiding behind being a good-looking leading man.

"Through the whole production, he was earnestly trying to work on the part, kept exploring it, refining it. He was a joy to work with from the beginning."

As vibrant and involved as Rock seemed, his physical appearance came as a shock to the director. "I was startled," said Englund. "He weighed much less than I'd ever seen him before. In a man that age, it produces a sort of haggardness. I realize now some of that must have been due to AIDS. I thought that what I was seeing was going to be rather startling for an audience, and I think to a lot of people it was. I was concerned about it, but there was nothing to do about it. In some of the film he looked wonderful, in other parts he looked very troublesome."

The director knew that Rock had had a bypass operation some two and a half years earlier and, "not having any inkling [about his AIDS], I attributed whatever it was to the heart operation. On the other hand, he didn't smoke any less or drink any less. He had a great deal of bustle about him, and energy."

Despite the way he looked, Rock assured Englund he felt fantastic. "I think everyone over fifty ought to have one of those operations automatically. That's how much better you feel," he said.

Early in the filming Rock's voice started going, causing great concern for the director and crew. He had to return to the project later to replace the dialogue that was lost because of his voice problem. At some stages of production, he looked so bad that he couldn't be filmed. During the long and tedious early days of shooting, Rock often perspired so heavily that the camera would have to be stopped so he could be dried off or changed.

At the end of the first week of shooting, Englund expressed his concern to Mike Greenberg, the line producer. "I'm really sad about Rock and concerned about him," Englund told Greenberg. "'I don't see him going a long way after this.' I thought it was just because Rock couldn't cure his habits. I didn't know how long Rock was going to hold up going this way."

Rock and the director would often dine together or have a drink at the end of the day. "I wouldn't call Rock's drinking excessive. I just thought it was sort of constant and taxing for somebody who'd had a bypass." Englund tried to do something about Rock's smoking, however. The director's son, Morgan, twenty-one, was working as a production assistant on the shoot. Father and son decided to ration Rock's cigarettes. Morgan held Rock's pack and doled them out to him as slowly as he could.

Twice during production Rock told Englund he had to go back to Los Angeles. He mentioned visiting his doctor. Englund didn't think there was anything unusual in that, considering the way Rock looked and the voice problems he was having. A couple of times Rock also saw the unit physician to treat his voice and may have gotten a vitamin shot or two. Rock was staying on location alone. At one point he asked to have his dialogue coach and friend Jimmy Dobson hired on, but the budget wouldn't allow it. When Englund explained the situation to Rock, he shrugged it off. "Don't worry about it, it's not important."

Having Dobson with him probably would have lessened the trauma he must have been experiencing.

Despite his dark secret, Rock kept up a cheerful front. When Englund asked Rock if it would be okay to have his mother-in-law, who was visiting from Chattanooga, Tennessee, play Rock's secretary and say a few lines, Rock said, "Oh, what fun."

Englund recalled: "It sounded like a great idea until you try to shoot it." It seemed that the poor woman suddenly realized she was shooting a scene with *the* Rock Hudson and she became a nervous wreck. It was the end of a very long and difficult day. Rock had just done a tedious scene with many pages of dialogue. But when he did the scene with the elderly woman, "he was a gentleman to the nines," said the director. "He was patient with her, helpful to her, and after a couple of takes, she was absolutely fine. This was the essence of Rock."

Rock stayed on location through most of July. When he was finished shooting, he told Englund that he was going off to Paris for a vacation. They made plans to get together, when Rock returned, to do the necessary soundtrack work and discuss promotional plans the network had for the film.

Before going to France, Rock was offered the role on "Dynasty," and an even bigger plum was tossed his way by the show's executive producer, Aaron Spelling. Rock was secretly offered the lead role on "The Colbys," the "Dynasty" spinoff.

Marty Baum had had a number of discussions with Rock about doing another television series, but Rock was ambivalent. He'd sworn he would never do a series after "McMillan," and he made the same claim after "The Devlin Connection" bombed. "The weekly shows are quite empty . . . it's dreadful, terrible," he declared. "It's the nature of the beast, really. TV gobbles up writers faster than they can be produced. They should put more effort into one show instead of just shipping them out."

Rock also blamed "McMillan" and "Devlin" for the high blood pressure and heart disease that resulted in his near heart attack and bypass operation.

"On the other side," said Baum, "the money and all the trappings that go with a successful show were something that he enjoyed—and being busy. Rock really did have a tough time with what actors have to learn to deal with—the fact that when they're not working they have to have other interests in life. It was obvious to me he didn't have that many to keep him emotionally sustained."

Spelling, who has produced a number of successful shows, including "Charlie's Angels," wanted to beef up "Dynasty" with a big-name star. Spelling was also represented by Creative Artists, and the agency suggested Rock. "I made the 'Dynasty' deal," Baum said. "Aaron thought hiring Rock was a great idea."

When Baum went to Rock with the proposal, the actor's initial reaction was negative. "He didn't like the kind of show it was," Baum recalled. "He didn't care how big 'Dynasty' was. He wanted to do material that tested him as an actor, that gave him a chance to do more, to win critical acclaim as against pop acclaim. He said he wanted to make a mark as an important actor rather than a personality star. But he recognized the broad commerciality of the show."

Spelling and Baum went to work on Rock to convince him to do the show.

"The advice I gave him—and remember, I had no knowledge of his being ill—was that 'Dynasty' was wildly popular, that the fans idolized the stars of the show, and that it would be a terrific shot in the arm for a flagging career. I felt from a career standpoint it would have some value—to be getting the money that he got out of it, to be seen on that show.

"Look at all the people who joined that show and have gone on to better things. Diahann Carroll's career went back into high gear because of that show. Almost every guest who appeared had something good happen to them. So I felt Spelling was a miracle man when it came to feeling the pulse of the American public, knew what the public was all about. I felt that being with Spelling was a marvelous thing."

Rock and Marty were invited to Spelling's office on the Hollywood-Warner lot, the old Goldwyn studio, where Spelling served an elaborate lunch. "The essence of the lunch," Baum said, "was for Spelling to tell us how much he wanted Rock to join the Spelling family. We both told Rock that if he was going to do television, he should do it with someone who really knew what he was doing—Aaron Spelling."

Rock took some time to think about it, and did not make his final decision until he got to Paris. While he was there, "Dynasty" creator and writer Esther Shapiro flew over to meet with him.

Baum said the "Dynasty" producers wanted Rock to sign for twelve shows, but he refused. "This was the first time," Baum said, "that I had a suspicion there was something wrong. Rock said that after the third show he would tell them whether he would do seven shows, which is the minimum they insisted upon, or twelve shows. He decided he was only going to do seven. He didn't want to do the twelve."

Rock eventually signed for ten shows (nine were finally broadcast). He was to get a whopping $100,000 per episode, working two or three days a week, for each of the episodes, Baum said.

Rock claimed that he didn't want to do a dozen shows because it would overexpose him. In fact, Rock didn't want to commit himself to a long-term run because of his disease, which neither Baum nor Spelling knew about. When Spelling offered Rock the lead role in "The Colbys," the actor shocked both his agent and the producer by turning down the part. "It was big bucks, prestige, everything, and he turned it down," Baum said. Rock said he didn't like the script. The role was offered to Charlton Heston. "Obviously," observed Baum, "Rock knew he physically couldn't do it. But he didn't tell that to me, so he told me he didn't like the script."

Rock was also offered another Spelling show, albeit an ill-fated one, "Finder of Lost Loves." He rejected the part because he claimed he didn't like the scripts. Again, the real reason was his health. Tony Franciosa eventually took the role that Rock turned down.

Before he left for Paris, Rock had told Christian about the "Dynasty" offer and asked for his advice. "He said he discussed the offer with Mark Miller, who thought he should do it, and that Marty Baum was on his case. He thought it might be okay to do it and take the money and run. I always had the feeling he was very reluctant."

* * *

In August, Rock Hudson told everyone he was going to France to take a vacation and to make an appearance at the film festival in Deauville, where a retrospective of his movies was scheduled.

He painted a glowing picture of his life to a *Los Angeles Times* reporter before he left: "I'm quite content. I'm not frustrated. I don't have any burning desires or burning revenges or burning loathings of any kind. I do the best I can."

Rock was accompanied to France by thirty-year-old Ron Channell, who had been his exercise coach since his heart bypass operation. Channell, a straight, good-looking, easygoing Floridian with a country twang, was trying to start a singing and acting career. He was going along strictly as a coach to make sure Rock stayed in shape during the trip.

En route to Paris, Rock stopped off in New York to take care of some important business. On August 23, 1984, he signed a codicil to his last will and testament dated August 18, 1981. Signing the document "Rock Hudson AKA Roy H. Fitzgerald," he declared: "I hereby delete in its entirety Article Fourth of my said Last Will and Testament. I purposely make no provision for the benefit of Tom H. Clark."

In the original will, Rock had given Clark "all of my automobiles, household furniture and furnishings, clothing, art objects, jewelry, motion picture equipment, my collection of motion picture films, cassettes and all other tangible personal property and personal effects of mine . . . Clark may retain for himself those items that he would like as a memento and may distribute the other items among such other friends of mine whom he may select and the persons and organizations named in the revocable trust created by me, dated April 3, 1974. . . ."

This is one of the few pieces of evidence that exists suggesting that Rock, some two months after his diagnosis, was getting his affairs in order. All of his actions and statements before and, particularly, after changing his will indicate a denial of the disease.

Christian claims that before Rock left for Paris, he had told Christian about his plans to change the will. He quoted Rock as saying, "I could be in a car crash and he'd get everything. I'm going to take him out."

In Paris, Rock checked into the Ritz Hotel. He immediately placed a telephone call to the Percy Military Hospital and asked to speak to Dr. Dominique Dormont, who was anxiously awaiting his arrival.

Dr. Dormont had been part of the team at the Pasteur Institute involved in AIDS research. He was one of the few doctors in France offering an experimental treatment with an antiviral drug called HPA-23. The French doctors believed that while it didn't cure the disease, the drug had shown itself to be somewhat successful in inhibiting the enzymes that caused the growth of the virus in a victim. The earlier the treatment was started, the greater the benefit to the patient.

"It basically can give an AIDS patient a chance to live longer, depending upon the clinical stage of the disease," said Dr. Dormont. "In the later stages of AIDS, it is impossible to get a benefit from the treatment."

Weeks before Rock's arrival in Paris, Dr. Dormont had received a transatlantic call from Dr. Michael Gottlieb, a nationally recognized AIDS expert based at UCLA Medical Center, who had diagnosed Rock's case.

"Dr. Gottlieb told me that a very famous actor was asking for the treatment, and the doctor asked whether I was willing to do it, and I said yes," Dr. Dormont said. "He told me that this famous actor wanted his disease to be kept strictly confidential. He didn't want his name to be used publicly in the hospital. Dr. Gottlieb said Mr. Hudson had heard about my treatment and asked him whether it was possible to get treated in Paris."

This shows that Rock was aware of the seriousness of his disease. He had discovered that an experimental treatment was available and was determined to travel halfway around the world to get those treatments, as long as he had assurances that his visit would be kept in strictest secrecy.

After receiving the call from Rock, Dr. Dormont

visited the actor in his suite at the Ritz. "I explained the drug to him. I told him how the treatment was conducted and what the side effects were. Sometimes the treatment can cause a drop in platelets that are involved in blood coagulation. So a blood test is done every two or three days to see if the platelet count is decreasing. If it is, the treatment is stopped until the platelet count increases. But there are no clinical side effects.

"I asked Mr. Hudson to think about whether he wanted the treatment and to give me an answer as soon as possible so we could begin the treatment. He called me back a few hours later and said he was willing to start as soon as possible."

On the first day that Rock arrived at Percy for the free treatments, Dr. Dormont conducted an extensive physical examination and ran tests.

"He had lost weight. He was somewhat tired. And he had had Kaposi's sarcoma lesions," Dr. Dormont said. "But before coming to Paris he had surgery to get rid of the lesions, which can be the first clinical signs of AIDS. When I examined him, the lesions had already been removed surgically. If there are only a small number of lesions, you can ask a surgeon to get rid of them.

"He was in the middle stages of AIDS. My feeling at that time was that he could benefit from a long-term treatment," Dormont said.

For the next six weeks, into mid-September, Rock left the Ritz almost daily and took a taxi to the hospital. Sometimes Dr. Dormont picked him up at the hotel for the drive. There is no evidence that Rock was ever noticed on the streets of Paris or in the hotel. There were no interviews with the celebrity press inquiring about his stay in Paris, no wire-service photos in American newspapers showing a smiling Hudson strolling alone by the Seine or posing next to the Eiffel Tower. Certainly, at the hospital it was not difficult to maintain secrecy, because he was treated as an out-patient. His traveling companion, Channell, thinking Rock was attending business meetings regarding film projects, never questioned Rock's daily disappearances.

Rock spent about three hours a day at the hospital,

lying in a bed, an intravenous tube sending the experimental HPA-23 antiviral drug coursing through his body. "He came in every morning, usually for four consecutive days, and then he would have a few days off," Dr. Dormont said.

Based on his examination and the fact that Rock was in the middle stages of the disease, Dr. Dormont felt that an intensive series of treatments would be beneficial and could extend Rock's life. "I felt he needed treatments for more than six months."

Dr. Dormont was shocked when, early in the process, Rock told him he could not continue the treatments beyond six weeks because he had an acting commitment to fulfill. Rock Hudson had decided to appear on "Dynasty"—despite Dr. Dormont's repeated warnings that this decision would cut short his life.

"Mr. Hudson told me he wanted to leave Paris after six weeks because he had to appear on a TV show—'Dynasty'—and he wanted to do his job. So he told me he could not stay in Paris. I told him that the treatment he was getting would not be efficient for a long time. But he wanted to go back and do the television show. I explained to him that it was a bad choice, and I explained to him that continued treatment would be better for him. We did the most we could do at that time."

Dr. Dormont, interviewed in December 1985, two months after Rock died, said, "I can only tell you that he would have had a better chance to be alive now had he continued the treatment for six months, but it's not sure."

Over the course of the treatment, Dr. Dormont spent dozens of hours with Rock. "This man was very nice. We got along well, but it was very difficult to have a conversation with him. He was not that kind of man." The AIDS researcher noted that Rock rarely spoke about the disease for which he was being treated, and never discussed his career. "He talked about everything but." It was almost as if Rock was attempting to hide his identity from the doctor—which he might well have thought he was doing. There also was never any discussion of Rock's sexual preference.

On the basis of his talks with Rock over the six weeks of

treatments, Dr. Dormont felt that Rock wasn't being realistic about his disease.

"He was a little bit too optimistic," Dr. Dormont observed. "It's my feeling that he felt Rock Hudson could not die. He did not feel AIDS would be fatal to him. If he had taken his disease seriously, he would have stayed longer in Paris, but he didn't want to. He was an intelligent man, and I explained to him that he could die, yet he still wanted to leave.

"He was not realistic. I told him that if he ended his treatment and went back to do 'Dynasty,' he could shorten his life. He said, 'But I have a job.' He was not afraid of dying. Perhaps for him it was not so important to prolong his life, I don't know. He never talked about life and death."

Hudson expressed himself candidly on the subject of death five months before he died. Still keeping his AIDS a secret, he talked about the heart-bypass operation he had undergone a little more than three years earlier.

"I'm a fatalist," he told interviewer Nancy Collins. "Whatever is going to be, is going to be. The night before the operation, I did have one moment of thinking, I hope I get through this. It was a very clear night and I looked out my window, over Los Angeles, and it was just beautiful, as L.A. can be on a clear night. I love it when the lights are sparkling. And I thought to myself, This might be the last time I ever see this sight. Then I thought, Oh, so what? I've seen it before. If I make it, terrific. If I don't, I'll never know the difference anyway."

Several months after Rock died, Marty Baum was still confused by Rock's decision to stop the treatments in order to do "Dynasty."

"I can't understand his thinking or his motivations," said Baum. "The show wasn't life-or-death. He didn't need the money. Making another half-million dollars or not making another half-million didn't matter to him. I don't know what his thinking was at that time. It's not like he was leaving the treatments for something of great artistic value or importance. I just don't know what was going through his mind. It's hard to fathom. There was no pressure about the show from me. I brought him the offer as I always do. He's

Denial 191

turned down things in the past, so it would have been another turndown. I didn't say, 'Rock, you must do this for your career, because it's very good money for what you're doing.' Now, if I had known he was sick, it would have been a totally different situation. But I didn't know it, and I don't think very many people did know it."

Esther Shapiro most certainly didn't know Rock had AIDS when she went to Paris to convince him to do the show. He deftly hid the fact from her that he was there seeing a doctor. When Spelling, Shapiro, and other "Dynasty" executives met with Rock earlier in the summer, it had been evident that he was thinner, but there was nothing to suggest he was ill. The subject of his weight loss did come up. Rock laughed it off, telling them he liked being thin, felt healthier being thin, and thought it was better for his heart.

Before Rock agreed to sign the contract, he wanted to see some scripts. The "Dynasty" executives were unwilling to write seven episodes unless he committed himself to do the shows. Shapiro went to Paris to describe to Rock in detail the story lines and the character he would portray. Rock liked what he heard and agreed to do the shows. A triumphant Shapiro returned to Los Angeles. Shooting would begin in October.

With the "Dynasty" deal concluded and his treatments ended, Rock went on to the film festival in Deauville. The star was being honored for his long career, and many of his films were being screened. Rock greeted fans, gave autographs, drank, and ate. He appeared happy and healthy to those who saw him. The treatments seemed to have had a positive effect. He gave no hint that anything was amiss in his life.

Rock had linked up with his friend Yanou Collart, a publicist in Paris, whom he had met some eight years earlier at the Beverly Hills home of Danny Kaye. Collart suspected nothing. "Nobody knew anything until [1985], when everything fell down. He said he was visiting Europe. . . . I just thought he was enjoying spending some time in Europe, where he hadn't been for a long time."

Collart handled Rock's publicity at the film festival and then arranged a trip for him to Rome. From Rome, Rock went to London. Collart confirmed that Ron Channell was traveling with Rock, was with him at the film festival and in Italy, and attended a dinner with Rock at Collart's apartment. "He was with him to help Rock with the exercises he was required to do after his heart surgery," she said. Collart met Rock again in Nice, where a good friend, writer Vivian Glenavy, lived. Rock spent a few days in Saint-Tropez, and then Collart arranged for him to appear on a TV talk show in Barcelona. Collart remembered that Rock, while thinner than usual, appeared healthy.

Shortly after the film festival, Collart gave a dinner party in Rock's honor at her Paris apartment. Rock announced to the other guests that he was going to be doing "Dynasty." "He was very happy," Collart said. "It was the first time I had heard about it. He said he was also thinking about doing a show on Broadway, La Cage aux Folles." Collart did not see Rock again until the following July—when she would become the person to tell the world that he had AIDS, an announcement that would be fraught with controversy.

Rock returned to Los Angeles early in October. He had exactly one year to live.

The honeymoon period between Rock and Marc Christian had ended, and there appeared to be growing tensions between them. They started to have arguments for the first time in their relationship. Christian was jealous of the camaraderie between Rock and Ron Channell, typical of Rock's relationships with his straight buddies.

"Rock and Ron were able to get along in a dumb way—they could just talk about dumb things and crack fart jokes. They would crack the dumbest jokes of all time. They had that kind of sense of humor they could share with each other," Christian maintained.

As 1984 drew to a close, Christian began tiring of Rock's friends, and they became increasingly bothered by him. "They'd camp and they'd hang out," he said with disdain.

Jon Epstein had met Christian at the house on several occasions and was not fond of him.

"I was never connecting with that kid in any way. We had nothing to talk about," Epstein said. "I didn't like what was coming out of his mouth. He talked about politics, for example, and the things he said, well, there was an attitude about it that I didn't care for. My feeling was, 'Who is he to be talking this way?'"

After Rock returned home from Paris, it became generally known in the industry that he would be doing guest appearances on "Dynasty." Producer Allan Carr, who still had hopes Rock would do *La Cage aux Folles*, heard the reports before Rock shot his first "Dynasty" episode on October 11.

Prior to hearing the trade gossip, Carr had called Marty Baum a few times because he hadn't been told whether Rock would do the show. Baum told Carr that Rock was still interested and that Rock would like to meet with the show's composer, Jerry Herman, and Arthur Laurents, the director, to talk and to do an informal audition.

"I was waiting for this to happen," Carr recalled, "when all of a sudden I read in the paper that he signed for 'Dynasty.' I think that he was torn between being able to live at home and do 'Dynasty,' which is an easier thing than living in New York and doing *La Cage*. But we never got an answer out of Rock. We were kind of left waiting."

Carr concluded that Rock never intended to do the show because he was aware of how much energy the role would have required and Rock knew that he was not healthy enough to commit himself. Rather than lie to Carr, he just left him hanging. "When I saw him on 'Dynasty,' he obviously didn't look well," said Carr. "I was really shocked by how different he looked in the six months between when I visited him at his house and when I saw him on 'Dynasty.'"

Carr believed that one of the reasons Rock was initially interested in doing the show was because of his homosexuality. "The public didn't know, and I think that's finally what was interesting—that he was brave enough to take this step. I think it was intriguing to Rock, and it may have been a step towards his being more open and honest."

At the same time, producer Jimmy Hawkins was hoping for a thumbs-up sign from Rock on the *Pillow Talk II* project he had pitched earlier in the year.

"The word was getting out that Rock wasn't looking so good on 'Dynasty,'" said Hawkins. "When we met with him, the guy looked like a million bucks. I thought maybe he looked a little thinner. Then I saw how he looked on 'Dynasty.' I thought maybe it was the way he was shot. People just can't fall apart that quickly. Apparently he had. People in the business thought he had cancer. He wasn't looking good, so we just didn't go ahead with the project."

Looking back on his meetings with Rock, Hawkins observed, "He must have felt very positive if I have a letter from him written in December. He must have felt he was going to get better."

Another piece of business Rock had to clear up after returning from Paris was to help promote "Las Vegas Strip Wars," which was scheduled to air on NBC early in November. The network wanted Rock to go to New York for a few days for a press appearance with the director-producer, George Englund. Rock, who usually never made a fuss over such things, demanded that his personal publicist and friend, Dale Olson, accompany him. NBC said no as a matter of policy.

When Englund assured Rock that he would try to make the trip as easy for him as possible, Rock relented on the issue of Olson and agreed to go. But he canceled at the last minute. He was doing "Dynasty," he said, and just did not feel up to making the trip. "He specifically said he wasn't feeling well, that it would be too taxing," Englund said. "I remember being surprised at that, because he knew how many arrangements had been made."

Several months after Rock died, Englund considered how difficult it must have been physically and emotionally for Rock, with his disease, to do the movie.

"If he really knew the cold, remorseless facts, he was made of stern stuff," Englund said. "If I was told something like that, I doubt if I could have gotten through a four-week shooting schedule with the affability and grace that he did. To me, the most incredible thing was that he could have been so involved in making the film, so courtly in it, so hard-working. He came to the screening and called me afterwards to say how pleased he was. 'I really learned things in this picture,' Rock told me. 'I want to thank you.'"

About a week before his fifty-ninth birthday, the last he celebrated, Hudson went to Dallas for an event honoring the film for which he had received his Oscar nomination, *Giant*. Rock's co-star, Elizabeth Taylor, could not attend because of another commitment. Rock was overjoyed when he got to the ceremony and found that Dorothy Malone, his friend and co-star from several early movies, was taking Taylor's place. He greeted her with enthusiasm. Malone was upset by his appearance and told him so.

"'Rock, you look terrible,'" Malone remembered saying in her blunt Texas style. "'You've got to put on weight.' He was emaciated-looking. He looked very wan. He looked tan, yet he looked gray. Rock told me he was doing 'Dynasty,' which I thought was great. But I said, 'Rock, you've got to stop running around the country this way. You don't look well. Please rest up before you do anything else.' He looked gaunt. I just said, 'Go to the beach or rest or do something.' I was very concerned."

Rock just smiled. He explained that his weight loss was the result of his open-heart surgery, giving Malone the impression that the operation had been recent. She had not seen him in a long while and was unaware that the surgery had occurred three years earlier. Rock had begun using the bypass operation as one of his excuses to explain away comments about his appearance.

"He told me to watch for him on 'Dynasty,'" Malone said. "He was very tickled about it, and I was tickled for him. He said it was time Blake Carrington had some competition. I said, 'Boy, won't that be good,' and we laughed."

Later, when Malone saw Rock on "Dynasty," she thought he had had eye surgery because his eyes looked so big. Actually, it was just that his face had gotten so thin that his eyes looked enormous.

Rock returned to Los Angeles the day after the Dallas event. Back at the Castle, a small group of friends had a birthday party for him. "He looked awful," said Christian. "The party was pretty low-key. Roddy McDowall was there and Dale Olson, Rock's publicist, and Matthew West and a few others."

Around that time Rock was invited to have dinner at the Burbank home of Lou Antonio. Rock came alone. The other guests included Rock's friend actress Lee Remick and her husband, producer Kip Gowan. Everyone commented on Rock's weight loss—it was impossible to ignore. "I did a movie in Israel, the food was terrible," Rock said in explanation. "So I lost weight. And I shot a movie in Las Vegas. You know how bad the food in Las Vegas is."

Remick and Antonio exchanged a look. It wasn't that hard to find a good meal in Vegas. Something was terribly wrong with Rock. When he left, they talked about it.

"Do you suppose it's cancer?" Remick asked, worried. Antonio didn't know. Maybe he was just proud about being thin, he thought later. Rock had always had a bit of a weight problem; maybe he was just trying to lose weight. But he had looked so drawn.

Rock, looking progressively worse, was working several days a week on the "Dynasty" set as if nothing was wrong with him.

While he told friends and colleagues he enjoyed doing the show, he complained constantly at home about the role and the work. "I like the actors, but it's the most unprofessional work I've ever done," he told Christian. Rock found the long hours especially fatiguing. Some shooting days required him to be up as early as 4:30 A.M. Some days he would not get home until seven o'clock. Rock had begun experiencing another symptom of the disease, a loss of appetite, making him even thinner and less energetic. He also increased his smoking and started drinking more because of the pressures of doing the show.

In promoting "Dynasty," Rock hid his true feelings and painted a glowing picture of the job.

"I took the role because the very wealthy neighbor I play is a good character," Rock said. "He's a maverick and he uses his money. He doesn't collect dollars like some wealthy people whose total objective is to make more money. He uses his money for rescuing people, that sort of thing.

"The people I work with on 'Dynasty' are terrific. I've known Joan Collins for years. She's an excellent pro. I don't see any similarities between Joan and the character she plays. Nobody's that bitchy.

"I've known Linda Evans for years. She worked as a guest star on 'McMillan.' Everybody's very nice, including the four hundred thousand producers of 'Dynasty.' I never saw so many producers in my life. They have a producer for this and a producer for that. If I have a problem, which one do I go to?" Asked whether he was a "Dynasty" fan, Rock said, "I don't watch TV much."

Seven months later, in the final stages of AIDS, Rock didn't bother to sugarcoat his feelings about being on the show. He described his "Dynasty" experience as "all right," and said that any future appearance "depends on the money. If they're willing to pay what I'm asking, they're fools. If it [the work] were great, I'd do it for free, wouldn't I? Well, I won't be doing it for free."

Rock played a character named Daniel Reece, a millionaire horse breeder who falls for Krystle Carrington, played by Linda Evans. One scene included a passionate kiss between Rock and Evans. That love scene caused a furor when it became public knowledge that Rock kissed Evans knowing he had AIDS. TV news programs showed clips of the segment, and the supermarket magazines and the daily tabloids ran stills of the kiss.

Everyone had a comment—from comediennes to sex therapists.

"Frankly, if I were Linda Evans I would be crazed now," declared an irate Joan Rivers. "If I had to kiss a co-star—because the disease is crossing over into the straight world—I'd want assurances he doesn't have AIDS. You have to protect yourself."

Dr. Ruth Westheimer, in a *Playboy* interview, said, "I feel sad for all of the thousands of women who fantasized about being in his arms, who now have to realize that he never really cared about them. I heard one older woman say, 'I used to dream about him; too bad that he really didn't like erotic relations with women.' But I do believe he should not have kissed anybody. If he knew he had a disease that was communicable, he should not have kissed. He should have found some excuse. He should have let a stunt man do the kissing."

While there was no conclusive medical evidence that AIDS could be transmitted by kissing, the turmoil caused by the "Dynasty" love scene between Rock and Evans sparked a change in Screen Actors Guild rules. Weeks after Rock's death, the union required the seven thousand producers and agents with whom it had contracts to notify performers in advance of any scenes that required open-mouth kissing.

After Rock died and Christian sued his estate, Christian's attorney, Marvin Mitchelson, added to the kissing-scene controversy. In an appearance with Christian on the Phil Donahue show, Mitchelson revealed that Rock was actually being treated by a nurse for open sores in his mouth on the "Dynasty" set. He claimed that the treatments had been investigated by health authorities. "It's documented," the lawyer stated.

After Rock's death, Esther Shapiro and other executives of "Dynasty" declined to be interviewed for this book. A lengthy list of questions given by one of the authors to a publicist for the show went unanswered. It was clear that the "Dynasty" people wanted the Hudson scandal to go away.

In April 1986, in a *TV Guide* article, several of the show's cast members and technicians spoke out for the first time, expressing fond memories of working with Rock. But the article noted that Joan Collins declined to be interviewed and that a publicist cut short an interview with Linda Evans when she sensed the star was growing uncomfortable with the questions.

One of those who talked was makeup man Jack Freedman. "He [Rock] didn't seem at all worried about his condition. He'd say, 'I'm eating everything, but I just don't seem to be putting on weight.' The only thing I did notice, when he sat in the makeup room, he'd never look in the mirror. . . ."

Guests were shocked at how bad Rock looked at the

round of Christmas Eve parties given in 1984, particularly at the one given by Nancy Sinatra, Sr.—Frank Sinatra's former wife. Former columnist Dorothy Manners was a guest at that traditional party. Much of the Hollywood crowd was there, and they couldn't believe how gaunt and ill Rock looked.

"I was absolutely shocked," said Manners, who tried to make small talk about "Dynasty."

" 'What's going to happen?' I asked him.

"He said, 'I won't tell you because you'll blab it all over town.'

"I said, 'I won't because I'm retired.'

"He said, 'People like you are never retired.' "

But what Manners really had her mind on was the "absolute overnight change in Rock's appearance. He had gone from being ungodly handsome to looking gaunt and haggard—a look he had never really had. The change in his appearance was not to be believed."

Manners noted that Rock hardly had the energy to stand. She watched as he went over to a corner and sat down.

"A friend came over to talk to him, and he was so grateful. Rock said, 'Oh, sit here and talk to me for a while.'

"The rumors started at the terrible, terrible, and very quick change in Rock's appearance," said Manners. "He had gone from a virile, healthy physique to almost a scarecrow."

Rock began the last ten months of his life at a party on New Year's Day, 1985. A magazine editor saw Rock chatting with producer Ross Hunter. The editor, who had known Rock and Hunter for years, crossed the room to wish both of them a happy holiday. "You know Rock, don't you?" Ross asked the man. "Certainly. Happy New Year, Rock," said the editor, extending his hand.

It was like a freeze frame. The man's hand hung in midair as Rock ignored it. Rock looked up at the ceiling and around the room, glancing everywhere except at the man. The smile on the editor's face faded, as did Hunter's.

"Rock?" the man prodded, his hand still extended. But Rock did not acknowledge the man's presence. "At the time I found it rude and embarrassing," recalled the editor. "Thinking back on it now, I believe the disease had begun affecting his mind. Rock never acted like that before. He always was a gentleman."

Shortly after the new year started, rumors that Rock had AIDS began to surface. The rumors circulated primarily among gays who knew Rock was a homosexual and were based on how bad he was beginning to look. These were people who had either noted his appearance on "Dynasty" or had seen him in person.

In one instance, Rock himself mentioned the rumor to Jimmy Dobson. While having breakfast with Rock at the Castle, Dobson became concerned about his friend's appearance and weight loss. He asked Rock about it.

"I wanted to lose weight," Rock responded. "I think I look better this way. I'm working out every day with a workout instructor, Ron Channell." Dobson had met Channell and knew Rock took the young man with him when he traveled. He accepted his explanation because Rock had been overweight many times in his career. Then Rock startled Dobson:

"This producer [a homosexual] who wants to get even with me because I wouldn't sign a contract he wanted me to sign has started a rumor that I have AIDS," Rock said. "It's ridiculous that I have AIDS." A worried Dobson said, "Yes, I'm sure it is." Rock said nothing more and Dobson asked no further questions.

Thinking about that conversation several months after Rock died, Dobson said, "Roy was normally a very honest person, but at the point we had that conversation he had had AIDS for a while. I think there was a little brain damage. Obviously this thing he said about the producer was crazy—although the producer Roy mentioned is a vicious man and he did want Roy to sign a contract. At the time I accepted it to be true because Roy told me. Now, in light of what I know, it sounds paranoid."

At about the same time, Marty Baum received a call from Mark Miller, who sounded very upset. Miller claimed that a longtime friend and former business associate of Rock was spreading rumors that Rock had AIDS and was dying.

"Miller asked me what we should do," Baum recalled, "and I asked him whether the rumor was true. He said, 'No, it's not true at all.' And I said, 'Forget about it, then. I don't care what —————— is saying. If it's not true, don't worry about it. If we take legal action and it gets out to the press, you're going to draw more attention to it. Then there's really going to be trouble.' I had not put together at that point yet that Rock was that ill. I thought, in seeing him, that he looked thinner than I would have liked to have seen him. But he looked good enough that Aaron Spelling wanted him, so he didn't look that bad."

Around the time Baum received the call from Miller, rumors were circulating that several major celebrities, including Burt Reynolds, had AIDS. The rumors about Reynolds had gotten so out of hand that he finally agreed to be interviewed by Rona Barrett on "Entertainment Tonight" just to put a stop to them. Looking drained and distraught, Reynolds denied the rumors.

Aware of what was going on, Baum felt the rumor about Rock "was simply the work of a spiteful friend doing something to hurt the guy." He said he never bothered to call the reputed source of the gossip because he didn't want to dignify the rumor. Baum never actually confirmed whether the person was, indeed, spreading the rumor. He only took Miller's word for it.

As early as January, Marc Christian had also started hearing rumors that Rock had AIDS. "I'd run into people and they'd say, 'God, Rock looks terrible. Is he ill? Does he have AIDS?' I'd say, 'No, he's okay. He's just trying to lose weight.' And they'd say, 'Well, we hear he has AIDS.' And I'd say, 'Oh, that's ridiculous.' At that time anyone who was gay and looked sick was thought to have AIDS."

Christian claimed at that point he had no reason to believe that Rock had AIDS.

In March, Rock was invited to dinner at the Beverly Hills home of actor Danny Kaye and his wife, Sylvia Fine. Rock had come a long way since those early days in Winnetka when he and Jimmy Matteoni would roll in the aisles watching Danny Kaye movies and memorizing his zany lines. By 1985, Rock and the Kayes had been friends and neighbors for well over a quarter of a century. As an indication of their closeness, the Kayes called Rock by his real name, Roy.

The dinner invitation was strictly for pleasure, but in the back of her mind Fine was thinking of Rock for a role in a production of one of her "Musical Comedy Tonight" specials for PBS; it would be taped in May and aired in the fall of 1985. Fine and a national television audience had been charmed and delighted in 1979, when Rock and Ethel Merman sang "You're the Top" as a duet on one of the first "Musical Comedy Tonight" shows. Though Fine, who wrote and produced that special, thought Rock was wonderful with Merman, Rock, characteristically, had been unhappy with his performance. He told Fine that he felt he had thrown away the bit. He was the only one involved in the production who was that critical. Everyone else thought he was wonderful, and Fine was eager to work with him again.

Rock arrived at the Kayes' looking thin and drawn. He looked almost as bad as he had immediately after his heart surgery more than three years earlier, but they never would have told him that. "Roy, you look wonderful. You're absolutely slim as a reed," Fine told him, hiding her concern. Not only was she worried about his weight loss, but she was struck by the way Rock's skin looked. There were numerous lines around his eyes and at the edges of his mouth, and his cheeks were sunken. Fine never asked Rock if anything was wrong, because he said he was happy that he was finally able to lose weight. After he left that night, she told Kaye, "There's something about his look that I just don't like. I know he doesn't take drugs, so it can't be that." The Kayes concluded that Rock's run-down condition was due either to a strenuous diet or to his continued heavy smoking.

Fine had all but forgotten how bad Rock had looked when she called him some six weeks later to ask him if he'd be interested in making another appearance on "Musical Comedy Tonight." Since Rock had played King Arthur in a road company of Camelot, Fine wanted him to do the funny eclipse scene from *A Connecticut Yankee* where the Yankee tells the king that he'll cause a permanent eclipse of the sun if they burn him at the stake. Rock would play the king, Fine proposed, and he would get no billing on the show. Rock's would be a surprise appearance in the tradition of the old Bob Hope movies, where Bing Crosby would unexpectedly show up at the end. "The audience will say, 'Who's that? Is that Rock Hudson?'" Fine explained to Rock, who chuckled into the phone and agreed to do it. He loved the mystery-guest routine.

Rehearsals began a short time later at the Wilshire Ebell Theater in downtown Los Angeles. When Rock arrived, he looked even worse than he had at dinner six weeks earlier. This time Fine told him so. "I think I'm getting the flu," was Rock's excuse. "All I did this weekend was sleep. I'm just tired and I just want to sleep."

Fine urged Rock to go home. The rehearsal was not that important. He'd have no trouble learning his part. Certainly, the important thing was to take care of himself. Rock refused. As run-down as he was, Rock came to every rehearsal. It was more than a job; Rock was doing his best to hang on to life.

Everyone in the cast and crew was distressed by how bad he looked, observed casting director Gus Schirmer, who worked on the show. Of course, they had all seen Rock on "Dynasty" not looking well, but his deteriorating appearance was even more striking in person. By this time the diesease was making daily inroads, wreaking terrible changes on the man they had known. Rock was now gaunt, with a pronounced florid complexion. He tired quickly. While Rock normally had a quiet demeanor, cast and crew members noted that he was now even less voluble. There were a lot of whispers—Rock has cancer; Rock's heart is causing problems again. Everyone knew he was gay, yet no one thought he might have AIDS, or at least, no one voiced the possibility. All they were sure of was that somehow, in some terrible way, Rock Hudson was literally wasting away before their eyes.

Looking at Rock, Schirmer remembered the first "Musical Comedy Tonight" special he had worked on with him. "Rock would come in, do his little bit with Ethel, and leave. He was so vital and busy."

This time, though, Rock seemed to be hanging around the theater all the time, which was unlike him. In the past, he'd rehearse and leave. Now cast and crew members began to notice him, after his part was finished, sitting by himself beyond the lights looking tired, lonely, and withdrawn. During breaks they'd come and sit beside him and chat, hoping to cheer him up from whatever was bothering him.

"It was as if he had no place to go," Gus Schirmer said. "We were all concerned. Elaine Stritch, who was doing the show, would call me at night and say, 'What's going on with him? He looks terrible.'"

Stritch had seen Rock after his bypass. She had come out to Los Angeles to do a "Trapper John" episode and gone to dinner with him. He had looked amazingly well at that time, she thought—anything but ill. Obviously he had weathered the operation beautifully.

But now, when Stritch first walked in to the "Musical Comedy Tonight" rehearsals and saw her friend, it was all she could do to keep from gasping audibly. It was as if she had suddenly turned a corner unaware and come face-to-face with a terrible accident. The effect was that strong.

"I don't think I've ever done that good an acting job, because I was so thrown I couldn't believe it. You could hardly recognize him. He looked so terrible," said Stritch.

Rock greeted Stritch as he always had. He grabbed her in his arms in an enormous hug, twirling her around. Stritch returned the hug, laughing up at him. Inside, her mind was racing. Her old friend was obviously deathly ill. She wondered whether he even knew. For one brief moment, a horrible specter flitted across her brain: AIDS. He has AIDS. She pushed it far back in her mind.

During the show's rehearsal period, Rock stayed very close to Stritch. In the morning, he would greet her and ask her to sit by him. They went out to dinner several times. They would sit together, two old friends, and Stritch would feel a tremendous yearning coming from Rock, an urge to talk. She knew how private he had always been about his personal life; she knew how much he hated any probing.

Yet the yearning she felt from him was so strong, it was all she could do to keep herself from responding. "What is it?" she wanted to say. "What's the matter? We've been friends for so long, don't you know you can trust me?"

She never did. It would have been too much of an intrusion, almost a violation of the respect they had always had for each other. "I couldn't burst that bubble," she said. Rock referred to his thinness, telling Stritch he was struggling to get over anorexia. Along with his heart bypass operation, the terrible time he had had in Israel shooting *The Ambassador*, dieting, and the flu, anorexia was one of the excuses he was using to cover the fact that he had AIDS. Stritch wanted to accept his explanation, and yet . . .

And yet, he had the look. She couldn't help recognizing it. Stritch's husband had died of cancer in 1982, and he too had had the look of death. A gray pallor, as ashen sheen. She had seen it on her husband, and now she was seeing it on her friend.

Over the years, Rock had called her from time to time, just to keep in touch. This time, he called her as soon as she returned home. She was walking in the door of her house in Nyack, New York, when the phone rang. It was nothing specific. He just wanted to see if she had arrived safely, he said. Two days later he called again.

Stritch became even more convinced: Rock wanted to talk to her, to let it all out, to tell someone what was happening to him. But all the years of enforced privacy, the secrecy of his life, prevented him from opening up now. Elaine Stritch learned the truth of Rock's condition the same way the rest of the world did: from television.

During the actual taping of the "Musical Comedy Tonight" special, Sylvia Fine sat at a piano on an extension of the Wilshire Ebell's stage, where she joked and narrated as the mistress of ceremonies. To her right was the audience of some seven hundred to eight hundred people. She was close enough to notice their reaction to the various bits in the show. Their responses helped her when she began editing the tape. They enabled her to know what worked and what didn't, what could be cut and what should stay.

When Rock Hudson walked on stage dressed as King

Arthur, Fine expected a few giggles, then laughter and applause from members of the audience as they recognized the star behind the makeup. Instead, there was no audience reaction at all. No one knew who the tall, skinny actor was—they had completely failed to recognize him. As they left the theater, they were dumbfounded when they were told that it was Rock. They could not believe how worn and aged he looked.

"The camera picked it up more than the naked eye," said Fine. "What went through my mind was that he was ill, but I didn't have the vaguest idea what he had. People suddenly age for all kinds of reasons. All he needed was a pair of bad kidneys to get that look, or a bad liver, or a bad gall bladder. So it never crossed my mind that it was anything spectacularly wrong with him. There was no hint that he had AIDS."

It was not until after Rock died that Fine decided to cut his *Connecticut Yankee* mystery-guest sequence from the show. "I saw all the morbid interest. They were running his picture in all the magazines and newspapers. There was a lot of bad journalism. They would run anything, any gossip. It was morbid and I didn't like it.

"If he had looked better, I would have kept him in the show. But the combination of the morbid interest and the fact that he didn't look well—and this was the last real work he did, the last real part he played—I didn't think that was the way he should be remembered."

Many of Rock's actions during the last months of his life are difficult—yet not impossible—to understand. This was a man doing his best to hang on to life by continuing to do exactly what he'd always done: work hard, show up where he was expected, and plan for future projects. This was his attempt to keep the demons at bay, and pathetic and ill-chosen as it might have been, there was nonetheless something valiant in it.

Toward the end, though, there were unavoidable signs that Rock was no longer capable of seeing reality as others saw it. Certainly he had no idea of how sick he looked, how much his appearance had changed. His desperate attempt to play one last role—to act as if there was nothing wrong with him—had succeeded only too well. He had managed to convince himself it was the truth.

In April, when nearly every friend he saw came away shocked by his appearance, Rock made plans to launch a publicity campaign. He instructed his publicist, Dale Olson, to set up interviews, and he himself made arrangements with a portrait photographer for a photo session.

The photographer, Greg Gorman, had met Rock several years earlier when the actor was starring in *On the 20th Century*. Rock went to Gorman's Beverly Hills studio on May 8 for an all-day session. Rock explained his weight loss by telling Gorman about his heart bypass operation. He also told him he was working out with a trainer to keep in shape. "I was not aware he was sick," Gorman said.

In the month following the photo session, Rock dropped by Gorman's studio several times to look at the photos. Obviously he enjoyed the young man's company. "He'd come over and look at the photos, sit down and visit," the photographer said. "Some days he probably didn't feel as strong as other days, but it didn't strike me as abnormal."

One of the photos, chosen by Rock, ran on the cover of the July issue of *Beverly Hills 213*, a local newspaper specializing in society news. The photo, a close-up in color, was obviously retouched, and it looks as if Rock had been embalmed. A false rosy hue hangs over the waxen cheeks. The hair is gray and sparse, the lips ashen. The famous eyes are huge, dark, impossible to read. It is a picture of a man who is close to death.

Denise Abbott, managing editor of the paper, interviewed Rock at the Castle in May. The interview had been held, then retrieved and run after Rock's collapse. The publication had not approached Rock. Olson had called and offered the interview. Abbott had every reason to expect a warm reception when she got to the house.

Instead, she found Rock in a suspicious, hostile state. "Questioning him is like psychoanalyzing a recalcitrant patient," Abbott wrote. "He grows restless and annoyed. His sentences drop off before they're finished. He hums, he yawns, he glares at you warily—volunteering almost nothing."

On April 29, 1985, a public-service spot sponsored by the Illinois Office of Tourism ran for the first time on stations around the country. It began with a close-up of a thin, pensive Rock Hudson sitting in a rocking chair, and ended with a shot of him entering a home, where he was embraced by an older gray-haired woman who called him "little Roy." "Chicago is calling you home," intones a voice-over. "No matter where you're from in America, Chicago is your hometown. Come home."

The spot was one of a series dreamed up a year earlier by Jan Zechman, who heads the ad agency of the Illinois Office of Tourism. Other spots featured celebrities like Ed Asner, Quincy Jones, Bob Newhart, Carol Channing, and Dick Butkus, stars either born in Chicago or associated with the city.

Linda Simon, managing director, was in charge of contacting the various stars. The fee was small by star standards—$5,000—and not every celebrity she reached agreed to do it.

Simon contacted Dale Olson sometime near the end of 1984. He assured her Rock would be able to do the spot, but there was a problem. Rock was involved in other projects, like "Dynasty," and not feeling well besides. Would they mind coming out to Los Angeles for the shoot?

It was the only Los Angeles shoot they would have to make—all the other celebrities agreed to come to Chicago. The ad agency decided it was worth the trip for Rock Hudson. "We wanted world-class stars," said Donna Shaw, a Zechman account executive. The shoot was scheduled for March.

Bud Davis, another Jan Zechman executive, liked the idea of using Rock. The two had been classmates years before at New Trier High School. "We weren't close friends, just good acquaintances. We doubled together once. He dated a good friend of mine, Sue Moulton," Davis said.

Davis wasn't surprised Rock had agreed to do the campaign. "If there was one thing he distinguished himself for in high school, it was being a nice guy. When I talked to Olson, I said, 'He was such a nice guy.' And Olson said, 'He still is, he hasn't changed a bit.'"

Simon flew out to Los Angeles to supervise the all-day shoot. She found Rock quiet, polite, and cooperative. He arrived late in the morning and stayed the whole day, even agreeing to pose for publicity stills, an extra favor many stars had balked at. He said very little. Olson was with him throughout the day.

"He looked thin, like he had lost weight, but he didn't look seriously ill. He was friendly, but not overly effusive." He did talk to her briefly about Winnetka. Simon had lived near the town for many years.

"He said, 'Is the skating rink still in Hubbard Woods?' There's a little park, and every winter they flood it for ice skating. He said, 'Do the kids still skate there?' I said yes. He asked if the place was still there across from the park, where you ate. I said, 'Yes, it's still there.'"

When Davis viewed the tape in Chicago, he noticed how thin Rock was and that his complexion seemed sallow. He too had been told about the heart surgery, and assumed that was the cause. "He came up fairly well in the spot, considering," he said. "He didn't look too well, but people chalked it up to the bypass."

The campaign was scheduled to run through the first week of August 1985. It didn't make it. As soon as the news of Rock's collapse flashed around the world, all spots were pulled. "I pulled the commercial after the first announcement, that he was dying of cancer," said Davis. "I pulled it out of respect. Period."

For several years Doris Day had not done any major work in movies or television. She was happy living in her beautiful home on the coast in Carmel, where she was involved in animal-rights causes.

Writers and producers were constantly trying to get her interested in projects—such as the *Pillow Talk II* deal

Jimmy Hawkins had proposed to Rock in 1984—but Day had rejected most of them out of hand.

There were unfounded rumors in the industry that Day had become a bit eccentric, possibly even agoraphobic, since she refused any work that involved leaving the immediate vicinity of Carmel. One tabloid even labeled her a recluse. But friends said that Day was fine, that after a long, successful career, she was finally content, staying close to the home she loved and working with animals.

Early in 1985 the Christian Broadcasting Network (CBN)—a cable network with a successful blend of religious programs and reruns of old westerns and sitcoms—approached Day's son, music producer Terry Melcher, with the idea for a new show to be called "Doris Day's Best Friends." It would be hosted by Day and feature celebrity guests and segments on animals. Best of all, CBN would shoot the show in Carmel so Day wouldn't have to leave home, and her son, Terry, would be co-executive producer. CBN got the gold ring.

When Melcher and the other executives on the show started discussing potential guests, Rock's name came up first. Day said Rock was a natural. What greater way could there be to kick off the program than by reuniting this famous movie team? At the same time, Rock loved dogs as much as Doris, so they could reminisce about the old movie days and chat about their beloved pets. It was decided that Rock would be invited to appear on the first show. Further, he would be at Day's side to promote "Doris Day's Best Friends" at a press conference scheduled for July 15. Doris hadn't seen Rock in a few years and had no idea he was sick.

Rogers & Cowan, a publicity firm in Los Angeles, had been retained by the Christian Broadcasting Network to handle lining up the guests for the show. Dale Olson also worked for Rogers & Cowan, so it was not a problem getting in touch with Rock. Rock accepted immediately. He would be there for the news conference and appear in the show's taping.

The question that was later asked by Rock's closest friends is why he had agreed to do the show, his last public appearance before he collapsed in Paris six days later. No one in Rock's condition, the reasoning went, would have risked exposing himself to reporters at a news conference, unless he was not in his right mind. At the time he agreed to make the appearance, Rock was in the very final stages of AIDS. He had lost so much weight that he had to purchase a new wardrobe—his waist size had dropped about six inches. He had no energy or strength left and spent long hours napping. He was sweating profusely and suffered constantly from nausea and diarrhea. His mind rambled and often his words were slurred, his statements incoherent.

Here was a man with only ten weeks to live, a man who had successfully hidden the secret of his terrible disease for over a year, who had kept the secret of his homosexuality from the world for a lifetime—about to allow it all to disintegrate by appearing at a routine news conference to announce a minor cable-TV show. It was an irrational decision made by a man whose mind clearly had been affected by the disease he carried.

Marty Baum was on vacation in Europe when Rock appeared at the press conference and taped the Day show. "I would have stopped him. He looked awful. I would have said, 'Rock, you don't look well. You're going to hurt yourself by doing it.'" But Baum wasn't around to give Rock that advice.

When director-producer Bob Finkel saw news clips of the Hudson-Day news conference, he was even more shocked. "I could understand him doing 'Dynasty.' Performers have great difficulty turning down parts like that. But I can't understand why he did the Doris Day thing. At that point he really looked awful. I can't believe he didn't look in the mirror and say to himself, 'I want to do every part. I'm an actor. But I really can't do this one because I look awful and this is all going to explode if I go on the air.'

"Something wasn't working up there," said Finkel, touching his head. "He might have been irrational at this point. He'd have to be. What a terrible degeneration. I got sick over it."

Marc Christian wasn't aware that Rock planned to do

Doris Day's show. He learned about it on July 14, the night before, while sitting in the kitchen with Rock and Mark Miller. When Rock mentioned the show, both Christian and Miller tried to talk him out of it. They knew how bad he looked and felt. But Rock remained adamant. Then Rock told Christian that a few days after the Doris Day show he planned to go to Europe again.

After Rock left the room, Christian asked Miller about the European trip. Miller claimed Rock was going to Switzerland where "a miracle drug" was available to treat anorexia, which is what Christian was led to believe Rock was suffering from. Christian was also informed that Ron Channell would accompany Rock to Europe.

Some two dozen reporters, cameramen, and sound and lighting technicians crowded into the airy meeting room of a lovely lodge on the ocean in Carmel late on the afternoon of July 15. When Doris Day entered the room around 4:00 P.M., the time scheduled for the press conference to start, she looked dazzling, just as bubbly and vivacious as she had years earlier when she had starred in three smash light comedies with Rock Hudson.

Doris smiled and shook hands with some of the reporters—several of whom had flown up from Los Angeles because it was such a good feature story: Rock and Doris together again. Day told the reporters that Rock was running a bit late, so she would begin answering questions about her new show. He would join her just as soon as possible.

CHAPTER SEVEN
Fallen Idol

While Doris Day fielded questions about her new show, there was growing impatience—first among the reporters, then among the CBN producers and executives—as to when Rock would show up. The first excuse was that his plane was late. Then word was circulated among the reporters that Rock was delayed because he wasn't feeling well, that he had the flu. Some crews had enough videotape of Day alone to start breaking down the gear and head back to their stations. It was approaching five o'clock.

Looking dreadfully ill, Rock had arrived at the airport in nearby Monterey with Dale Olson. They were met by a CBN talent coordinator, Nellie Bryan, who had a limousine waiting. Rock said little on the drive to the Quail Lodge, in Carmel Valley, where he was staying. On the way, Rock asked the driver to stop at a drugstore. Because he looked so ill, Nellie Bryan thought Rock wanted to pick up medicine. Instead, Rock asked her to buy him mousse for his hair. He was then driven to the lodge, where he fell into a short, fitful nap.

At the press conference, Day decided to take a break when reporters started repeating questions. During the lull, some of the reporters got testy. They threatened among themselves to ask Rock some hard questions when he finally showed up—why he looked so bad on "Dynasty," whether there was any truth to rumors that he had cancer. A few reporters even mentioned AIDS.

213

Their get-tough attitude soon changed. There was an audible, collective gasp—and then a hush—as Rock, his face a virtual death-mask, his body gaunt and hollow under baggy pants and jacket, was ushered into the room by Dale Olson. In contrast to his grim appearance, Rock was wearing a cheerful yellow, blue, and white plaid shirt with the top three buttons undone, showing his bony chest; a charcoal jacket; and tan slacks.

"Everyone knew the minute he walked in that he was real close to death," declared reporter Kimberly Hunt of KMST-TV in Monterey. "We knew he had something very seriously wrong with him, probably AIDS. We knew he was a homosexual."

"I was stunned," exclaimed "Entertainment Tonight" reporter Jeannie Wolf. "In walked this gaunt, scary-looking figure. It was scary. You knew you were seeing someone who looked horrible and who was disoriented. The reporters were all whispering, 'God Almighty, this guy has cancer. They must have him drugged or something.'"

Doris Day's face was frozen into a sickly smile. She didn't skip a beat. She threw her arms around him, giving him a hug. She started talking about how good it was to see him again. She was an actress, trying to look composed, playing to her audience.

The reporters could only stare in disbelief, the sound of the video- and audio-tape machines whirring in the background. This was not the Rock Hudson they remembered—his cheeks were hollow, his eyes lifeless, his voice weak. He looked a thousand times worse than he had on "Dynasty." He stood very close to Day—she actually seemed to be holding him up. He placed his left hand on the podium to help support himself. The static smile remained on Day's face.

Finally, the reporters began asking questions, but none of the hard questions they had threatened earlier. The videotapes that were shown that night and the next day and then for weeks to come told the whole story: Rock Hudson was dying. The man didn't have to say anything, and the reporters were too embarrassed and felt too sorry for him to ask.

"I love dogs as much as Doris does," Rock said weakly, trying to smile. "I have three—a doberman, a golden retriever, and a shepherd." A few moments later he looked at Day lovingly, one bony arm around her shoulder, and said, "This is just like a stroll down memory lane. I think I can even remember some dialogue from *Pillow Talk*."

Kimberly Hunt caught Rock's eye. "We've been told you have the flu today and that's why you were late. How are you?" But Rock's gaze drifted away from the reporter's direction, as Day jumped in to answer another, less pointed question. Finally someone gave the nod that the press conference was over, but Rock started talking again, explaining somewhat incoherently why he was late. The story he told indicated as much about the state of his mental health as his appearance reflected his physical condition.

Rock addressed the reporters. "Before I go, I'd like to apologize to everyone for being so late. You see, I was leaving the airport and I realized I had forgotten my luggage. So I went back inside to find it. I grabbed the bag and got into the car. Then I realized it wasn't my bag. I thought someone else had taken my bag by mistake . . . then I realized I never even packed any luggage, and some poor woman is wondering where her makeup kit is." He smiled weakly. The reporters couldn't believe what they were hearing and seeing. They were having difficulty processing what was happening. They didn't know what to say or ask at that point. Day took the opportunity to lead Rock out of the room.

Time magazine had made a special request to photograph Rock and Doris outside on the grass with a dog. The two went out on the lawn and someone spread a blanket on the grass. Everyone watched with sadness as Rock, like a man years older, struggled to sit down and then to get up.

Dale Olson told a reporter after the press conference, "Rock was not his usual bubbly self. I didn't want him to go. But he's the kind of person who's very loyal. He said, 'Doris expects me. I want to go.'"

Olson, in the first of what would be many contradictions over the next weeks, maintained that the man who had just appeared before the press was "in perfect health. Everybody says does he have cancer, does he have whatever. I've asked his doctor. He's just thin. He loves it. He just threw out all his clothes and bought a new wardrobe." From that day, Olson contended that he never knew Rock had AIDS until it was revealed in Paris.

Kimberly Hunt rushed her videotape back to her station in Monterey. "I walked right in the door and said, 'You guys have to look at this. He doesn't have the flu, he's dying.' And everyone said, 'Yeah, he is.'" The piece she put on the air emphasized the positive part of the story— Day's new show. She noted that Rock Hudson made a late appearance. He was on her tape, but nothing else was said about him.

Nor did the ninety-second piece put together by "Entertainment Tonight"'s Jeannie Wolf deal with Rock's condition. When she got back to Los Angeles, Wolf talked with her editors and producers about checking into Rock's health, but they decided against it. "The decision was to leave it alone. The poor guy's got cancer. This isn't our kind of story. We don't chase ambulances," Wolf said. After the announcement was made that Rock had AIDS, her footage would be used over and over.

Those first reports of the press conference, along with gossip from the reporters covering it, soon spread throughout the entertainment industry. Everyone whispered that Rock Hudson was dying. He might have AIDS.

After the reporters left and Rock was driven back to the lodge, where he fell into a deep sleep, Day was overwhelmed by her emotions and cried. "The dear man, he's really very ill," she sobbed to co-executive producer Dave Freyss. "We should see what we should do for him."

Freyss was also concerned about whether Rock was in any condition to begin two days of taping. "I really thought he had cancer. His eyes looked strange to me. I've seen that look, that stare in cancer victims. I felt very concerned. I was really wondering whether we should do the show."

The next day, July 16, an 8:00 A.M. call had been scheduled to begin shooting, but that was canceled to allow Rock time to rest and to have a decent breakfast. "Boy, if we could just feed him, because he looks so underweight," Day said. As Day; her son, Terry Melcher; CBN executive Tim Robertson; and Freyss waited for Rock to come to breakfast, they speculated on what might be wrong with him—cancer, anorexia. Someone even asked what the symptoms of AIDS were, but that possibility was never seriously considered. Finally, Rock showed up for breakfast, still appearing very tired. He said he was getting over a virus.

Because CBN is a Christian organization, its staffers normally start the workday by saying a prayer, so Robertson asked Rock, "Could we pray for you and with you?" Rock did not say yes or no. He only murmured what was taken to be an assent. So he was ushered into the dining room, where he was asked to sit at the head of the table with Doris on one side of him. The others also took seats. They all held hands, their heads bowed, as Robertson prayed aloud, asking the Lord to bless the time they had together and to give Rock healing and to help him regain his strength.

The shooting location for the day was at Stone Pine, a lovely French chateau on several hundred acres used as an executive retreat. Interior and exterior scenes were to be shot there. The first scene was a parody of the split-screen technique used in *Pillow Talk*, in which Rock and Doris shared a party line. When Rock arrived on the set, he was exhausted before shooting even started. He managed to get through a bit of the taping but then told everyone he was very tired and went upstairs and took a nap. "I just want to lie down," he said.

About an hour later he returned and appeared to be a bit rested. He was able to finish taping the scene. When the day's shooting ended at about 4:30, Rock was taken back to his room by Dale Olson. Freyss remembered that Olson had spent much of the day fielding calls from reporters inquiring about Rock's health, telling them, "There's nothing wrong with him. He's tired and he has the flu."

The next day, July 17, Rock seemed like a new man, Dave Freyss recalled. "He arrived early in the morning ready to go to work. He was peppy, laughing, seemed to be having a good time. He put in a full day shooting."

After he returned to Los Angeles that night, Day talked

about Rock a good deal, staff members said. "What a dear man to come. I wish I knew what was really wrong with him," she said. "Maybe I could help him."

CBN executive Earl Weirich said that when the news broke in Paris only days later that Rock had AIDS, a decision had to be made whether to air the show. Eventually "Doris Day's Best Friends" with Rock Hudson became the second show in the series. It was aired eleven days after Rock died, and then again a week later. Doris prepared a special memorial opening for the program. It is one of the most heartrending sequences ever broadcast.

Day, her voice choked with emotion, tears clearly visible, said she had to have Rock as her first guest on the show.

"So I called him and he said, 'Eunice!' That's what he called me. Don't ask me why. But he said, 'Whenever I think of you as Eunice, it makes me laugh.' So it was okay. And he said, 'I'll be there, you can count on me.' And that was the truth. All his friends, and there were so many, could always count on Rock Hudson. Not only was he a very talented dramatic actor, as we all know. His favorite thing was comedy, and he always said to me, 'The best time I've ever had was making comedies with you.' And I really felt the same way. We had a ball.

"As I reflect on his arrival in Carmel, I can only tell you, my friends, that it was a heartbreaking time for me to see him. He didn't talk about his illness, not one time. He just said, 'Eunice, I've had the flu and I can't gain weight.' And I said, 'You've come to the right place, my darling, because I'm going to put weight on you. I'm going to force-feed you.' And we laughed. And he said, 'I just can't gain and I have no appetite.'

"And, of course, I felt that he wasn't feeling well enough to work. And I told him, I said, 'You know nothing is as important as your health. You don't have to do this show, and I don't want you to. I want you to forget it. I want you to just stay in Carmel for a while and relax and enjoy it,' and he said, 'Forget it. I came here to do your show and that's exactly what I'm going to do.' And he did. That's what he did, and he was wonderful.

"And I feel that without my deep faith I would be a lot sadder than I am today. I know that life is eternal and that something good is going to come from this experience."

Rock returned to the Castle on the night of July 17 and collapsed in his bed, exhausted from the trauma of the press conference and the two days of shooting. The next morning Christian passed Rock's bathroom and heard him vomiting. He was more convinced than ever that Rock was anorexic, as Mark Miller had claimed.

From the time Rock returned from Israel after shooting *The Ambassador* in winter of 1983 to the eve of his departure to Paris, Christian maintained, he confronted Rock at least four times with suspicions that the actor had either cancer or AIDS, and Rock denied them each time. Rock's extraordinary weight loss, his general weakness, malaise, and sudden aging, pointed to those diseases. Initially, Christian suspected lung cancer because his father, like Rock, was a heavy smoker and was dying of it. But Rock assured him he had been to the doctor and had had his lungs checked and everything was fine.

Besides the weight loss, Christian had noticed that Rock had heavy night sweats, which were a symptom of AIDS. When Christian mentioned AIDS to Rock, he got angry. "How can you accuse me of that?" he bellowed.

Whenever Christian told him how bad he looked because of his weight loss, Rock became defensive. "I want to keep the weight off," he'd say. "I want to have the same kind of physique I had when I did *Pillow Talk* with Doris."

Christian claimed that at one point Miller told him a rumor was circulating that Christian had AIDS and had given it to Rock, which was why Rock looked so bad. On the Phil Donahue show, Christian told the story of the confrontation that ensued. "I went into the kitchen that afternoon and I said, 'Rock, have you heard the latest rumor?' And I was kind of joking about it because I thought it was so fantastic. He said, 'What is it?' I said, 'People say that I have AIDS.' He looked at me very sternly and said, 'Well, do you?' And I said, 'Of course not.' I looked back at him. I said, 'Do you?' He said, 'No, I told you no.' I said, 'Okay, but what do you have? There's something wrong with you.' And he said, 'There's nothing wrong with me. I'm just exercising.' He just didn't want to admit anything was wrong. He was very proud."

With all the strident denials, Christian said, he had finally been convinced that Rock was not dying of AIDS. He said he felt assured that Rock really was going to Switzerland to get a "miracle drug" to cure anorexia, as Miller had told him.

In fact, Rock was not going to Switzerland. He had secretly set up an appointment with Dr. Dormont in Paris in hopes of resuming HPA-23 treatments. It was a sad, unrealistic, last-ditch attempt by Rock to try to halt the devastating disease that was now uncontrollably ravaging his body.

Rock would have left for Paris earlier but delayed the trip because of his pledge to Doris Day. As sick as he was, he still would not break a professional commitment, a trait of his that went back to the old studio contract days.

Rock's decision to make the trip to Paris was a tragic mistake. He was so debilitated at that point that he was in no condition to travel—the trip only served to deplete him even more. Further, Dr. Dormont had told Rock that while he would see him, it probably was too late for him to benefit from more treatments.

Most important, the trip succeeded in doing what Hollywood and Rock himself had managed to prevent for so many years. In Paris, the secrecy this intensely private man had spent his life maintaining was abruptly shattered. Rock Hudson—worldwide celebrity, the "Beefcake Baron," the matinee idol—was exposed to the world as a homosexual dying of AIDS.

Rock and trainer Ron Channell were booked on an Air France flight leaving Los Angeles International on the evening of July 20. Christian remembered that producer Ross Hunter had come to the Castle to visit Rock earlier that day. Christian was sitting on the patio listening to music when Rock asked Hunter if he wanted to take a ride in the Mercedes. Rock got behind the wheel, almost immediately lost control of the car, and smashed its side. Rock managed to get out of the car and stormed past Christian, hollering at him to turn down the music. He marched into the house as Hunter watched, alarmed and confused at his friend's behavior.

Late that afternoon Mark Miller and George Nader arrived at the house to help Rock get ready for his flight. "Rock was so weak he couldn't even dress himself," Christian said. "He was so weak he could hardly get out of bed. I felt that it might be the last time I would ever see him again. I really felt that he might just die of starvation." Christian wanted to go to the airport with Rock, but Miller advised against it, saying that photographers might be there. Miller, Nader, Channell, and Rock got in the car and left for the airport, leaving Christian standing in the driveway.

At the airport, Air France representatives were initially reluctant to allow Rock on the plane because of his physical condition. They were persuaded, finally, but only after they had been told who he was. Terribly weak, almost unable to stand by himself, Rock boarded the plane with the help of his staff. He was lowered into his seat in the first-class cabin, dazed and sickly.

Air France flight 4, nonstop to Charles de Gaulle Airport, left LAX at 10:00 P.M. It was in the air ten and a half hours. The flight is an exhausting experience for a healthy person. For Rock, whose body was ravaged constantly by bouts of nausea and diarrhea, it was hellish. He said little; he slipped in and out of consciousness.

Early on the evening of July 21, shortly after his arrival in Paris, Rock Hudson walked into the lobby of the elegant Ritz Hotel and collapsed. It was the beginning of the end.

Rock was helped to his room, where the hotel doctor examined him. Opening Rock's shirt, the doctor spotted the zipperlike, long vertical scar from the bypass operation and made a tentative diagnosis that Rock's collapse had been caused by a heart condition.

Someone made an emergency transatlantic call to Mark Miller. Rock was rushed to the famed American Hospital, where he was immediately seen by a cardiologist. Rock was admitted to the hospital's cardiology section and tests were begun. Miller left for Paris on the twenty-second, arriving on the twenty-third.

Even as Rock was being examined in Paris, reporters in the United States were beginning to probe into his condition as a result of rumors that had begun after the Doris Day news conference.

"This is about the twenty-fifth call I've gotten," an irritated Dale Olson told the New York Post in a story that ran on the twenty-second. "He was very tired when those pictures [of him and Day] were taken. He hadn't slept for forty-eight hours because he had the flu. I know he's okay. I talked to him Saturday. As far as I know, it's nothing. I saw him the day before. He seemed all right. He's going on a vacation."

On July twenty-third, word leaked out in Paris that Rock had been hospitalized. At the same time, in Los Angeles, Daily Variety columnist Army Archerd broke the exclusive story that Rock had AIDS.

The short item read:

Good morning. The whispering campaign of Rock Hudson can—and should—stop. He was flown to Paris for further help. The Institute Pasteur has been very active in research of AIDS. Hudson's dramatic weight loss was made evident to the national press last week when he winged to Carmel to help longtime friend Doris Day launch her new pet series.

His illness was no secret to close Hollywood friends, but its true nature was divulged to very, very few. He left for France and possible aid from scientists there over the weekend. Doctors warn that the dread disease AIDS is going to reach catastrophic proportions in all communities if a cure is not soon found.

Archerd, a veteran show-business columnist, said deciding to print the story was the most difficult decision he had ever faced. "There's no question it was the toughest. Number one, it's a very terrible disease. Number two, I've known him for so long—since he began working at Universal. It took two months to check it out and decide whether or not to break it."

Archerd noted that, for the next forty-eight hours, one could not turn on a TV or radio without hearing the word AIDS.

Once the word was out that Rock was in the hospital, American, French, and Italian reporters in Paris began calling Rock's friend and European publicist, Yanou Collart, demanding a comment. Besieged with calls, she telephoned Dale Olson in Los Angeles. "My God, I was just trying to reach you!" Olson said. "Could you call a person at the Ritz Hotel named Mark Miller? He needs your help desperately."

Miller asked Collart to come right over. It was late afternoon, around 6:30 on the twenty-third; Miller had just arrived from Los Angeles. Collart grabbed a cab and rushed to the hotel, where she found Miller in a state of panic. Reporters had already tracked down his room number and were calling him with questions. One press report in France later erroneously identified him as Rock's lover. The media circus was just beginning to gather force.

Miller ushered Collart to a sofa and sat beside her. "I have to tell you that Rock has AIDS," he told the stunned publicist. "I am the one who told the doctors at the American Hospital this morning that he has AIDS."

"I knew Rock was gay," said Collart, "but what shocked me the most is when Miller told me that Rock knew he had AIDS and that was the reason he was here a year ago, to get the treatments. I was surprised. Miller knew Rock had AIDS from the beginning, which was June 1984. He told me that Rock found something wrong behind his ear and they did a biopsy and they found out he had AIDS."

With that statement to Collart, Miller acknowledged for the first time to someone outside Rock's inner circle that he was in on Rock's deepest secret. He acknowledged that he knew Rock had AIDS and was aware that he had been to Paris the year before to get secret HPA-23 treatments. Collart, who had entertained Rock and handled publicity for him during that visit, had been led to believe that he was there for a vacation and to attend the film festival at Deauville. No wonder she was left dumbfounded when Miller filled her in.

The old myth was beginning to unravel; a new one was about to be woven.

Based on information he received from Miller in Paris, Olson told reporters on July 23 that Rock's doctors at the American Hospital "have diagnosed that he has cancer of the liver and that it is not operable. The doctor also said there were indications of cancer in his blood." Olson also said that "we have reports from other doctors" that Rock was suffering from AIDS. "We simply don't know. The reports have been confused."

Months later, Collart explained what had happened. When Rock was admitted to the hospital Sunday night, a test determined abnormalities in his liver, but it was impossible to determine whether it was an infection or cancer. A biopsy was put off because Rock was too weak to undergo surgery.

When Miller, who does not speak French, arrived in Paris and went to the American Hospital, he met with a doctor who was not very fluent in English. The doctor explained that a liver scan had shown an abnormality, but that they could not operate—that is, perform a biopsy— because Rock was so weak. Miller understood this to mean that Rock had inoperable liver cancer and passed on that information to Olson, who released it to the press.

Miller, of course, also knew that Rock had AIDS, but presumably withheld that information when he talked to Olson. By that time, Miller had told Collart. "I'm quite sure that Dale didn't know Rock had AIDS," Collart said. "Only four people knew: Mark Miller, Rock's valet [whom she said she didn't know by name], the doctor, and Rock."

The first person Miller asked Collart to contact was Dr. Dormont, to see if he could see Rock. In late June or early July, Rock, his condition swiftly deteriorating, had telephoned Dormont to ask for an appointment.

"He knew at that time that he was worse and worse every day," said Dr. Dormont. "He wanted to know if I could do something for him. He wanted advice on whether he could begin treatments again. When he called, I didn't know the answer. My feeling was that if he wanted to come back, he probably was in very bad condition. He made an appointment for August, but he came in July. I didn't know he was coming over. I was very surprised when I heard on the radio that he was at the American Hospital. Then I got four messages on my answering machine."

Collart reached Dormont that night. Dormont told her he had already sought permission from his commanding officer at Percy Military Hospital to transfer Rock but had been refused because of red tape. Dormont was even being denied permission to visit Rock at the American Hospital. Collart used personal influence with defense officials, and late on July 24 Dormont was finally given permission to see Rock.

Collart visited Rock for the first time on the twenty-fourth. Rock was sitting in a chair as a nurse changed his linen. He smiled when his friend walked in. "Look how strange life is," Rock said. "Here I am back in my favorite city but in the hospital."

Collart told him that she didn't think he would be in the hospital very long, and Rock said, "No, certainly not. What I want to do as soon as I get out is for you to have another dinner party for me and have that incredible chocolate mousse" (the dessert Collart had served him at a party she'd held a year before). Rock seemed to have no real awareness of the seriousness of his condition, and Collart did not feel she should mention it. She stayed only a few minutes.

Sporting gold-framed aviator sunglasses and smiling broadly for television cameras, Mark Miller left the hospital after a visit with Rock and told a reporter, "He looks wonderful, I must say. He said to me, 'How are you?' I said, 'I'm fine,'" said Miller, chuckling.

Around this time, Miller placed a telephone call to Los Angeles, to Sylvia Fine, who was in the process of editing the "Musical Comedy Tonight" special. "Roy asked me to call you and tell you he is here in the hospital in Paris to get treatment for AIDS," Miller told Fine, who was stunned. "Can I call any of the doctors, can I exert any pressure on anyone, is there anything I can do?" Fine asked. Miller said no, there wasn't.

Upset by the call, still disbelieving what Miller had just told her, Fine telephoned a mutual friend who confirmed the news. " 'Yes, I know he has AIDS,' my friend said. This was a person who knew a lot more than almost anybody, because very few people knew he had AIDS. What I was doing was verifying the report for one thing, and for another, we commiserated with each other. It was god-awful from then on in." Fine declined to reveal the friend's name.

Later, Fine questioned the motivation behind Miller's call. "I'm not at all sure that Rock suggested that he make the call, because I was told that he was not in very good shape, and that he was not conscious of what was going on."

Later, after Rock's return to the United States, Fine talked to his doctor, AIDS expert Michael Gottlieb. "He told me Rock never had a chance."

In Los Angeles, Dale Olson, interviewed by CBS, said, "Rock Hudson was aware of rumors that were circulating that he was ill. His reactions to those were really negative reactions. He kept saying, 'Forget it. It's none of their business. It's my business and I'm feeling fine.'"

The next morning, July 25, Dr. Dormont visited Rock for the first time. He had not seen him for a year. Rock was dozing when Dormont entered his room. He recognized the doctor and exchanged a few words with him, but that was about it. Dormont looked at Rock's body, made a few tests, and performed a clinical examination. He concluded that Rock had collapsed because of generalized weakness.

"He was in very bad shape," the doctor reported. "He was very tired. It was too late for him to get any benefit from the HPA-23 treatment." Collart, who was outside Rock's room while he was being examined, said, "Rock was in terrible shape. He was totally dehydrated and he had constant diarrhea."

That same day a major decision was made: to announce to the world that Rock Hudson had AIDS. Whether Rock actually was involved in making that decision or whether it was made for him without his knowledge—or understanding—is still being questioned long after his death.

One fact is indisputably clear: at no point between the time of his collapse and the end of his life seventy-three days later did Rock Hudson ever stand before a television camera or say directly to any reporter, "I have AIDS." The announcement from Paris was handled with such finesse that the general public never questioned that Rock himself had mouthed the words.

"We decided to tell," Collart said. "Rock said we will tell everybody what happened." She said that the press release, written in both English and French, was put together with a number of people present, including herself; Miller; Dr. Dormont; a doctor from the American Hospital; Bruce Redor, the hospital's spokesman; and a friend of Rock's, Lady Vivian Glenavy, a writer.

After the release was written, Miller told Collart that she would be the one to read it to Rock. No one else would be present in the room. "The only thing that Mark Miller told me was not to show any tears," she said.

Collart claimed that she then went into Rock's room and stood at the foot of his bed and read the statement, which began, "Mr. Rock Hudson has Acquired Immune Deficiency Syndrome, which was diagnosed in the United States. He came to Paris to consult with a specialist in this disease. Prior to meeting the specialist, he became very ill at the Ritz Hotel. . . ." Collart said that Rock was "lucid" as she read him the statement.

"I must tell you that it was a very hard moment to read that, because his eyes were on me and he knew that by telling the world that he had AIDS he was destroying himself," Collart said. "I believe I will never forget his eyes. It was like his whole life was flashing before him. I will not forget it. When I finished, he said, 'Go and give it to the dogs.' That was the phrase he used, because he hated journalists."

Collart subsequently used these exact words—with no variation—every time she described what happened in Rock's room to a reporter. She used them again, exactly, when interviewed for this book. Her recounting has a mythic quality about it. Only two people know what happened in that room, and one of them died. The man who reportedly told Collart to go with the story went to his grave without ever once meeting face-to-face with the public or the press to acknowledge his disease.

For Rock to have given the green light would have meant going against the grain of his whole life, a life of intense privacy, a life in which he was able to conceal his homosexuality for decades, his disease for over a year. It's doubtful that such a man would suddenly change, want the world to know his secrets. Even when he was admitted to the American Hospital, he did not let the doctors know he had AIDS, which resulted in the confusion about liver cancer. It was Miller who finally told them. "I like to keep my secrets to myself, and I guess they will die with me," Rock said a few weeks before his collapse.

Assuming Rock did, in fact, authorize release of the statement, one must consider whether he was mentally competent to do so, whether he was completely cognizant of the words Collart was reading to him.

Dr. Thomas Hewes, the cheif of medicine at the American Hospital, who examined Rock, talked with him, and performed a liver biopsy on him, was asked about Rock's condition. "He was a very, very sick man during the whole time that he was here. He was very confused and very acutely ill. He was in bed. He wasn't able to get out of bed. He was very mentally confused, so he was unable to look after himself."

When asked if Rock could have made such an important decision, Dr. Hewes stated, "I'm unable to answer that question. I mean, I'm literally unable to answer that question—not that I'm evading the question, because I'm not able to judge from my personal contacts with him. He was a very sick man, very weak and bedridden."

Dr. Dormont, who was present during the preparation of the statement and was outside Rock's room when Collart read him the press release, said, "Mr. Hudson was not in very good condition, and sometimes with that kind of patient you have to repeat a question just to be sure they are willing to do what they say they are willing to do. He could have said yes the first time and then, thinking it over, said, 'I don't want to.' You can ask a patient something important like that two or three times."

After leaving Rock's room, Collart was instructed by Miller to meet with some two dozen reporters, photographers, and TV cameramen who were gathered in the parking lot outside the hospital awaiting the statement. With microphones thrust in her face by the hungry media horde, Collart read the statement and then began fielding a barrage of questions. All the hard work that had gone into preparing and approving the press release began to fall apart.

Amid the chaos of the press conference, Collart caused more problems by declaring that Rock's AIDS had been "cured." She said that "the last test made in America before he came here showed that he was not having any trace of AIDS . . . any virus." When questioned further, she insisted "he had been cured."

Later, Collart denied the foul-up ever happened. "I don't know if you know what it is to be in front of two hundred fifty journalists all fighting. They always try to get more. It was really a misinterpretation of what I said to them. I never said that he was cured. Never!"

As Rock Hudson lay in his bed, the news of his illness, now officially confirmed, flashed around the world. By that evening, hundreds of telegrams and phone calls had been received at the hospital, showing support for the stricken idol. In all, some five thousand telegrams and letters arrived. "They say you are gay, but we feel you are a real man" was the overall message.

Celebrities lined up to voice their love for and support of Rock.

"I've always loved Rock very much," said Doris Day, who finally learned why her friend had looked so bad a week earlier, "and I'm praying for him." Elizabeth Taylor said, "All my love and prayers are with him." "Dynasty" executive producer Aaron Spelling said, "We're stunned and depressed. He never missed a day of work. We didn't know anything about this. When he appeared on 'Dynasty,' he looked terrific, displayed great energy, and, as always, was a consummate professional."

In Los Angeles Dale Olson said he did not know whether Hudson was a homosexual. "There have been reports to that effect for many years, but our relationship has been purely business and the subject has never come up. Hudson is a very private person."

Members of Rock's inner circle contended that Rock had contracted AIDS from blood transfusions administered during his heart-bypass surgery several years earlier. Dr. Dormont said such statements were "hypothetical." The doctor said he knew how Rock got the disease but declined to discuss it.

When Mark Miller learned that Rock had collapsed, he called Marc Christian at the Castle to tell him he was going to Paris. Miller, according to Christian, said that Ron Channell had telephoned him from Paris in a panic to report what had happened and wanted to be relieved of the responsibility. "But Mark didn't tell me Rock had AIDS," Christian said. "He just said he was going to Paris to relieve Ron." Collart said that as far as she knew, Rock had come to Paris alone, and she never saw Channell.

When Army Archerd's story ran, the phone at the Castle started ringing off the hook. The calls were mostly from friends of Rock. Christian told those he hardly knew that Rock had gone to Paris to try to quit smoking; he told others he knew better that Rock might have anorexia. But he denied the AIDS report to all. He had no reason not to. "I was still legitimately defending him because I knew nothing else," Christian said.

Christian was alone in the house, sitting in the playroom watching the evening news, when he saw the report that Rock had AIDS. He couldn't believe what he was hearing. At first he thought they were just repeating rumors that had been floating around since the "Dynasty" appearances. When he heard the reporter say that Rock had been in Paris a year earlier for treatments, Christian said to himself, "No, he hadn't. He was over there for the film festival. I still hadn't realized that I had been lied to."

Two days later Miller called Christian, who was still

waiting for some official confirmation from Paris, not knowing what to believe. According to Christian, Miller said he hadn't told him Rock had AIDS on the advice of Rock's physicians. "Mark said, 'The doctors told Rock and myself never to tell you because they did a study on partners of people with AIDS and the partners became so depressed that they wound up in mental institutions. Rock forbade me to tell you.'"

Christian never believed that Rock authorized the press release in Paris.

"He never had any intention of letting anyone know he had AIDS," Christian said. "At that point, Rock had no long-term memory. I don't think he knew what they were talking about. He might have understood for about ten seconds and then thought about a steak. He might have thought he had measles."

As soon as Miller hung up, the phone rang again. This time it was Dale Olson, who apologized to Christian. "I forgot to call you before the press conference. I was going to soften the shock by telling you first, but I got busy."

Christian was in a state of panic. He realized now that he himself risked getting AIDS—since, he claimed, he had slept with Rock on and off between the spring of 1983 and February 1985.

Marty Baum was vacationing in England when the story broke that Rock had AIDS. Shocked, he returned to Los Angeles the next day and began getting calls from Miller and Olson.

"They were telling me up until he went to UCLA [Medical Center] that the AIDS was under control," Baum said angrily. "They were telling me that he was going to be okay, that he was going to beat it. Miller told me in a long conversation that he was confident Rock was going to lick this disease."

In fact, in Paris, Dr. Dormont told Rock he was in no condition to benefit from a new series of HPA-23 treatments. He gave Rock two options. One was to stay in Paris and try to rebuild his strength, with the possibility of getting treatments in the future. The treatments, however, would depend on the results of tests that were still being processed.

The other option was to return as soon as possible to the United States. Dr. Dormont gave Rock two days to make a decision. The next day Dormont was told that Rock wanted to return home.

Late on the afternoon of July 29, Yanou Collart was instructed by Mark Miller to start making preparations for the secret evacuation of Rock Hudson from Paris. Rock, Miller told Collart, wanted to leave that night. Collart said the doctors thought it would be advisable for Rock to fly on a nonstop flight and for the plane to be equipped with emergency medical equipment. A decision was made to charter a jumbo jet to fly Rock, Miller, and a small medical team to California. The cost: a reported $300,000.

Collart indicated that the decision to charter the jet was Rock's. "There was no reason not to do what Rock was wishing, because it was his money," she said.

However, Dr. Dormont said, "It was not him. He could have been transported on a normal flight. The people around him did not want the press to disturb him." Dr. Dormont, who was constantly battling for AIDS research funds, was upset by the huge amount of money spent for the charter flight. "In France," he said, "we always have problems getting money to run our labs. So when we see somebody spending a lot of money which is wasteful, this can get to you. I wanted to let them know that they were spending too much to bring back a person to the U.S."

Marty Baum said he was dumbfounded when he heard that a plane had been chartered for "a preposterous sum of money, an enormous amount of money" to bring Rock home. "I never could understand the need for that, because he was ambulatory. For a guy who lived conservatively— and he lived very conservatively—chartering that plane was totally out of character for him."

To avoid the press, Collart planned Rock's evacuation with military precision. Since Rock looked terrible, Miller decided that photographers were to be avoided at all costs. Miller was aware that certain publications would be willing to pay six figures for "the exclusive last photo" of Rock. He did not want Rock to be remembered that way. In fact, the last news photos ever taken of Rock were those shot at the Doris Day press conference.

Initially, Collart called the Ministry of the Army to see if a military escort could be provided for the ride from the hospital to Charles de Gaulle airport, where a chartered Air France Boeing 747 was waiting with a crew of eight. She rejected that idea because it would allow the press, still gathered outside, to follow.

Her next plan was to hire a helicopter to land at the hospital and evacuate Rock, but she was told that this was not possible.

Finally, she arranged for a helicopter to be waiting at a nearby pad. An ambulance brought into the rear of the hospital drove Rock, Miller, and Collart to the chopper. Luckily, a heavy shower struck as the ambulance raced away from the hospital. When the rain caused the reporters to run for cover, they never noticed the ambulance. "It was only when we were flying in the helicopter to the airport that we heard the news on the radio that Rock was flying back to the U.S.," Collart said. "Somebody who was in charge of chartering the plane at the airport must have leaked the news. But they never could get any pictures of Rock, because by that time we had landed at the airport and were boarding the plane to fly to L.A."

Rock arrived in Los Angeles before dawn on July 30 and was taken by ambulance to the UCLA Medical Center.

Shortly after Rock was hospitalized there, the results of the tests conducted in Paris were made available to Dr. Gottlieb. Bringing Rock home had been the right decision. The tests showed that nothing could be done for him. "He was in the very last stages of AIDS," Dr. Dormont said. "The tests showed he was about to die." Rock Hudson had about two months to live.

Rock required immediate and proper medication, rest, nourishment, and around-the-clock observation at UCLA. He was severely debilitated. His condition was serious but stable. The doctors knew he was dying—the tests conducted in Paris confirmed that. With proper care, his last days could be made comfortable.

Shortly after Rock was admitted, Marty Baum had a telephone conversation with Rock's New York attorney, Paul Sherman. Miller had led Baum to believe that Rock had a chance of beating the disease. "What's going on?" Baum asked Sherman. "Rock's finished," the lawyer told the agent emphatically. "It's over."

Mark Miller put together a select list of about twenty people who were authorized to visit or telephone Rock. Phone calls were limited to people on the list and were carefully screened. Security was so tight that Rock's long-time friend Jim Matteoni could never get through by phone. Eventually he wrote a detailed letter explaining who he was but got no response until after Rock's death.

Miller choreographed visits to Rock's private suite with the clockwork precision of a Busby Berkeley dance number. He would schedule the time precisely and usually accompany the visitors to Rock's room, where he would announce them. This was done so that there would be no embarrassment for Rock, who was often confused and unaware of what was happening around him. Many times Rock didn't recognize his visitors, all of them old friends. Other times he'd quickly forget they had been there at all. Sometimes he'd nod off as they stood at his bedside. He couldn't remember who he saw from one day to the next.

On good days, when he was conscious most of the time, Rock would have two visitors in the afternoon and one or two at night. Among the VIPs on the list were Elizabeth Taylor, Carol Burnett, Doris Day, Martha Raye, Nancy Walker, and Roddy McDowall. The reason for the list was to maintain tight security around Rock—to keep away scoop-hungry reporters and zealous fans and, for a time, Marc Christian.

To get to Rock's room, visitors reportedly had to pass through several checkpoints manned by hospital and private security guards. The elevator would stop one floor below his suite, where visitors would get off and identify themselves to a security guard. They would then walk up a flight of stairs to Rock's floor, where there was another guard, who would clear them.

Jon Epstein, one friend on the list, was called by Miller a few days after Rock entered the hospital. "You're on for two o'clock tomorrow," Miller said. Epstein didn't understand. "You can see him at the hospital," Miller explained. "You're on the list of people he'd like to see." Epstein was taken aback by what he termed the "quite bizarre" brisk and businesslike tone of Miller's call. Other friends felt the same way. If he wanted to see Rock, Epstein was instructed to pick up Miller at the Castle and drive him to the hospital, where he could "spend five minutes with him" before returning Miller to the house.

Not only was Epstein put off by Miller's officious tone, but he was still reeling from the shock of the news from Paris and wasn't emotionally prepared to visit Rock so soon. "But I figured this is what's done. I was being scheduled, so I just accepted it," he said.

"Well, guess who's here? Jon Epstein has come to see you," Miller announced brightly to the bedridden Hudson, who was propped up against a pillow, his face gaunt, his skin flushed from having just received a blood transfusion.

"It was quite pathetic," said Epstein, realizing that Miller had to go through the show-and-tell because Rock's mind was not tracking. Later, after he had gained some strength in the hospital and returned home, there were times when Rock seemed totally lucid, his memory clear. But in those early days at the hospital, he was more often vegetablelike.

The day Epstein visited, Rock seemed to recognize his old friend and offered a weak "hi." "He looked awful," Epstein said. "I just chatted away about how glad I was to see him, about how he was going to be fine and just blah, blah, blah for a couple of minutes. He just nodded and kind of half smiled."

The last time Epstein had seen Rock was in December, when he had gone to the Castle to watch a Rams-Giants game. At the time, Epstein had feared that Rock was ill— he suspected cancer, not AIDS. He had hoped that Rock would open up to him about his illness because, Epstein thought, it might help for him to talk about it.

That day they sat in the playroom and reminisced

about the "McMillan" days and watched the game. Rock made tuna-fish sandwiches for lunch. At the time, Epstein was himself recovering from an illness and was aware that Rock had heard about it through the grapevine. "I told him I was fine and on the mend," said Epstein, "but he never opened up to me. How difficult it must have been to carry this within him as long as he did and as privately as he felt he had to."

Epstein, like most of Rock's friends, learned what was wrong with Rock from the six o'clock news.

Actor Tony Perkins visited Rock and noted that he had lost so much weight that he "looked like the young Roy. It was uncanny." Rock was happy to see Perkins but told him that some days "I wish people would go away and leave me alone."

George Robotham was in Munich when the story broke that Rock had AIDS. He toyed with the idea of going to Paris but realized how difficult it probably would be to see Rock. Instead, he sent a telegram. "I tried to put something together . . . what do you say to a guy who's on his way to the gas chamber?"

When Robotham returned from Germany, he arranged to visit Rock at the hospital with their other pals, Pete Saldutti and Mark Reedall. They joked with Rock and talked about some of the good times they had had. "But Rock would get a little vague at times," Robotham said. "He was just as thin as a rail."

Jimmy Dobson visited the hospital about a week after Rock got back from Paris. To see him, Dobson had to go through the same routine with Miller that Epstein had. Miller announced Dobson and then left the two men alone. "Roy looked so terrible," recalled Dobson. "He was very quiet and gentle, like a little animal that had been whipped."

Dobson felt it was important to touch Rock, because he was aware of how afraid people were of the disease and how that must affect its victims. He put his arms around Rock's neck and held him for a moment. To keep things light, he had brought Rock a roll of joke Hollywood toilet paper that said "Cut and Print" on each sheet. On another visit, he brought him a dozen balloons of different colors because Rock always loved them.

"I said, 'Roy, I don't know if you know it, but in a way you're a hero.' He said, 'No, I didn't know that.' And I showed him a banner some people had been carrying outside the hospital that said WE LOVE YOU ROCK." Dobson also told Rock about a newspaper story that had praised Rock's courage for admitting he had AIDS.

Later, when Tom Clark returned to care for Rock, he warned visitors against such conversations. "You must never discuss AIDS with Rock," Clark told them. "Never at all." At the hospital, there were strict instructions not to allow Rock to look at any newspapers or magazines for fear he might see stories about himself. Television programming was also monitored so that Rock wouldn't see any newscasts. The same rules applied once Rock got home. Fearing he might see *People* magazine or *National Enquirer* commercials, which were then trumpeting stories about him, Rock was permitted to watch only cable television or videotapes.

So many people, friends and fans alike, were sending flowers to Rock that they were distributed among other AIDS patients or to child patients at the hospital. Rock only kept one red rose—a fresh one was placed in a simple glass vase each day.

Marc Christian, fearful for his own health after learning that Rock had AIDS, went home to Orange County to be with his mother. No one called Christian to tell him that Rock had returned and had been admitted to UCLA. He heard about it on the radio and immediately drove to the Castle.

Christian was told that he should leave as soon as possible for Paris to be tested for AIDS. "They told me to go the very next day because Rock insisted that I be tested," he said. "I was scared. I didn't know what to expect." Christian spent about ten days in France. The tests were negative.

Before returning, he visited Vivian Glenavy, Rock's writer friend. During the visit, Miller called and asked her if she would be interested in writing Rock's biography. Christian was surprised by the call because Rock had once told him he never wanted such a book. "I don't want a book written until I can write it myself," Rock told Christian. "I don't want to write about Rock Hudson. I want to write about Roy Fitzgerald, and I don't know who Roy Fitzgerald is yet."

Only a short time before he collapsed in Paris, Rock declared, "I believe that if you write one [an autobiography], you should tell the truth, not butter it up. What do I want people to know about me? Nothing. It's none of their business. As far as correcting misconceptions, good luck!"

There was a time in the mid-to-late 1970s—at the height of the so-called Gay Liberation Movement—when Rock toyed with the idea of coming out of the closet and telling his story. The subject came up during visits with writer Armistead Maupin. "One of these days I'm going to have a lot to tell," Rock told Maupin.

"Rock seemed kind of fascinated by the idea that such a book would have an enormous impact," Maupin said. "He felt that by writing it he would be in charge of his life for once, that he wouldn't be the stick figure that the studio was cranking out, that he would be Roy Fitzgerald getting to say something.

"I don't think Rock was ashamed of being a homosexual, but he was given enough conflicting reports about what he could and couldn't show the world that it was troublesome to him at times."

Once, at dinner, when the idea of the book was brought up, Tom Clark tried to shoot it down, Maupin recalled.

While Rock may have considered a book back in the 1970s—when the mood of the country was more liberal and receptive—he had definitely rejected the idea by the 1980s, when a greater conservatism permeated the country. Asked blatantly in 1980 by the London Daily Mirror whether he was a homosexual, Rock skirted the truth: "I know a lot of gays in Hollywood and most of them are nice guys. Some have tried it on with me, but I've said, 'Come on, now. You've got the wrong guy.'"

In August, with Rock's death imminent, Mark Miller and several other intimates were pushing for an "authorized" book. They claimed that Rock's share of the royalties would go to benefit AIDS research.

According to Christian, Glenavy didn't like the way Miller wanted her to write Rock's biography. "They wanted the book written fast," Christian said. "They were desperate to get it written even before he died." Glenavy told Miller she would have to interview hundreds of people to get a true picture of Rock, but they wanted to control her work. So she flatly refused. Another writer, Sara Davidson, agreed to do the book.

Christian returned to the Castle in mid-August. He had not seen Rock since the day Hudson had left for Paris. When Christian got to the hospital, he was told he could not see Rock because his name was not on Mark Miller's list of approved visitors. Christian was furious. His anger must have aroused the suspicion of security guards because, he claimed, he was stopped and questioned as he left the building.

Back at the Castle, Miller told Christian he would have to move out within forty-eight hours. "Rock wants you out," Christian said he was told by Miller. Christian was tired of being pushed around. "If Rock wants me to leave, have him call me, and if he really wants me to go, I will go," Christian told Miller. Miller reiterated, "He won't speak to you." Christian said, "Well, I'm not going to leave. If he can't be a man and tell me to leave, I'm not going to leave." Christian felt that Miller personally wanted him out of the house but was throwing the blame on the hospitalized Hudson.

A couple of days later, Miller relented and gave Christian permission to visit Rock.

At 1:00 P.M. Christian walked into Rock's room. Rock was lying in bed. To Christian he looked even worse than he had when he went to Paris. His body was even thinner, his complexion had a gray cast to it. But Rock seemed lucid. Christian felt like crying but held back the tears. He asked Rock how he was feeling, how the food was. Rock asked Christian about his dogs and if everything was okay at the Castle. Finally, Christian moved closer to Rock, placed his hand on his arm, and said, "Why didn't you tell me you were sick?" Rock let his eyes wander, then turned his focus on Christian and said, "Well, you know, when you've got a disease like this, you are all alone."

"Well, you're not," Christian said. "Not unless you want to be." Christian went on to tell Rock that he should never have ended his treatments in Paris in 1984 to do "Dynasty." He told him he should have gone back for treatment; Christian would have gone with him had he known.

Rock began to nod off. Before he left, Christian said, "I've been told by Mark that you want me to leave the house. Is that true?" Rock said, "No. Why should you leave?" Christian touched Rock's hand and said good-bye. Rock turned over and went to sleep.

"But Rock never admitted anything," Christian said. "He never apologized." Despite that, Christian could only feel pity for him.

As Rock's hospitalization dragged on, he became increasingly depressed. Lying in his bed, he would watch as orderlies wearing masks, rubber gloves, and gowns gingerly handled his bedclothes and bedding, which would be destroyed to avoid possible contamination. Nurses recalled seeing tears in his eyes whenever he caught his gray, gaunt reflection in a mirror. He felt a sense of isolation and despair and began to view himself as a leper. Rock started pleading to go home to the house he loved so much. Since no more could be done for him at the hospital, the doctors agreed to discharge him. They felt that being in familiar surroundings would help lift his depression and make his last days happier. Rock was discharged on August 24. He had a little more than a month to live.

It had been almost two years since Tom Clark had moved from the Castle. Like everyone else, Clark knew or strongly suspected after the Doris Day press conference that Rock had AIDS. When Rock collapsed in Paris and the world knew he had AIDS, Clark felt he had to do something for his dying friend. Miller and Clark talked. It was decided that Clark would return to the fold to aid and comfort his longtime companion during his final days.

"Tom had always put Rock first, above anything or anyone," Susan Stafford said. "He always wanted the best for Rock. In the last days, Tom put Rock first instead of his own needs, or pain or hurt. He showed his love right to the end without any qualifications."

The nurses who cared for Rock once he returned home said that if they were sick, they would want a friend like Clark. "He would do whatever was needed," one of them said. "He was always there for Rock. He just wanted the very best for him. He tried to cheer him up, keep him going, right to the end."

To avoid the press, Rock was moved out of the hospital at dawn. Clark helped bring him home. To be closer to Rock, Clark moved into Christian's bedroom, and Christian moved into the theater, an annex of the house.

Christian claimed that one of the first items on Clark's agenda, once he had taken charge of the Castle again, was to tell him not to see Rock, that it would upset him. According to Christian, Clark and Miller told him that Rock was already under the impression he had moved out of the house. But Christian ignored their orders and would sneak up to Rock's room to visit him when Clark was out on an errand. "He was pretty far gone," Christian said. "He'd ask about the dogs, or ask me what was on television. He never talked about his disease. I got the impression he had no idea he even had AIDS. He just kept saying he was tired of not feeling well."

With Rock back, a routine was established at the Castle. Miller and Clark, along with the butler, James Wright, ran the house, escorting guests in to visit Rock, helping to plan for a scheduled AIDS benefit, and assisting Sara Davidson, who was writing Rock's book.

There had been "no love lost" between Miller and Clark when Clark left in 1983, Susan Stafford observed. "But whatever love was lost was found during Rock's last days. There was a unity between Mark and Tom like I've never seen before." Stafford noted that Miller never had the same commitment to Rock that Clark did.

Rock was being given around-the-clock care by a team of four private nurses, all of whom were, coincidentally, born-again Christians. All of the nurses came to love Rock. "It was like being with a friend," said Toni Phillips, who suffered a deep sense of loss when he died. "Rock was a pleasure to be around. It wasn't like being at work. If things got bad or there were a lot of demands, I really didn't care, because he was such an easy person to love. He was really down-to-earth. He wasn't like some people who have a lot of money and are really obnoxious. He seemed like one of the guys."

If he was conscious, which he was less frequently now, Rock would watch old movies on cable or on tape. He would sometimes make a comment to one of the nurses about a particular actor or actress with whom he had worked on a film. He refused to watch "Dynasty." And he never talked about his disease or about dying. From the time he got home from the hospital until his death, Rock was never on strong medication or heavy pain-killers. Shortly after he arrived home, he asked that no heroic measures be taken to save his life.

In the first week or two after his return from the hospital, Clark and the nurses brought Rock down from his room every few days to sit in the garden. He sat quietly patting his dogs for a half hour or so, but he tired quickly and had to be taken back to his room.

Although Christian had tested negatively for AIDS in Paris, doctors warned him that he could develop the disease because he had been repeatedly exposed to the virus through sexual contact with Rock. They told him that the disease could hide in his bone marrow and might appear several years later. Upset over the prognosis and angered at the shabby treatment he claimed he was getting from Miller and others at the house, Christian decided to seek legal counsel.

Late in August he quietly contacted Marvin Mitchelson, the flamboyant Beverly Hills attorney. In the early 1970s the lawyer had gained worldwide notoriety representing actor Lee Marvin's live-in girl friend, Michelle Triola, with whom Marvin had broken up. In a landmark case,

Triola won the same kind of settlement a divorced wife would have received. The media dubbed her award "palimony," instead of alimony, and Mitchelson thereafter became known as "the famed palimony attorney."

The Marvin case stunned the Hollywood community. How many more girl friends—and boyfriends—were ensconced in the hills of Hollywood and Beverly ready and willing to file similar suits? Ironically, one of the stars who expressed concern was Rock Hudson. "What a can of peas you've opened!" he remarked to Michelle Triola at a party.

Christian's fourteen-million-dollar suit, which was not to be filed until after Rock died, was based on the premise that he had been exposed to AIDS by Rock, who kept the disease a secret from his lover. As Mitchelson so succinctly put it: "If you invite someone into your home and you know you have a hole in the living room and you don't tell them it's there and they fall through, that's actionable."

Christian also sued Miller; Wallace Sheft, Rock's business manager; two doctors who were not named; and a number of other unnamed persons on the grounds that they "consciously and callously disregarded [his] safety . . . his right to life and his right to be informed that the person with whom he was having sexual relations was afflicted with a fatal disease transmitted by such relations."

Christian kept his contacts with Mitchelson a secret from Miller and the others in the Castle. When Miller flew to New York late in August for a meeting with Sheft, Mitchelson called to inform them he was representing Christian in an action against the estate.

The next day Miller flew back to Los Angeles and confronted Christian. "Well, I guess you know by now that I know what you've done," he said. Christian accused Miller of only caring about himself and told him he had to get a lawyer to protect his interest, too.

Christian's threatened lawsuit was kept from Rock during the remaining days of his life. There was no reason to burden him with the impending scandal. Not even Christian wanted that.

Friends continued visiting Rock. They'd call Clark to see if Rock was awake, and if he was, they'd be invited up to the house to spend time with him. Under Clark, visits were less regimented than they had been with Miller. If Rock was asleep, friends would be invited up anyway just to hang out. Martha Raye, Nancy Walker, producer John (*Prizzi's Honor*) Foreman, and others would gather in the kitchen and reminisce about their friend.

"It was like sitting shivah in the Jewish religion," observed Jon Epstein, who was there several times. "People come over after the death of a loved one and sit around and talk. That was going on while Rock was still alive."

Matthew West visited Rock several times during the last month of his life. On one occasion, he sat beside the bed telling Rock about a recent vacation he had taken in his native New Zealand. It was a beautiful day, and a gentle breeze came through the opened windows. Rock smiled, and his eyes looked alive as West recounted stories about the boating and fishing he had done.

"He loved hearing all that," said West. "He mostly just sat there and listened. I told him about the bougainvillea that was climbing through the window behind his bed. I kept it very light. I'd joke about things—little, silly things, just to get him to smile, that's all. He seemed happy to just listen. That was a very good visit. There were other times when I could see him only a few minutes because he was tired. I never asked him any hard questions, because I knew he was dying."

Not all visits were as pleasant. The only time Jimmy Dobson saw Rock at home was a depressing one. Not realizing how Rock's condition had deteriorated, Dobson offhandedly asked his friend whether he had been visited by Betty Abbott, who had remained friends with Rock over the years. Rock looked quizzically at Dobson, not seeming to comprehend the simple question. Finally, Rock responded, "We don't have much fun anymore." Dobson looked puzzled and asked Rock what he meant. "Well, nobody drinks anymore," Rock said. "I don't drink. Betty doesn't drink. So when we go out, we have nothing to drink. It's no fun at all." Rock was out of touch with reality.

At times, though, Rock seemed to gain strength. One night Jon Epstein was in the kitchen watching television when Rock, accompanied by one of his nurses, made an unexpected appearance. Wearing a silk robe and pajamas, he sat at the table and made some small-talk. "He was kind of weak but he was totally aware," Epstein recalled. "He just seemed so normal that night, but I knew he was dying and I presumed that he knew the same thing."

Epstein said his other visits were much shorter and, during them, Rock always stayed in bed. Once Epstein went to Rock's room and started talking to him and Rock fell asleep.

One night Martha Raye and a few other friends were sitting in the kitchen when Raye, who spent hours at Rock's bedside, made some critical remarks about Christian. She was aware that he had seen an attorney and was contemplating filing a suit. At that moment, Christian popped his head in the doorway and Epstein tried to introduce the two. Raye refused to acknowledge his presence. Christian, who had apparently heard what Raye was saying, snapped, "Keep your opinions to yourself." After Christian left, Raye was furious. "It was not a pleasant moment," said a friend who was there. "Martha was very emotional and she was talking on that level."

Once Roddy McDowall came to visit and Rock didn't recognize him. McDowall became so upset by Rock's condition that he had to be escorted from Rock's room.

Marty Baum made a difficult decision after he learned that Rock was dying of AIDS. He decided that he would not visit him either at the hospital or at the house.

"I felt my presence would be an embarrassment for him," Baum said. "I thought he would have felt guilty seeing me. Out of compassion for the problems he had, I didn't want to add mine to them. He'd have to be embarrassed because there was nothing but a succession and a string of lies for two years. Every time he would turn down a television series, he didn't tell me why he was turning it down.

"He was telling me he wouldn't take this job or that job because the script wasn't any good, when the script was good. He was lying. He couldn't say to me, 'Hey, I'm sick. I can't do it.' He wanted me to get him work for as long as he felt capable of working. He didn't want anything to interfere with that. He wanted to be functional and make money and do his job professionally for as long as he could get away with it.

"There was so much bullshit going on that I didn't want to go to that house and look at Miller."

Early in September the telephone rang in the North Hollywood offices of the Pierce, Hamrock, Reed Mortuary. The caller identified himself to assistant manager Beth Burr as a Mr. Miller. He made an appointment to discuss an impending death.

Three days later Mark Miller and George Nader arrived at the funeral home. Miller asked Burr general questions about cremations and costs. "At first they did not tell me who it was they were talking about, except that he was well known," Burr said.

Miller asked about the company's philosophy toward handling AIDS victims, and Burr explained to him that it was illegal for a mortuary to refuse a case. Miller indicated that another mortuary had at first refused to handle the case and then tried to charge him more money to take it. "I told him it would be illegal to charge more, and we can't refuse him," Burr recounted. "He finally said, 'Now we'll tell you that we are here talking about Rock Hudson.' I had a feeling that's who it was."

Burr went on to explain to Miller that because Hudson had no relatives living in California, the mortuary was required by law to report his death to the Los Angeles County public administrator. The office protects the rights of the deceased from such illegalities as someone trying to keep a death a secret. The office also protects the deceased's estate. "It's there to make sure one or two people don't run off with all the money when they're not entitled to it," Burr explained. Miller and Nader said they understood.

Miller demanded tight security to keep the media from finding out when and where the cremation would be. "We talked about logistics of what would transpire at the time of his death," Burr said. "I told him that we would use an unmarked van to pick up the body. We would not use a hearse, anything that would be obvious. I told them the men who would pick up the body would be dressed casually, just like workmen, rather than in suits, which is the normal attire. Again, this would be done so as not to attract attention. I told them that the cremation would be done as soon as possible, but that if the death occurred in the middle of the night, we would have to deal with the situation at that time."

Miller and Nader were satisfied. The cost to cremate Rock Hudson's body would be $285. They gave Burr a deposit. She also said there would be an additional cost of four dollars for a certified copy of the death certificate. Large estates like Hudson's require more than one copy, usually a couple of dozen. Miller eventually ordered two hundred. Despite the tight security promised by the funeral home, the press would soon discover the plan and Beth Burr's life would become a nightmare.

On the night of September 14, Rock's favorite nurse, Toni Phillips, was working the 7:00 P.M. to 7:00 A.M. shift. The born-again Christian had often chatted with Rock about religion when he was lucid. Sometimes she would turn the cable-TV dial to a religious program called the "700 Club"—and Rock would watch. Or she'd put on an audio cassette of contemporary religious music or a tape with a religious message. Sometimes as he lay in bed she would talk about God in a general way. Over the weeks, she felt she had established a close enough relationship with Rock to ask him directly whether he wanted to accept Jesus.

As Rock came out of the bathroom that night and sat on the edge of his bed, Phillips moved next to him. She asked him a few questions to test whether he was aware and coherent. Believing that he was, she started telling him about patients she knew who had gotten well after they developed a relationship with the Lord. Rock listened.

"Then I just asked him whether he knew Jesus personally," Phillips said. Rock said he didn't. "Then I asked him whether he wanted to know the Lord, or invite the Lord into his heart." Rock said, "Well, I guess it's about time." Phillips told Rock to hold her hand and to repeat her words: "Jesus, come into my heart and be my Lord and savior." Rock followed her instructions. He continued holding Phillips's hand, and she eventually had to tell him to let go. She helped him get into bed. "Well, it looks like you're stuck with me for eternity," she said. "It looks that way," said Rock, who fell asleep immediately.

A cynical Marc Christian was aware of what happened that night and scoffed. "Rock would have taken Muhammad Ali or Khadafi into his heart at that point. Rock was an atheist. He was just too out of it to know what was going on."

Phillips eventually told her congregation what had happened. A member of the congregation was the daughter of Representative Robert Dornan, a California Republican. She called her father. A day or two later, standing on the floor of the House, the ultraconservative Dornan told the story of how Rock Hudson had found Jesus.

". . . in the last eighteen days of his life," the congressman declared, "Rock found more riches than he had ever known in all his years as a star in the Hollywood motion-picture community." Dornan's office would also tip off the "700 Club" staff, and Phillips would be invited on the show to offer her testimony. As a result, she would jeopardize her job in the service of Jesus. The company she worked for took a dim view of their private-duty nurses disclosing confidential information about their patients.

CHAPTER EIGHT
Ashes

After word was officially released in July that Rock Hudson had AIDS, his Hollywood friends—led by Elizabeth Taylor—had found a new cause. The glitz-and-glamour set suddenly discovered the killer disease that had been swept under the carpet for so long. Now that one of their own, a screen idol, had become a victim, it was time to take AIDS out of the closet. Activism would replace apathy.

"Rock's illness helped give AIDS a face," actress Morgan Fairchild proclaimed as she and other celebrities prepared for a star-studded AIDS benefit on September 19 that was to raise about a million dollars. The money went to the AIDS Project L.A. "Sometimes people will listen more to celebrities than to a doctor somewhere in a newspaper," Fairchild added.

It became *the* event of the fall season, and tickets, which ranged from $250 to $500 a seat, were sold out before invitations were even issued. So many people were on the waiting list for seats that the event, billed as a Commitment to Life benefit, had to be moved from the Century Plaza Hotel to the Bonaventure.

Comedienne Joan Rivers, who always had a large gay following, was stunned by the turnout: "Two years ago when I hosted a benefit for AIDS," she said in an interview, "I couldn't get one major star to turn out. It ended up being just me and a transvestite on stage. I received death threats and hate mail. Rock's admission is a horrendous way to

249

bring AIDS to the attention of the American public, but by doing so, Rock, in his life, has helped millions in the process."

The biggest names in Hollywood backed the fund raiser. Co-sponsors included Taylor and Shirley MacLaine. Honorary benefit committee members were Yoko Ono, Roddy McDowall, Richard Pryor, and Brooke Shields. Performing at the event were Carol Burnett, Sammy Davis, Jr., Diahann Carroll, Cyndi Lauper, and Rod Stewart. The big finale would see Bette Midler performing with a gay men's chorus via a remote voice-over from Germany. It was like Oscar night.

The most important part of the evening was a statement from Rock read by actor Burt Lancaster. To make the moment even more dramatic, "Dynasty" star Linda Evans made the introduction. This was her way of showing that she was not angry with Rock for having kissed her on the show in a scene with which the news media was having a field day.

Rock's statement, read by Lancaster, said:

I regret the circumstances of which you are all aware that prevent me from being with you tonight. But please be sure that I am with you in thought and spirit. I am particularly proud to learn that there is such a significant turnout of people from my industry present and extremely proud of my good friend, Elizabeth Taylor, who organized this event.

People have told me that the disclosure that I have been diagnosed as having Acquired Immune Deficiency Syndrome helped to make this evening an immediate sellout, and that it will raise some one million dollars to help the battle against AIDS.

I have also been told the media coverage of my own situation has brought enormous international attention to the gravity of this disease in all areas of humanity, and is leading to more research, more contribution of funds, and a better understanding of this disease than ever before.

I am not happy that I have AIDS. But if that is helping others, I can, at least, know that my own misfortune has had some positive worth.

Thank you, Elizabeth. Thank you to all my friends who are attending this evening, and to the thousands who have sent their prayers, thoughts, love, wishes, and support.

It was a heartfelt statement, and there were people at the benefit with tears in their eyes as Lancaster's resonant voice carried Rock's message. The next day newspaper headlines would read ROLE IN AIDS FIGHT GRATIFIES HUDSON and HUDSON HOPES HIS ILLNESS WILL HELP OVERCOME AIDS.

It was not enough that Rock be shown simply as the decent human being he was—a warm friend, a loyal colleague, a person of sensitivity and humor, a man with faults and virtues who had contracted a terrible disease. It was now necessary to present him to the public as a star dying a star's death, a larger-than-life presence, more heroic, more valiant—in short, a mythic hero.

In fact, as Lancaster stood at the dais reading the statement, Rock Hudson, his weight down to ninety-seven pounds, lay virtually comatose, an I.V. in his arm pumping life-sustaining nourishment into his body as a nurse sat at his bedside. It would not have been a pretty picture to show to the Rodeo Drive crowd at the hotel.

The fact is, Rock Hudson never wrote the words read by Lancaster. Moreover, he was not even aware that there was a benefit. By this point, he didn't even know what AIDS was. He wouldn't have known the difference between Elizabeth Taylor and one of his nurses. His mind was not tracking and had not been for weeks. No one was even permitted to talk about the disease with him, nor were television, newspapers, or magazines allowed in his vicinity.

Tom Clark finally told the truth the day after Rock's death. "The statement was not written by Rock," he said. "But can't we just say they were his thoughts? Those words have been so encouraging to so many millions. Let him have those words as his legacy."

A spokesman for the AIDS Project L.A., John Latham, acknowledged that the statement had come from the office of Dale Olson, Rock's publicist. Eventually Olson confirmed to a *Los Angeles Herald Examiner* gossip reporter that the words were not Rock's, but he insisted they "were written for Rock Hudson, gone over very carefully when he was in a totally lucid state by Rock Hudson, and had the complete approval of Rock Hudson."

Elizabeth Taylor's spokeswoman, Chen Sam, confused the issue by claiming that Mark Miller had recorded Rock's statement. Sam said she didn't know whether anyone else was present when Miller took the statement because Rock "was not seeing very many people."

After Rock's death, producer Ross Hunter charged that Rock was being manipulated by people who wanted to use the star's name against AIDS. "Rock never, never publicly acknowledged he had AIDS," Hunter angrily told syndicated columnist Marilyn Beck. "All those statements made in his name were lies. He knew nothing about any of them. He fought all his life to stay out of the limelight, and the last thing he would have wanted was to have been thrust into it the way he was."

Hunter told Beck that he and others close to Rock had done all they could to shield Rock from the media blitz surrounding his illness. "I'm sure he didn't know what was going on; he couldn't have known. He was in no condition to know. Ninety-five percent of the time he wasn't lucid."

Hunter had spoken out against the myth makers of his own industry and was treated for a time like a pariah, intent on destroying Rock's heroic stature. Reluctantly, with obvious misgivings, he decided against talking further. Hunter had consulted with Nancy Walker before making that decision. She, too, questioned what had been going on but decided to be silent. Walker advised Hunter to do the same.

"Every time I try to tell the truth, people have misquoted me," he said in a brief conversation several months after Rock's death. "My friend is at peace, and that's the way I'd like to leave it. I can't get it out of my mind. It's been like a ghost following me. Can you imagine what would happen if I said anything that was against what Elizabeth said, or any of the others?"

Perhaps it should not be surprising that Rock Hudson, who lived his life in a haze of myth, should have a myth surrounding his death as well. But such a myth can be unfair, not only to the man himself, who was a real person and not just a studio prop, but to the thousands of people, their families, and friends, who are currently struggling with the disease that killed him—and deserve better than to be asked to judge themselves against a Hollywood hero.

By mid-September the doctors determined that Rock Hudson had only a very short time to live. Preparations secretly began for his death.

Rock's friend Susan Stafford placed a call to Father Terry Sweeney, a forty-year-old Catholic priest whom she had known for about eight years. A Jesuit, Sweeney lived at Loyola of Marymount University in Los Angeles. His principal work in the church was communications. He was a veteran television producer with some forty shows to his credit, ranging from religious programs for Paulist Productions to cartoon features for Hanna-Barbera. He had also been a consultant on "The Thorn Birds," which featured the character of a priest in the leading role.

Stafford told the priest to expect a call from Tom Clark regarding Rock Hudson, who was failing fast. "I think it would be a good opportunity for you to do whatever is necessary as a priest to help him. This is a very important opportunity for Rock to be reconciled, if that's possible," Stafford told Father Sweeney.

Knowing that Stafford was an active born-again Christian and had close ties to the religious community, Clark had sought her advice on what to do for Rock from a religious standpoint. Clark told Stafford that Rock was a baptized Catholic but had not been a practicing Catholic since he was very young. "I don't know what to do," Clark told her. "Rock's dying and he hasn't been part of any real church for a long time."

Stafford gave Clark several options. She mentioned

Shirley Boone, wife of singer Pat Boone, who was an active born-again Christian. Stafford also suggested Father Sweeney.

"At this particular point," said Father Sweeney, "there was no indication of how much longer Rock Hudson was going to live. It was just that things were getting very critical. The desire was to get Rock at peace with God. There was a desire to make sure that Rock would be ready to die."

The priest called Clark and told him he was available to help. "I'm not exactly sure what to do at this moment," Clark said. "I will talk to Rock and see if he wants you to come up, but already he's starting to go in and out of consciousness." Clark asked the priest to call back. The next time he telephoned, Clark said that Rock was not in any shape to be seen. However, the next day, September 26, Clark made an urgent call to Father Sweeney. "Come up today. I'm sorry it's short notice, but it's very important," he said.

It was a warm and sunny afternoon between 1:00 and 2:00 P.M. when Father Sweeney, unnoticed by several reporters and photographers staked out outside Hudson's house, turned off Beverly Crest Drive and into the driveway of the Castle. He was greeted by an obviously agitated Tom Clark.

"I really appreciate your coming," Clark told the priest. "I don't know how much clarity Rock is going to have." Clark led the priest upstairs. "I'll introduce you and leave you alone," he said.

Entering the room, Clark said, "Rock, I want you to meet Father Terry Sweeney. This is Susan Stafford's friend." Clark waited a few seconds to make sure Rock had connected with Father Sweeney, then quietly left the room. The nurse who was with Rock followed him out. The priest and the movie star were alone.

Except for a towel around his waist, Rock Hudson was nude, sitting bolt-upright in a thinly padded straight-backed chair, tugging helplessly at an intravenous needle stuck in his left arm. The needle was attached to a clear plastic flexible tube and a bottle hanging from a stainless-steel stand next to the chair. The apparatus was to the right of Hudson's enormous four-poster bed.

If Father Sweeney had not known he was in Rock Hudson's house, he would never have recognized the shadow of the man sitting in the chair. The full, handsome face that had caused millions of women to swoon had been replaced by a death-mask. Rock's cheekbones and jawbone were pronounced. His once tanned face and "beefcake" body were a sickly brownish-yellowish hue. The chest and shoulder bones and the rib cage were clearly evident. The hair, what was left of it, had gone white.

"The only thing distinctive about him, recognizable, were his eyes," the priest said. "Otherwise I didn't recognize him as Rock Hudson, and I had seen many of his pictures. It was a shock to me in terms of what sickness can do to the human body. How it can ravage the human body and leave only a shell. I had been in hospitals before, so I was personally able to do what I needed to do, but I felt a tremendous amount of empathy."

Rock did not appear to be aware of what was going on. He had lost the ability to focus. His eyes drifted around the room. He appeared to be nodding off and would then slowly come back to consciousness. He would mumble one or two syllables at a time.

As the priest gently talked, Rock tried continually to pull out his I.V. with his bony fingers. Father Sweeney had to tell him twice before he understood that he should leave the needle alone.

Father Sweeney continued talking to Rock, trying to test his awareness, his attention and response levels. "Well, I've known Susan Stafford for many years and, you know, she is very concerned," the priest said. "Rock didn't comment. The only thing he would do is say, 'Uhm, hum.' He'd look at me and say, 'Uhm, hum.' And I realized within a minute or two that he was not going to speak in sentences whatsoever.

"I also realized from the movement of his eyes that his attention was drifting constantly, and I realized that I was not going to be in a position to have any kind of conversation with him. So I decided that it was important just to get to the essentials."

The priest asked Rock if he wanted to receive the sacrament of the sick, which includes anointment, confession, and communion. Whether he understood or not, Rock mumbled an assent. Father Sweeney anointed Rock's forehead with oil and then heard his confession. Since Rock was unable to speak in sentences, the priest asked him a couple of general questions, to which Rock responded with a yes or no.

After confession and absolution, Father Sweeney asked Rock if he wanted to receive communion. Rock looked at the wafer for a long while, then turned to the priest with a blank stare. It was apparent that Rock wasn't sure what he was looking at or what he was expected to do. "Do you want to receive the body of Christ?" the priest asked Rock twice. Rock finally said yes but did not open his mouth to receive the wafer. Finally Father Sweeney asked Rock whether he should break the wafer into smaller pieces and Rock said yes. "I guess he was looking at the host, thinking he couldn't swallow it, but he could not formulate the sentence 'It's too big,'" concluded the priest, who then gave Rock communion.

"Lord, I'm not worthy to receive you, but only say the word, and my soul shall be healed," the priest prayed aloud. "After I said the prayer, I put the host on his tongue and he swallowed it. We just sat there quietly for a few minutes, and then I said, 'God bless you.' I noticed a calmness. He looked at me, and then his eyes drifted off again."

Father Sweeney got up and went into the hallway, where Tom Clark was waiting. "I can't thank you enough for coming," Clark told the priest. "I really didn't know what to do. I told Susan Stafford that Rock had not been to church for many, many years and was not really particularly a religious man, so I was really happy that you would come here."

As they walked downstairs, Clark told the priest, "Some days Rock is clear as a bell and other days he is not, and he's been going in and out today. Were you able to communicate?" Sweeney said, "Minimally."

Father Sweeney would be asked to preside over the star-studded memorial service held at the house after Rock died.

Burt Hixson, owner of the fashionable waterfront Warehouse Restaurant in Marina del Rey, was given his assignment early in September: find a suitable boat for Rock's services at sea. The key requirements were that the boat be big enough for several dozen passengers and that it be laid out in such a way that celebrities on board would have security from the telephoto lenses of paparazzi. Hixson had to find the right boat and get the owner to lend it to him but could not tell the owner why the boat was needed. Tight secrecy prevailed.

Hixson had known Rock since the early 1970s, when the actor had started frequenting the Warehouse with friends. Ever so often Rock would ask Hixson to look around for a new boat, something interesting.

Hixson didn't find another boat for Rock, and eventually Rock gave up looking. But now, in September 1985, Hixson was again being asked to find a boat for his friend— a boat that would take Rock's ashes to sea.

"One of them called me from the house and said, 'It looks very bad. Can you find us a boat? His wish is to be spread over the water off Marina del Rey.' No one knew the severity of Rock's condition. When they called, I was really surprised. I started going around to various boat owners saying, 'Can I borrow your boat?' And everyone wanted to know why. I couldn't tell them why. I had to say, 'I'm looking for a boat, preferably for a Sunday, in the next three weeks or so.'"

Shirley Boone was a lifelong fan of Rock Hudson, like millions of other women. Rock was a real matinee idol, she'd say, even more so than Clark Gable. Pat Boone felt the same way. He thought that Rock, more than anyone in Hollywood, still typified what a movie star, an idol, should be—handsome, debonair, sexy. Over the years, the Boones had heard the rumors that Rock was a homosexual, the Jim Nabors story, and others. Boone spent one afternoon at Western Costumers near Paramount trying on costumes with Rock and found him to be such a great guy with a hearty sense of humor, so masculine, that he and Shirley wrote off the stories, until they learned Rock had AIDS.

Over the years the Boones had seen Rock at various celebrity functions and would say hello and chat. Although they lived only about ten minutes from each other—Rock in the hills and the Boones just below on Sunset—they never socialized.

In his last days, Rock was brought together with the Boones in what was the most bizarre—and the final—episode of his tragic illness.

The Boones, like everyone else, learned of Rock's illness on the six o'clock news and were stunned and deeply saddened. As born-again Christians, they felt they could help him. Shirley and the members of her prayer group, which met weekly, decided to begin praying for Rock. The prayers began a few days after the news of Rock's illness came from Paris. A short time later the prayer group was delighted to learn through the grapevine that the nurses caring for Rock were also born-again Christians. As a result, Toni Phillips was invited to join them.

Toni's presence intensified the prayers because the group was now getting in-depth, on-the-scene reports of how Rock was doing. It was at this time that Phillips began the proselytizing that resulted in Rock's reported "acceptance of Jesus" on September 13.

Around this time, another person entered the picture—a mystery woman who showed up unannounced at the locked front gate of the Boones' home. The woman rang the bell and, through the intercom, asked Shirley whether she could help get her in to see Rock Hudson because she wanted to pray with him. Boone explained that she didn't have any personal contact with Rock, but gave the woman directions to the Castle. Later, the woman reported to the Boones what had happened.

"I've come to pray," she said she told a startled Tom Clark a few minutes later when he confronted her in the driveway. "I'd like to pray with Mr. Hudson. I believe God wants to heal him," she said. Clark told the woman to leave. "I'll just wait," she said meekly.

"Well, you'll have to wait outside, not here in the driveway, but outside the gate, because we have business to do here," Clark said, leading the woman to her car.

That night Clark went outside and spotted the woman again, sitting in her car. He was furious. He had enough problems without having to deal with some religious nut. "Mr. Hudson can't see you," he told the woman. "I understand," she said. "But I believe I'm supposed to be here, so I'll just wait."

Clark returned to the house. Watching from a window, he saw that she was determined to stay, so he went back outside and invited her in.

Later that night she showed up at the Boones' claiming that Clark had allowed her to go into Rock's room and pray for him. As a result of all this fervent activity, Pat Boone said, "Shirley felt led to go on an eight-day fast with a lot of praying. As it turned out, this was eight days before he died, but we didn't know that, of course." Eventually, about twenty people joined the fast.

One night during the fast, about two or three days before Rock died, the prayer group took communion, which Boone presided over. They were sharing grape juice and bread. Two of the nurses were there that night, and they suggested that it would be nice to share the communion with Rock. One of them called Clark, who invited Rock's nurses to the house. "Rock was cogent of what was happening," Boone said. "He was in and out of consciousness, but at this time he was cogent and he did partake of the communion."

When the nurses returned to the Boone house and reported the good news, Boone said, "Everyone was really excited, believing there was going to be a turnaround in his condition."

The fast ended on October 1, and Shirley Boone felt compelled to visit Rock. The mystery woman also felt the same way, Pat Boone recounted. They wanted Rock to make prayers of forgiveness—"to his parents, to the person who was responsible for transmitting AIDS to him, to whomever he might have any unforgiveness toward in his whole life—to get that washed out of his whole life. It was important for his physical healing," Boone said.

Pat Boone and the others believed that people who harbor grudges are susceptible to chronic diseases. They wanted Rock, for example, to forgive his father for having abandoned the family because, Boone said, "so much homosexuality is traced back to some lack in the relationship with the father. It often seems that the male is looking for that male affection that he lacked while growing up. A guy can really feel that his dad abandoned him and rejected him and hardly ever vocalize it." Boone was convinced that was the case with Rock.

The Boones called Clark early on the evening of October 1 to ask if they could come up to the house and pray for Rock. Clark agreed, but warned them that Rock was unconscious most of the time.

At 8:00 P.M. Pat and Shirley Boone, two of the nurses, and the mystery woman arrived at the Castle and were welcomed by Tom Clark, who ushered them up to Rock's room.

"He was lying there on the bed with breathing tubes in his nose," recalled Boone. "I was shocked at how gaunt and really wasted he was. He didn't look like a Rock Hudson that I'd ever known. He still had some color. I don't know whether Tom was taking him out and letting him sit outdoors, because he looked like he had a little tan, which I found odd.

"But otherwise he was just skin and bones. His cheeks were sunken, the sockets of his eyes hollow. It was distressing to see what he looked like. He was out, unconscious. We just stood around the bed and prayed. I walked toward him, leading us in our prayer time, and put my hand on his chest and on his forehead.

"I did something that the Bible recommends. When someone's sick, it calls for the elders of the church—and I happen to be one of the elders in our home church [Church on the Way, in Van Nuys]—to anoint the sick person with oil, and pray. The prayers will raise him up, and if he has any unforgiven sins they will be forgiven. I brought a little bottle of oil—olive oil or something—and I put a little of the oil on his forehead and a little oil on his bare chest and put my hands on it and prayed for him. And the ladies also prayed. We asked God to heal his body and to forgive him any unforgiven sins.

"I had a feeling that if Rock were to recover miraculously that he would then have not only a wonderful story to tell about God's goodness but he would have hope to offer other AIDS victims and other homosexuals. That's what I hoped to see happen. I prayed that he would be healed and that God's love and power would be demonstrated through the situation."

During the session Clark came in and out of the room to make sure Rock was all right. At times he would stop and listen to the rites. The praying lasted about twenty minutes. Then the Boones and the nurses left the mystery woman alone with the unconscious Rock.

From the hallway, she could be seen sitting at his bedside speaking to him and asking him if he would be willing to pray prayers of forgiveness. About a half hour had passed when Boone noticed that the woman was talking more urgently.

"I looked into the room and Rock was looking at her," Boone said. "He had evidently stirred out of his comatose state. I saw him take her hand. She was holding one of his hands, and his other hand came over and held hers. He was looking intently at her. He couldn't talk. I guess the disease robbed him of any ability to speak.

"But he would grunt and make noises, and he was nodding and grunting assent as she would ask him, 'Do you forgive your father? Can I pray with you to forgive your father of anything he might have done to harm you, or any way that you feel he neglected you?' And Rock would sort of give a little nod of his head and grunt, and so she would pray that prayer."

The woman spent about fifteen minutes praying with Rock. "We were all delighted and praying outside," Pat Boone said. Finally the woman stood up. She was finished. The Boones and the nurses walked into the room and found Rock wide awake.

"He looked at us and seemed startled to see so many people. But he also seemed delighted. There was sort of a glow in his face. He eventually raised up, looked at every one of us—like a gaze—and I felt he was saying to me, 'I'm glad you're here. It's good to see you. Thank you for coming. Thank you for caring so much.' Of course, we could talk to him but he couldn't talk back.

"I said, 'Rock, we want you to get well. We want you to know that God loves you even more than we do, and we think you're going to be okay.'

"Tom came in and said, 'Rock, you're going to be fine. I told you you were going to recover. I told you you were going to get well. These people believe and I believe you're going to get well. You're going to be okay.'"

The mystery woman had another idea. "Get some bright clothes for him," she ordered. "He's tired tonight, but he's going to feel better in the morning, so get him some happy clothes to put on!" Clark, caught up in the fervor of the moment, rushed to a closet and brought back Rock's favorite yellow slacks, a handsome blue-and-yellow sweater, and a pair of canvas shoes. "Okay, Rock," the woman said, "we'll put these on in the morning. You're going to feel good." The clothing was laid out at the foot of Rock's bed so he could put them on the next day.

"We wished him well," Pat Boone said, "and I squeezed his feet and left feeling extremely good."

Around seven o'clock the next morning, October 2, one of the nurses awakened Rock from a deep sleep. Excited by, and believing in, what she felt was the profound experience of the previous night, she sat the deathly ill man up and dressed him in the yellow slacks and blue-and-yellow sweater. Then she moved him from his bed and into a chair.

About 7:30 Clark looked into Rock's room and was horrified to see Rock fully dressed and sitting up in the chair. "Oh, no! No!" he yelled. "Put him back in bed. He's not able to sit up. Put him back in bed! He's too weak! He's too sick!" She followed his instructions and undressed Rock and put him back into bed. He fell asleep instantly.

Marc Christian awoke that day at about 8:00 A.M. He was getting dressed to go to a dental appointment when Clark knocked on the door of the theater, the old converted garage where Christian was living. "We're having a hospital bed brought in," Clark told Christian. "It'll be better for Rock to sleep in." Christian asked Clark if he needed any help, and Clark said no.

At about 8:30, Gary Sweat, an employee of Life Support Home Health Care, a medical-supply company, drove his white Chevy van into the driveway of the Castle. He was there to deliver a hospital bed that had been ordered by the nursing service. Everything was peaceful. A gardener was working on the grounds. A handsome blond-haired young man was buffing a white Mercedes outside the garage. Near the pool were a couple of hand-lettered signs that read WE LOVE YOU ROCK. The only thing Sweat found odd were the strange statues of nude young boys that were on the grounds.

Sweat was met by Clark, who looked tired, as if he had been up all night. Sweat asked to see the room where the bed was to be placed, and Clark led him upstairs to Rock's bedroom. The actor was sleeping on his left side in a pair of light tan pajamas, a blanket pulled up to his chest. The sweater and slacks were still draped over the chair.

"He was totally unconscious," Sweat recalled. "He was slightly moaning and gurgling. I could hear the mucus, like from an asthmatic. He was in a coma. He was very pale. His skin was drawn. It looked like he had aged ten years since the Doris Day show. He looked like a man in his eighties. I knew this was a man who was dying."

To make way for the hospital bed, Clark helped Sweat move a massive sofa that was at the foot of Rock's giant four-poster. Clark was very concerned about the way Rock was breathing. One of the nurses asked Sweat whether a suction machine to remove mucus had been ordered and he said no. Sweat had to make several trips to bring various pieces of the bed into the house. He set it up and left the house a few minutes before 9:00 A.M..

Tom Clark went back upstairs and looked into Rock's room. The nurses were gathered around the bed crying.

Clark felt a chill. He pushed his way past the weeping women and looked at the bed. Rock Hudson was dead. He had passed away in his sleep just minutes after Sweat had left. There were no last words. Clark, too, began sobbing. After a few moments he managed to pull himself together. He went downstairs and told Christian that Rock had died. Christian asked Clark if he was okay. "No, I'm not okay," he said angrily, and walked away, saying he had to make a telephone call.

A number of calls were made during the next few minutes by Clark, Toni Phillips, and others in the house. There were calls to the mortuary, which sent a van for Rock's body, and to Rock's doctor, Rex Kennamer, who came to the house to pronounce him dead and sign a death certificate. Phillips called the Boones. Clark also contacted Rock's lawyer, his business manager, the publisher of his authorized biography, and "Good Morning America."

Clark called Jim Matteoni in Illinois to inform him of Rock's death. To diminish Matteoni's anguish, Clark painted a serene picture of how Rock died. "Tom told me Roy wasn't in pain when he died," Matteoni said. "He said the dogs were up in his room and he was playing with them. Tom said he asked Roy if he wanted some coffee and he said no, drifted off to sleep, and died."

Pat Boone was in his car, about to drive over to 20th Century-Fox, where he was doing a TV movie with Lee Majors, when the call from Phillips came. "I've got to get up there," Shirley Boone said, rushing to her own car and driving off.

"Shirley felt that sometimes people are pronounced dead and they are not, so she wanted to be there if that was the case," Pat Boone said. "Besides, she left her Bible there the night before and was going to have to get it anyway."

Boone sat in his car, disbelieving the news. "I must say I was stunned. I didn't particularly feel that I wanted to go up there. I wanted to digest what this meant, because it certainly wasn't what we expected, not after we'd been there the night before with evidence of a real turnaround. I was not eager to go running up there, because I knew it would be a scene of some confusion. He was dead. What else could be done?"

Shirley Boone had other ideas. She arrived at the Castle about the same time as the mystery woman, who apparently had also been telephoned by one of the nurses.

Boone and the woman walked up the driveway and ran into Clark. "Tom, I left my Bible here last night," she told the distraught man. Clark stared at her for a moment, speechless. "It's upstairs in Rock's room," he said finally. "If you don't mind seeing him dead, you can go up." His pain was visible.

Boone and the woman raced upstairs and into Rock's room. The nurse was upset and explained to Boone how she had dressed Rock earlier that morning, as instructed, in the "happy clothes" that had been laid out the night before. She told Boone that Rock "seemed glad" to put on the clothes, but that Clark had become furious when he saw what she had done and ordered her to put him back in bed. Rock, she said, had died a short time later.

Rock was lying stretched out on the bed. Boone put her hands on his feet. They were cold and rigid. She and the mystery woman began to pray fervently for him. The prayers were loud and attracted the attention of Clark and Christian. "Lord, what is your will in this matter?" Shirley Boone asked. The mystery woman wailed, sounding as though she were talking in tongues.

Finally, after about twenty minutes, Clark came into the room and told Boone and the woman they would have to leave because the men had come for Rock's body. Shirley Boone grabbed her Bible, thanked Clark, and left. Although Rock had not stirred during her ministrations, she told her husband she had felt his feet grow warmer.

The next day Pat Boone wrote Clark a letter thanking him for "being concerned about Rock the person, Rock the living soul and not just Rock the star, Rock the idol, and Rock the handsome guy."

"I wrote that I really believed the night of our visit that we were at Rock's going-away party. He was conscious and able to participate in it. We were part of his bon-voyage party and he was awake and he knew we were there to see him off and those happy clothes were his going-home clothes, not his coming-back clothes. I really believe this is what happened."

The day after Clark received Boone's letter, Susan Stafford was helping out at the Castle. She found the letter in the trash can, where Clark had tossed it. Stafford smoothed it out and gave it to the woman writing Rock's book because, Stafford said, "it was so beautifully written."

Although the first news of Rock Hudson's death had been upsetting, several months later, Pat Boone was absolutely convinced that the prayers and the visit had been all to the good; in fact, they had put Rock in heaven.

"We don't feel the anguish and the sadness that some of the others did. There was some very serious business done between him and God, and somebody had to come into his life to help that happen."

The next person to arrive at the house after Shirley Boone was Rock's longtime personal physician, Rex Kennamer. He stated on the death certificate that the time of death was 9:00 A.M. and that the immediate cause of death was "cardiorespiratory arrest." He listed the underlying causes as "lymphoblastic lymphoma," which, he stated, had started four months before the death, and "Acquired Immune Deficiency Syndrome," which had onset sixteen months earlier. The death certificate listed his marital status as divorced and his primary occupation as actor, and said that he had spent thirty-five years in that profession. It gave the name of his father, Roy Scherer, and mother, Katherine Wood. Under "disposition" was the word *cremation*.

At about 9:20 A.M., Beth Burr answered the phone at Pierce, Hamrock, Reed Mortuary and heard the strange clicking on the line that had been there for several weeks. She suspected that her line was tapped, that her calls were being monitored by a news organization intent on finding out when Rock died and where, and when the cremation would take place. (People at the Castle had the same suspicion about their phones.) The call was from Tom Clark. He told Burr that Rock had died. She immediately called the firm's downtown Los Angeles mortuary. "We put our game plan into effect," Burr said.

That plan called for the firm's two managers, Larry Rentz and Chris Kremins, to "make the removal." As soon as Rentz got the call from Burr, he told his secretary, "Don't give any information out under any circumstances to anyone. Period." He hoped that they could keep Rock's death a secret. But as Rentz and Kremins were preparing to weave their way through early-morning rush-hour traffic to Rock's home in the Hollywood Hills, the first reporters and photographers were already gathering there. They had gotten the word that Rock Hudson had died.

Next, Rentz and Kremins gathered the gear necessary for the removal of an AIDS victim. The disease had led to the development of a new and lucrative market—the sale of "AIDS Removal Kits" by medical-supply firms to funeral homes and fire and police departments. The kits, which cost twenty dollars each, came in sealed red plastic bags and contained a gown, shoes, gloves, a hat, and a face mask. After the removal, the apparel was placed in the plastic bag and incinerated.

Rentz threw two of the kits and a collapsible gurney into the back of the unmarked 1982 beige Dodge Ram van. He and Kremins took off their ties, rolled up their sleeves, and put on old pants—a disguise they thought would fool any reporters who might be at the house.

A story-hungry mob of about a hundred and twenty-five reporters, photographers, cameramen, and various crew people were at the front gate to greet them as they pulled up. The deathwatch that had been going on since July was over. Now the press wanted all the details of Rock's last moments. Photographers knew they could be paid huge sums for the coveted final shot: a picture of Rock Hudson, dead. Final shots of Elvis Presley and John Lennon had earned photographers tens of thousands of dollars.

Rentz blew the horn but got no response. He got out of the van and waded through the mass of media people. He managed to get to the speaker-phone. "This is the mortuary," he said above the din. Reporters heard what he said and passed the word. Rentz had to fight his way back to the van. Two minutes later someone came out and opened the gate, and Rentz maneuvered the van inside the grounds and into the garage. Under instructions from Mark Miller, Rentz parked in a position that would make it impossible for a photographer to grab a shot, or so he thought. A photo did appear the next day of Rock's body in a rubber bag on the floor of the van—the closest anyone would get to a final shot of Rock Hudson.

As Kremins went over the removal plan with Miller, Tom Clark led Rentz to the stairway. "He's upstairs in the master bedroom," Clark said. Nearby, several people were sobbing quietly. A young Latino woman, probably one of the nurses, was crying loudly. A tall, blond-haired young man, probably Christian, stood quietly with his arms folded over his chest.

Rentz went upstairs and looked into the bedroom. Rock's body was on the bed, covered by a sheet except for his face. Rentz didn't go into the room because he hadn't put on his protective clothing. He went back downstairs to talk to Clark about the easiest and least conspicuous way of bringing the body down and out to the van. Once that was settled—the body would be brought from the bedroom and directly into the garage through the house—Kremins called Rosedale Crematory, in downtown Los Angeles, where they planned to take the body. But there was a problem. The people at Rosedale told Kremins that their retorts—the ovens used to cremate a body—"were down." Kremins then called the crematory at Grand View Memorial Park, in Glendale, and alerted them that they should have a retort and a cremation container ready. He did not tell Grand View who the deceased was.

Rentz and Kremins put on their AIDS outfits and went upstairs, putting their collapsible gurney beside the bed. They removed the sheet from Rock's body, which was nude.

"I just felt so bad for the man," Rentz said. "I felt pity because he had wasted away—especially in the face—to practically nothing. He had been such a big, robust man and a good-looking guy and a real good actor."

Rentz and Kremins wrapped the body in a couple of sheets, put a cotton cover over it, and placed it on the gurney, strapping it down to keep it from falling or sliding off. The two men then got out of their AIDS outfits and placed them in the plastic bags, which they gave to one of the nurses, who said she would dispose of them.

Rentz and Kremins wheeled the gurney to the head of the stairs. Clark, Miller, Christian, the nurses, and several other people rushed over to grab the cot. "They all wanted to help, but I asked them to please stand back," Rentz said. He was afraid somebody might trip and fall. Removal of the body was a two-man operation, and they knew what they were doing. As Rentz and Kremins began carrying Rock's body down the stairs, one of the nurses began crying. Clark, Miller, and Christian had tears in their eyes.

The body was carried through the playroom, where for years Rock had screened movies for his friends, and into the garage. It was placed in the van, and the rear doors were closed. With Tom Clark in back, watching over the body, Rentz drove to the crematory. As Clark waited outside by the van, Rentz wheeled the body into the crematory building.

Rentz placed the gurney alongside the cremation unit. He slid Hudson's body off the gurney and into the cremation container—a corrugated cardboard box. The sheets and the cotton cover were placed inside the box with the body.

Rentz put a lid on the box and pushed it to the entrance of the retort, an ovenlike device filled with gas burners that were fired up. As the crematory workers stood to one side, Rentz pushed the cardboard box containing the body of Rock Hudson into the retort and closed the door. Someone in the room pulled a switch, and the flames, which could be seen through a window, accelerated. "I saw it take off and start consuming the container," Rentz said, "and at this point everyone left the room." It was noontime.

Outside, Rentz nodded to Clark, indicating that his friend had been cremated as he had wished. "I'm glad it's over," Clark said, and thanked Rentz for handling the situation so well. Rentz gave Clark back the towels and the chair from the van, and Clark left the grounds to return to the Castle with a driver who had come for him.

By 2:00 P.M. the cremation was completed. All that

was left were the ashes of Rock Hudson's skeletal structure, which were gathered from a trough in the center of the retort after it had cooled down. The ashes were placed in a green plastic urn and turned over to Beth Burr the next day. They were kept in a safe at the mortuary's downtown office until they were scattered at sea some days later.

All Hollywood, America, and the world mourned for Rock Hudson. One of the great screen idols had died. His death was the lead story on the network evening newscasts and on newspaper front pages from Los Angeles to Sri Lanka.

"Nancy and I are saddened by the news of Rock Hudson's death," a one-time fellow actor, President Ronald Reagan, said in a statement released from the White House. "He will always be remembered for his dynamic impact on the film industry, and fans all over the world will certainly mourn his loss. He will be remembered for his humanity, his sympathetic spirit, and well-deserved reputation for kindness. May God rest his soul."

Dozens of other celebrities were quoted in the papers saying how much they loved and respected Rock. Magazines and newspapers were filled with articles about his life. Rock Hudson's photograph on magazine covers resulted in record newsstand sales. Even in death, Rock Hudson was a bankable commodity.

As the tributes to Rock were being made, the struggle to keep Christian from filing his suit was continuing. On the afternoon of Rock's death, Christian met Susan Stafford for lunch at Butterfield's, a trendy health-food restaurant on Sunset Boulevard. She had made the date with Christian before Rock's death, and both of them decided to keep it because nothing more could be done at the Castle.

Stafford made the date because she had learned from Mark Miller that Marc Christian was planning to sue and she hoped to talk him out of doing so. She had also heard allegations from Miller that Christian had been working as a prostitute while living at the Castle.

"Marc arrived looking stunning," said Stafford. As they played with salads, Christian reiterated to Stafford all the reasons why he intended to sue. Stafford told Christian there were allegations that he had worked as a prostitute while living with Rock. She warned him the allegations would become public if he sued. Christian denied the charges, and the two parted company.

As it turned out, Susan Stafford's predictions were accurate. The allegations of prostitution eventually appeared in a lawsuit.

Meanwhile, preparations were being made for some kind of memorial service for Rock, since there would not be a funeral. Father Terry Sweeney, who had given Rock the sacraments in September, was on retreat when he died. He returned three days later to find a message inviting him to a meeting at Elizabeth Taylor's Bel Air home on the evening of October 8.

At first, Miller and Clark considered having the memorial service in a church, but rejected that idea because Rock had not followed any religion since he was a child. They felt it would be hypocritical to pretend he was a pious man when all his friends knew he wasn't. So they decided on a more informal ceremony that would be held at the Castle.

Clark, Miller, George Nader, and Stockton Briggle, a longtime friend of Rock who had directed him in *Camelot*, were at the meeting to plan the service. Taylor and the others wanted a sense of spontaneity in the service to reflect Rock's warmth and friendliness. They wanted to give his friends an opportunity to speak and sing and reminisce. It would be a joyous occasion with drinks, food, and music.

"He didn't want anybody to be sad," said Yanou Collart. "He wanted everybody to be happy because he had a good life. Rock loved parties. He left orders to have champagne, caviar, and mariachi bands."

It was decided, then, that Father Sweeney would start the service by welcoming everyone and giving a brief opening prayer. He would then turn the program over to Taylor and Rock's other friends. The service would conclude with Taylor inviting everyone into the patio area to toast Rock with margaritas as a Mexican band played.

Jim Matteoni recalled that Rock always felt funerals should be for the living rather than the dead. "The march played at my funeral will be played in boogie," Rock had joked as a teen-ager. "That's why they had the mariachi band at the memorial service," added Matteoni. "Rock would insist on it being a party."

While there would be no way to hide the memorial service from the news media, a plan was made to try to keep secret the time and day of the scattering of Rock's ashes at sea.

A wire-service story that ran in newspapers around the country on October 13 quoted Beth Burr as saying, "The ashes have been scattered in the ocean. It was within the last few days." Taylor's spokeswoman, when asked by the *Washington Post* about the ashes, said, "I was told that had all been taken care of." Both were phony stories to mislead the press corps. Rock's ashes were still in the safe at the mortuary. They were not scattered until the morning of October 20, the day after the memorial service.

Tight security prevailed outside the Castle gates as one hundred and fifty of Rock's friends began arriving around 5:00 P.M. under a warm sun and clear skies. A parking area was filled with limousines—Rolls-Royces and Mercedes-Benzes. Both ends of Beverly Crest Drive were closed off, and only those with invitations—telegrams had been sent by Elizabeth Taylor—were permitted through the mob of reporters and photographers. Guests were stopped by security people at several checkpoints leading into the house—up to the very front door, where they were greeted by Clark and Taylor.

Overhead, a low-flying helicopter was making sorties, with a cameraman hanging out the door shooting videotape. Another photographer wearing camouflage fatigues was caught by security guards after he climbed up the side of Coldwater Canyon and onto the property.

Adding to the carnival atmosphere, a neighbor of Rock, twenty-two-year-old Myra Hall, offered reporters and photographers front-seat tickets to Rock's wake. For three hundred dollars each, they could rent a space on the property and observe all of the comings and goings. Hall called her offer "free enterprise."

A mob of cameramen cornered Father Sweeney, wearing a black suit and Roman collar, when he drove up to the house. "Are you the priest that saw Rock Hudson before he died?" several shouted in unison. "Can you tell us what he said, or what his emotional attitude was?" others asked. The priest was saved from the mob when a security person banged on the hood of his car, shouting, "Leave the newspeople! Get in! Get in!" Inside the house, several of Rock's female cousins from Illinois thanked the priest for seeing Rock before he died.

Once inside the house, the guests were ushered to the garden area, where folding chairs were arranged in a semicircle under a canopy. On each seat was a memorial folder with Rock's name and the dates of his birth and death on the cover. Inside was a photograph of Rock and a poem by Khalil Gibran. From their seats, the guests had a view of the valley below and the setting sun.

"There are two things that we all have in common regardless of race and belief and cultural background," Father Sweeney said, starting the service. "One is that we are born, and the other is that we die. What matters is what we do with the life we have on this earth.

"Rock Hudson was a man of great talent and courage. I would like to suggest that we spend a moment of silent prayer and think about Rock Hudson's life and his gift to us." All heads bowed for a moment of silent prayer. "May his soul and the souls of all the faithful departed rest in peace," the priest concluded.

Taylor then stood and talked about her friendship with Rock and her fond memories about working with him in *Giant*. She laughed remembering how one night they invented a new drink, chocolate margaritas.

Carol Burnett, her eyes filled with tears, told stories of the fun she had touring with Rock in *I Do! I Do!* Her tears mixed with laughter when she noted the courage Rock displayed when he went out on stage and danced, not one of his better talents.

John Schuck, one of Rock's co-stars in "McMillan and Wife," and actress Constance Towers sang two of Rock's favorite tunes from the play—"My Cup Runneth Over" and "Roll up the Ribbons."

Leonard Stern, who had been executive producer of "McMillan and Wife," remembered how Susan Saint James was chosen for the part of Mrs. McMillan. He told the story of their dinner, and Rock's punch line, "I gained seven pounds, hire her."

Elaine Stritch was unable to attend, but sent a message. It was simple and moving:

> Let's raise our glasses in thanks that Rock will not have to wake up every morning from now on and know that he is going to die—and with the hope that he is waking up as we speak every morning and is glad that he did.

There were other remembrances from Roddy McDowall, Tab Hunter, Angie Dickinson, Lee Remick, George Grizzard, Kip Gowan, Linda and John Foreman, Robert Wagner, Esther Williams, Susan Saint James, Dr. Rex Kennamer, Glenn Ford, Dr. Michael Gottlieb, Tom Clark, Mark Miller, Ricardo Montalban, Jack Scalia, and Marc Christian, among others. Ross Hunter apparently did not attend and neither did anyone from "Dynasty."

"Now, let's all go upstairs to the patio and lift a glass in memory of our friend," said Taylor after the final guest had spoken. "I'll have my Perrier and you all can have anything you want." The mariachi band struck up the music, and everyone moved off to eat and drink, the way Rock would have wanted it. "What a turnout it was," said Jon Epstein. "It was a marvelous affair." By 8:30 everyone had left. The Castle was quiet. There would be no more parties there.

Around ten the next morning, Beth Burr picked up Rock Hudson's ashes at the mortuary, placed them in the trunk of her car, and drove toward Marina del Rey. Looking in the rearview mirror, she spotted a car that seemed to be following. She confirmed that fact a few minutes later when she led the car, driven by a woman, into a dead-end street. Burr made a quick U-turn and lost her. But as she pulled into the parking lot of the Warehouse Restaurant, Burr again spotted the woman parking nearby. The woman turned out to be a reporter. Rock's friends would not be able to scatter his ashes unobserved.

It was cool and slightly overcast at the pier as Burr waited with about thirty of Rock's friends to board the boat. Warehouse Restaurant owner Burt Hixson had actually needed to find two boats for the ceremony—the first one had suffered a broken crankshaft three days earlier. Luckily, at the last minute, he'd been able to round up another one. Hixson had only that day told the crew what they were to do. They were all surprised—they had read and believed the phony story in the papers that Rock's ashes had been scattered at sea a week before.

The group filed slowly on board. Because the small size of the boat made security difficult, Rock's celebrity friends had decided not to attend. Elizabeth Taylor sent two of her security people to help, though. The group included a number of close friends, members of Rock's house staff, and several of his cousins from Illinois. Clark, Miller, Nader, Christian and his friend Liberty, and Susan Stafford were present.

Hixson wanted to get an early start, before noon. "After that, the sea starts picking up, and I didn't know how seaworthy some of these people were," he said. About 11:30, the boat pulled slowly out from the pier and moved into the channel. The mood on the boat was quiet and somber. There was little talking. "Everybody obviously had his or her own thoughts about Rock," said one of those aboard, Jon Epstein.

Later the group would return to the restaurant, where Hixson had given orders for a huge buffet brunch to be ready, a Warehouse feast. Champagne would be served and they would all raise their glasses in a toast to Rock. The group would settle in to eat at one long table overlooking the water, choosing among eggs Florentine, ham, bacon, sausage, blintzes, prime rib, and twelve different international salads. The mood would become very jovial, with most of the guests going back for third and fourth helpings. Everyone would be sharing stories of Rock. At the finale, a big birthday cake for George Nader would be served—white cake with orange filling—and the whole entourage would join in singing "Happy Birthday."

As the boat pulled out of the harbor, though, there was silence. Everyone on board was conscious of the solemnity of the occasion. It was very unlike the lively, festive mood of the memorial service the day before. That had been a celebration of Rock and the way his friends remembered him—laughing, happy. His spirit had seemed to hover over the festivities. Now the air hung heavily.

The boat had pulled out into the channel and turned around, facing land. Quietly Hixson gave the skipper the order to shut off the engine. Susan Stafford, at the behest of Clark and Miller, read the Twenty-third Psalm aloud from her Bible. It was very quiet as Beth Burr carried the urn to the stern of the boat. She gave the ashes to Clark to scatter. The only sound was the lapping of the waves against the side of the boat, and the occasional rumble of a jet taking off from the airport several miles away. The small group stood motionless, waiting. Overhead, a lone sea gull flew by.

At the precise moment the ashes were dumped, against all laws of probability, science, or good taste, the lone sea gull far up in the sky took aim and scored a direct, massive hit all over Mark Miller.

Miller, standing up on the fly bridge with several others, glanced down at his ruined jacket, then up at the sky. "All right, Rock," he said, managing to grin. "You got the last laugh."

No one who witnessed it, or heard about it later, doubted for a moment that he had. It was all in the timing. No one but Rock could have timed it that well, his friends later agreed. The mood had been too solemn and dignified, not like him at all. It was Rock's signature.

The brief ceremony concluded with the group throwing flowers into the water, over the ashes. The boat circled the entire area for two turns, then headed back to shore. The ceremony was simple and moving, and many people had tears in their eyes. Clark sobbed unabashedly.

Epilogue

Despite intense lobbying, none of Rock's friends could stop Marc Christian from filing suit against the estate. On November 12, five days before what would have been Rock's sixtieth birthday, the suit caused a sensation. For the first time, Marc Christian's name became a matter of public record. He was an instant celebrity. His photo and story were featured in newspapers and national magazines. Christian got top billing on the Phil Donahue and Larry King shows. The *National Enquirer* hit the supermarket check-out counters with ROCK'S BOYFRIEND: WHY I'M SUING FOR $10 MILLION. *People* was on the racks with A LAWSUIT OVER ROCK'S ESTATE EXPOSES SCANDAL. There was even a widely publicized story, quickly discounted, that the federal government wanted Christian to give lectures about AIDS.

Wallace Sheft and Mark Miller denied Christian's assertions that he had been exposed to AIDS because they hid from him the fact that Rock had the disease. They claimed that Christian was aware of Rock's deteriorating condition and knew the symptoms of AIDS. By continuing to have "sexual relations with Rock Hudson after June 1984," Christian "assumed the risk . . . he would expose himself to contract AIDS," they declared in court papers. Further, Sheft and Miller charged that Christian had engaged in sexual activity with one or more (unnamed) persons other than Rock who were "afflicted with AIDS." If Christian con-

277

tracted AIDS, it would happen because "of his own promiscuous behavior and not as a result of any sexual contact with Rock Hudson. . . ."

Early in March 1986, acting as executor of Rock's estate, Sheft filed a two-million-dollar countersuit, charging that Christian had extorted money from Rock by threatening to publish love letters he received from Rock and to reveal him publicly as a homosexual. The complaint accused Christian of taking money for sexual activities while Rock was in Israel in late 1983. Christian allegedly admitted these actions to Rock, and Rock then tried to end the relationship. In response, the suit charged, Christian blackmailed him. Sheft claimed Christian "forced" Rock to let him stay at the Castle and pay him more than seventy thousand dollars. He charged that Christian stole more than sixty thousand dollars' worth of Rock's phonograph records and audio, video, and film equipment. Other items allegedly stolen included a needlepoint rug and pillow made by Rock and a silver-framed autographed photo given to Rock by Carol Burnett. Christian denied all the allegations. His lawyers called the charges "scurrilous and perjurious."

Tom Clark went home to Oklahoma City for the Christmas holidays. He was depressed and dejected. "Rock's death was a real bad blow to Tom," his stepmother said. "It was difficult for him to get over it. He was sad. He talked about it." The family had a traditional Christmas dinner and open house, and Tom accompanied his stepmother to Christmas Eve services at St. Luke's Methodist Church. When friends asked, Clark told them he thought Rock had contracted AIDS from blood transfusions he had received during his open-heart surgery four years earlier. After the holidays, Clark returned to Los Angeles to do publicity work.

Rock's will was filed in Los Angeles Superior Court, becoming public information. There were more headlines, revealing that Rock had changed his will to cut Clark out. The more important news was what the will didn't disclose. The bulk of his estate went to a trust he had created some years earlier. The beneficiaries were not named, and the value of the estate was not given. It is possible that Tom Clark was named a beneficiary of the trust. Various publications reported that Rock had left the bulk of his estate to George Nader. Values of fifteen million dollars to thirty-five million dollars were placed on the estate by insiders, but no one knew for certain.

Miller and Nader remained at the Castle, which was put on the market for $4.7 million. Miller was in charge of helping to show the house to prospective purchasers and handling the day-to-day business of the estate.

The apartment that Rock shared with Clark in New York City was sold for two million dollars. Despite the fact that it overlooked Central Park and was in the prestigious Beresford, the apartment was not snapped up when it went on the market. Insiders said that potential buyers were put off when they learned that the apartment had belonged to an AIDS victim.

Some of Rock's belongings were auctioned early in April 1986 at William Doyle Galleries in New York. Among the items was a footstool inscribed by Elizabeth Taylor in lavender ink. The inscription read *E.T. stood here, she had to because she couldn't reach the sink. R.H. is a love and I thank him always—even tho he is one foot taller. Your always friend, Elizabeth.* There was a silver-plated cigarette box engraved *Dynasty, 100th Episode,* and a sword used by Rock in *Camelot.* The furnishings included an African spear, a steel milk bucket, stereo equipment, two needlepoint pillows made by Rock, and a leather loving cup.

In spring 1986, the number of reported AIDS victims in the United States had approached twenty thousand, and about 50 percent of the victims had died. Neither a cure nor a treatment appeared imminent.

Filmography

Fighter Squadron, Warner Bros. (1948).
Seton Miller, producer; Raoul Walsh, director.
Edmond O'Brien and Robert Stack co-starred.

Walsh gave Rock his first break in this picture. Rock flubbed one of his few lines dozens of times, but he looked great in a pilot's uniform. Rock didn't even show up in the screen credits.

Rock said he didn't appear in a single picture for the first 12 months he was at Universal. Instead, he did publicity stunts and went to acting school. When he started doing bit parts, they were so incidental he was often not even mentioned in the screen credits.

Undertow, Universal (1949).
William Castle, producer and director.
Scott Brady starred.

This was Rock's first screen credit at Universal. Rock played a minor detective in this gangster story filmed on location in Chicago.

I Was a Shoplifter, Universal (1950).
Leonard Goldstein, producer; Charles Lamont, director.
Scott Brady and Mona Freeman co-starred.

In this story of a shoplifting gang, Rock continued his minuscule bit parts as a contract player. An actor named Anthony Curtis had a bit part, too.

One Way Street, Universal (1950).
Leonard Goldstein, producer; Hugo Fregonese, director.
James Mason, Marta Toren, Dan Duryea, and William
Conrad co-starred.

Mason portrayed a doctor involved with a gang of
hoods. Rock was a truck driver.

Winchester '73, Universal (1950).
Aaron Rosenberg, producer; Anthony Mann, director.
James Stewart, Shelley Winters, and Dan Duryea co-
starred.

Stewart took a percentage of this top-grade western.
Rock skulked in the background as Young Bull, wearing
wig, war paint, and a built-up nose. Tony Curtis played a
minor character.

Peggy, Universal (1950).
Ralph Dietrich, producer; Fred de Cordova, director.
Diana Lynn and Charles Coburn co-starred.

This was Rock's romantic debut. He played an Ohio
State fullback in this Rose Bowl saga and missed Diana
Lynn's mouth on his first attempt to kiss her.

The Desert Hawk, Universal (1950).
Leonard Goldstein, producer; Fred de Cordova, director.
Yvonne De Carlo and Richard Greene co-starred.

Rock was a minor Arab in this remake, his first
"Easterner." The original Persian epic had starred Jon Hall.
Jackie Gleason played Aladdin.

Shakedown, Universal (1950).
Ted Richmond, producer; Joseph Pevney, director.
Howard Duff, Peggy Dow, and Brian Donlevy co-starred.

Rock played a doorman in this story of an evil,
blackmailing photographer.

Air Cadet, Universal (1951).
Aaron Rosenberg, producer; Joseph Pevney, director.
Stephen McNally, Gail Russell, and Richard Long co-
starred.

This dull postwar story of three pilots in training featured glimpses of Rock, as an upperclassman, clad in a jumpsuit.

Tomahawk, Universal (1951).
Leonard Goldstein, producer; George Sherman, director. Van Heflin, Yvonne De Carlo, Preston Foster, and Jack Oakie co-starred.

Rock moved up to eighth billing in this cavalry-and-Indians story, in which he played a trooper.

The Fat Man, Universal (1951).
Aubrey Schenck, producer; William Castle, director. J. Scott Smart and Julie London co-starred.

Rock made the leap to third billing in this detective story, and Julie London, who played his girl friend, believed his solid performance stopped Universal from dropping his option. In this one, Rock danced with London, who is only five-foot-three.

The Iron Man, Universal (1951).
Aaron Rosenberg, producer; Joseph Pevney, director. Jeff Chandler, Evelyn Keyes, and Stephen McNally co-starred.

Rock trained hard for this macho boxing picture, and it remained one of his favorites. Rock, a lefty, had to learn to box right-handed. James Arness had a minor role.

Bright Victory, Universal (1952).
Robert Buckner, producer; Mark Robson, director. Arthur Kennedy and Julie Adams co-starred.

Rock played a minor role in this top-notch drama about a blind war veteran.

Here Come the Nelsons, Universal (1952).
Aaron Rosenberg, producer; Fred de Cordova, director. Ozzie, Harriet, Rick, and David Nelson co-starred.

Rock played a friend of Harriet Nelson who becomes embroiled with radio and TV's popular family at a centennial celebration with them.

Bend of the River, Universal (1952).
Aaron Rosenberg, producer; Anthony Mann, director.
James Stewart, Arthur Kennedy, Julie Adams, and Lori Nelson co-starred.

This western marked the first time Rock's name appeared above the picture's title and the second time he worked with James Stewart. Rock played a gambler in this slick production, with outdoor scenes filmed on location in Oregon.

Scarlet Angel, Universal (1952).
Leonard Goldstein, producer; Sidney Salkow, director.
Yvonne De Carlo and Richard Denning co-starred.

Rock found himself poised for leading man status after this film, for which he moved up to second billing as the old boyfriend of Yvonne De Carlo, a Civil War-era saloon girl trying to rise in the world. George Hamilton and Amanda Blake had minor roles.

Has Anybody Seen My Gal?, Universal (1952).
Ted Richmond, producer; Douglas Sirk, director.
Piper Laurie and Charles Coburn co-starred.

Rock shared top-billing in this 1920s period piece with his fellow acting student from Sophie Rosenstein's school, Piper Laurie. But Coburn stole all the scenes. James Dean had a bit part. This was the first of many pictures Rock made under the direction of Sirk.

Horizons West, Universal (1952).
Albert Cohen, producer; Budd Boetticher, director.
James Arness, Robert Ryan, and Julie Adams co-starred.

Rock played one of three Texans returning home after the Civil War. Despite the fine cast, which also included Dennis Weaver and Raymond Burr, this paceless plodder never even broke into a trot.

The Lawless Breed, Universal (1953).
William Alland, producer; Raoul Walsh, director.
Julie Adams co-starred.

As a result of this performance, George Stevens picked Rock over William Holden and others to play the lead in

Giant. Rock portrayed western outlaw John Wesley Hardin in this solid piece of outdoor entertainment directed by his old mentor Raoul Walsh. Rock was artificially aged in the lifelong saga. His high school classmate, Hugh O'Brian, was numbered in the supporting cast.

Seminole, Universal (1953).
Howard Christie, producer; Budd Boetticher, director.
Barbara Hale, Anthony Quinn, Richard Carlson, Hugh O'Brian, and Lee Marvin co-starred.
In this Everglades epic Rock played a shavetail fresh out of West Point and full of progressive ideas. He tried to stop his commanding officer—Richard Carlson—from exterminating the Florida Indians. Quinn got the Indian role this time and Marvin played a sergeant.

Sea Devils, RKO (1953).
David Rose, producer; Raoul Walsh, director.
Yvonne De Carlo and Dennis O'Day co-starred.
Rock went to England to headline this old-fashioned swashbuckler worthy of Errol Flynn.

Gun Fury, Columbia (1953).
Lewis Rachmil, producer; Raoul Walsh, director.
Donna Reed, Lee Marvin, and Neville Brand co-starred.
Once more on loan-out, Rock again worked with Walsh in this western scripted by Irving Wallace.

The Golden Blade, Universal (1953).
Leonard Goldstein and Richard Wilson, producers; Nathan Juran, director.
Piper Laurie and Gene Evans co-starred.
Acting schoolmate Piper Laurie and Rock headlined this "Easterner," in which Rock slashed about with the magic sword of Damascus. Anita Ekberg was a handmaiden.

Back to God's Country, Universal (1953).
Howard Christie, producer; Joseph Pevney, director.
Marsha Henderson co-starred.
Rock portrayed a sea caption stranded on the snow-

drifts with a busted leg, all the while dog-sledding across Canada.

Taza, Son of Cochise, Universal (1954).
Ross Hunter, producer; Douglas Sirk, director.
Barbara Rush and Gregg Palmer co-starred.

Rock accepted the mantle of Cochise from Jeff Chandler in the first few minutes of the movie and went on to woo Barbara Rush as a dusky maiden named Unga. This extravaganza was filmed in color and in 3-D on location in Utah, but the script was baby talk. Rock had to say "Unga bunga wunga" to Rush and forever after referred to her as "Unga Dos Tres."

Magnificent Obsession, Universal (1954).
Ross Hunter, producer; Douglas Sirk, director.
Jane Wyman, Agnes Moorehead, and Barbara Rush co-starred.

This remake of the 1935 tearjerker did the same thing for Rock that it did for the original star, Robert Taylor: it catapulted him to real stardom. It was the improbable—but moving—story of a playboy who blinds a widow (Jane Wyman), reforms, goes to medical school, falls in love with her, and saves her sight. Once again, Rock worked with the winning Hunter-Sirk team.

Bengal Brigade, Universal (1954).
Ted Richmond, producer; Laslo Benedek, director.
Arlene Dahl and Dan O'Herlihy co-starred.

Despite his midwestern accent, Rock played a soldier of the British empire in India. Uncharacteristically, he also let it be known he hated the script.

Captain Lightfoot, Universal (1955).
Ross Hunter, producer; Douglas Sirk, director.
Barbara Rush, Jeff Morrow, and Dennis O'Day co-starred.

This nineteenth-century Robin Hood story was shot on location in Ireland in Technicolor and Cinemascope.

One Desire, Universal (1955).
Ross Hunter, producer; Jerry Hopper, director.

Anne Baxter, Julie Adams, and Natalie Wood co-starred.
Natalie Wood portrayed an orphan girl adopted by Rock, who played a reformed gambler going respectable.

All That Heaven Allows, Universal (1956).
Ross Hunter, producer; Douglas Sirk, director.
Jany Wyman co-starred.
Hunter and Sirk tried to bring back the magic of *Magnificent Obsession* and stumbled into the realm of the ridiculous, casting Rock as a tree surgeon and Jane Wyman as an older woman who falls in love with him. However, the film was a box-office success.

Never Say Goodbye, Universal (1956).
Albert Cohen, producer; Jerry Hopper, director.
Cornell Borchers and George Sanders co-starred.
This was another of Universal's remakes, a turgid tearjerker in which Rock once again portrayed a doctor who operates to save the female lead, German actress Cornell Borchers.

Four Girls in Town, Universal (1956).
Aaron Rosenberg, producer; Jack Sher, director.
George Nader and Julie Adams co-starred.
Rock appeared briefly as himself in this story about chasing women and success in Hollywood. His friend George Nader had top billing.

Giant, Warner Bros. (1956).
George Stevens, producer and director.
Elizabeth Taylor, James Dean, and Mercedes McCambridge co-starred.
Director Stevens won the Oscar for this Texas epic and Rock got his only nomination. Rock formed his lifelong friendship with Elizabeth Taylor on the set. James Dean played the foil to Rock's Bick Benedict, then crashed his silver Porsche and died just before the last scenes were wrapped. This Warner masterpiece remained Rock's favorite of his own movies. The superlative supporting cast included Rod Taylor, Sal Mineo, Earl Holliman, Carroll Baker, Jane Withers, and Dennis Hopper.

Written on the Wind, Universal (1956).
Albert Zugsmith, producer; Douglas Sirk, director.
Robert Stack, Dorothy Malone, and Lauren Bacall co-starred.

The "good guy" role went to Rock in this oil-family saga and precursor of TV's "Dallas." And the glory went to the seedy characters. Dorothy Malone got an Oscar for best supporting actress, and Robert Stack was nominated for his role as a psychotic.

Battle Hymn, Universal (1957).
Ross Hunter, producer; Douglas Sirk, director.
Martha Hyer and Dan Duryea co-starred.

Rock starred in the true-life story of a pilot who is making up for accidentally bombing an orphanage in Germany by saving Korean war orphans.

Something of Value, MGM (1957).
Pandro Berman, producer; Richard Brooks, director.
Sidney Poitier, Dana Wynter, and Wendy Hiller co-starred.

"Moments in bhwa-nality," sniffed *Time* magazine at this rendition of the Robert Ruark novel about the Mau Mau uprising in South Africa, filmed on location.

A Farewell to Arms, 20th Century-Fox (1957).
David O. Selznick, producer; Charles Vidor, director.
Jennifer Jones, Vittorio De Sica, and Mercedes McCambridge co-starred.

Selznick teamed Rock lifelessly with his beautiful wife, Jennifer Jones, and then proceeded to make what turned out to be his own swan song. After rendering this classic Hemingway love story into dullness, Selznick decided he'd lost his touch. Selznick hired Vidor after John Huston quit as director.

The Tarnished Angels, Universal (1958).
Albert Zugsmith, producer; Douglas Sirk, director.
Robert Stack, Dorothy Malone, and Jack Carson co-starred.

Universal hardly ever failed to follow up on a success. Here, the studio brought the old *Written on the Wind* team back, minus Bacall, for this Faulkner story about barnstorming pilots. Rock got to play a drunken reporter—a mistake.

Twilight for the Gods, Universal (1958).
Gordon Kay, producer; Joseph Pevney, director.
Cyd Charisse, Arthur Kennedy, and Leif Erickson co-starred.

This was Rock's first crack at the new genre cropping up, the disaster picture. John Wayne had scored in *The High and the Mighty,* and Rock followed up as a troubled (and sometimes drunk) skipper trying to make landfall in Hawaii.

This Earth Is Mine, Universal (1959).
Casey Robinson and Claude Heilman, producers; Henry King, director.
Jean Simmons, Dorothy McGuire, and Claude Rains co-starred.

Wine, not oil, was the juice of this production sprawling with subplots and characters. Rock played a second-generation grower in California's Napa Valley.

Pillow Talk, Universal (1959).
Ross Hunter, producer; Michael Gordon, director.
Doris Day, Tony Randall, and Thelma Ritter co-starred.

History was made (and Universal was saved) by Ross Hunter's teaming of two unlikelies in a romantic comedy. Doris and Rock found an enduring style in this frisky romance of a career woman and a songwriter-playboy—sexy stuff for its time. Tony Randall scored as Doris's unsuccessful square suitor. Stanley Shapiro and Maurice Richlin won an Oscar for their script.

The Last Sunset, Universal (1961).
Eugene Frenke and Edward Lewis, producers; Robert Aldrich, director.
Kirk Douglas, Dorothy Malone, and Joseph Cotten co-starred.

A turgid western in which Rock played a lawman chasing bad-guy Douglas as the murderer of his brother-in-law. The heavy script was by Dalton Trumbo.

Come September, Universal (1961).
Robert Arthur, producer; Robert Mulligan, director.
Gina Lollobrigida, Sandra Dee, and Walter Slezak co-starred.

Writer Stanley Shapiro, who won an Oscar for *Pillow Talk*, thought this one was even better. Rock's second romantic comedy had a European flavor, and Gina Lollobrigida provided the love interest. Joel Grey had a minor part. Rock's agent, Henry Willson, was credited as assistant producer.

Lover Come Back, Universal (1962).
Stanley Shapiro and Martin Melcher, producers; Delbert Mann, director.
Doris Day, Tony Randall, and Edie Adams co-starred.

Third in the *Pillow Talk* series, this time Doris and Rock were rivals in the ad business. And Tony Randall was back playing the nebbish.

The Spiral Road, Universal (1962).
Robert Arthur, producer; Robert Mulligan, director.
Burl Ives and Gena Rowlands co-starred.

Rock said he studied harder than ever before for this role as a young doctor pitted against a witch doctor in the jungles of Java, but the movie bombed anyway. Burl Ives played a brilliant but gin-soaked old doc.

Marilyn, 20th Century-Fox (1963).
Pepe Torres, editor.

Rock narrated this early documentary of Marilyn Monroe's life, rushed out shortly after her death, composed mostly of film clips from her movies.

A Gathering of Eagles, Universal (1963).
Sy Bartlett, producer; Delbert Mann, director.
Rod Taylor, Barry Sullivan, Kevin McCarthy, and Leif Erickson co-starred.

The industry had not yet found the right mix in this docudrama, in which Rock played a colonel in the Strategic Air Command.

Send Me No Flowers, Universal (1964).
Harry Keller, producer; Norman Jewison, director.
Doris Day and Tony Randall co-starred again.

This was the last of Doris and Rock's romantic comedies, which were growing progressively weaker. By this time they were married, and Rock was a hypochondriac who mistakenly believes he is dying.

Man's Favorite Sport, Universal (1964).
Howard Hawks, producer and director.
Paula Prentiss and Maria Perschy co-starred.

Prentiss chased Rock around a fishing resort. He played a bumbling angling intellectual. In retrospect, Rock decided he was too big to play a fall guy, because he looked like he could handle anything, whether he really could or not.

Strange Bedfellows, Universal (1965).
Melvin Frank, producer and director.
Gina Lollobrigida, Gig Young, and Terry-Thomas co-starred.

Gig Young played a PR man charged with cleaning up Rock's image, including his tempestuous marriage to an Italian bombshell. The London locale was actually Universal's "European" set in California.

A Very Special Favor, Universal (1965).
Stanley Shapiro, producer; Michael Gordon, director.
Leslie Caron, Charles Boyer, and Walter Slezak co-starred.

This was Rock's last romantic comedy. Rock asked Michael Gordon to tone down the sex.

Blindfold, Universal (1966).
Marvin Schwartz, producer; Philip Dunne, director.
Claudia Cardinale and Dean Stockwell co-starred.

Rock entered the domain of the modern thriller for the first time in this confusing caper film about a psychiatrist involved in a plot to kidnap a scientist patient. The chase scenes were filmed in the Florida Everglades.

Seconds, Paramount (1966).
Edward Lewis, producer; John Frankenheimer, director.
Salome Jens and John Randolph co-starred.

Rock always needed a good director and got one with Frankenheimer, who chose arty black-and-white to film this scifi-ish story about a corporation that gives people plastic surgery, a new identity, and a second chance at life. The film became a classic without ever being a success, and thus one of Rock's finest performances was buried.

Tobruk, Universal (1967).
Gene Corman, producer; Arthur Hiller, director.
George Peppard and Nigel Green co-starred.

Rock was back boiling in Universal's pot in this churned-out tale of a German-Jewish column defying all odds to blow up Rommel's fuel depot at the Mediterranean port of Tobruk. Peppard played a German officer.

Ice Station Zebra, MGM (1968).
Martin Ransohoff, producer; John Sturges, director.
Ernest Borgnine, Patrick McGoohan, and Jim Brown co-starred.

Rock was stuck here in another stodgy role—the captain of a nuclear sub ferrying a couple of agents under the polar ice to a station containing secrets capable of ending civilization as we know it. This was the last of Rock's big money-makers.

A Fine Pair, National General (1969).
Francesco Maselli, producer and director.
Claudia Cardinale and Thomas Milian co-starred.

This Italian production represented Rock's fourth romance with a European flair. He played a U.S. police captain who becomes involved with Claudia Cardinale and—unwittingly—in a robbery.

The Undefeated, 20th Century–Fox (1969).
Robert Jacks, producer; Andrew McLaglen, director.
John Wayne co-starred.

Both Rock and Wayne played colonels—Rock in gray, Wayne in blue—in this Civil War drama shot in Mexico.

The Hornet's Nest, United Artists (1970).
Stanley Canter, producer; Phil Karlson, director.
Sylvia Koscina co-starred.

After surviving a Nazi ambush, Rock enlists the aid of some war orphans to blow up a dam in Nazi-occupied Italy.

Darling Lili, Paramount (1970).
Owen Crump, producer; Blake Edwards, director.
Julie Andrews co-starred.

Writer-director Edwards turned his wife and America's singing sweetheart, Julie Andrews, into a German spy for this one. William Blatty collaborated on the script.

Pretty Maids All in a Row, MGM (1971).
Gene Roddenberry, producer; Roger Vadim, director.
Angie Dickinson, Telly Savalas, Roddy McDowall, and Keenan Wynn co-starred.

Rock fulfilled his ambition of playing the villain—looking uncharacteristically sleazy in mustache and sideburns—in this film about a high school coach and counselor who murders his girl students.

Showdown, Universal (1973).
George Seaton, producer and director.
Dean Martin and Susan Clark co-starred.

Rock broke his vow not to do any more westerns and played a sheriff chasing a train robber, in turn played by Dean Martin.

Embryo, Cine Artists (1976).
Arnold Orgolini and Anita Doohan, producers; Ralph Nelson, director.
Diane Ladd, Barbara Carrera, and Roddy McDowall co-starred.

This one provided Rock with one of his most wooden roles: a doctor who finds a way to drastically speed up the maturation process. He creates a monster, albeit a pretty female one.

Avalanche, New World Pictures (1978).
Roger Corman, producers; Corey Allen, director.

Mia Farrow and Robert Forster co-starred.

This was a formula disaster picture about a group of people—each burdened with his own personal problems—trying to survive an avalanche at a winter sports paradise.

The Mirror Crack'd, EMI Films (1980).
John Brabourne and Richard Goodwin, producers; Guy Hamilton, director.
Elizabeth Taylor, Tony Curtis, Edward Fox, Geraldine Chaplin, and Kim Novak co-starred.

This rendition of an Agatha Christie mystery was a reunion of sorts. Rock turned in the best performance of all. The cast was super, but the plot didn't translate to film.

The Ambassador, Cannon Films (1984).
Menahem Golan and Yoram Globus, producers; J. Lee Thompson, director.
Robert Mitchum, Ellen Burstyn, and Donald Pleasance co-starred.

For the first time in three decades, Rock accepted second billing in this, his last movie. He played the CIA man in a subplot, while Mitchum got the top role as the idealistic ambassador. The film was previewed in selected cities and then put in mothballs. After Rock died, it was released for home video and cable TV.

TV MOVIES

"Once Upon a Dead Man," NBC (1971).
Paul Mason, producer; Leonard Stern, director.
Susan Saint James, John Schuck, and Stacy Keach co-starred.

This was the ninety-minute pilot movie for the "McMillan" series.

"Wheels," NBC (1978).
Roy Huggins, producer; Jerry London, director.
Lee Remick, Ralph Bellamy, and Tony Franciosa co-starred.

Based on Arthur Hailey's best-selling book, this auto-dynasty movie was shown in five parts, as a miniseries.

"The Martian Chronicles," Charles Fries Productions (1980).
Andrew Donally and Milton Subotsky, producers; Michael Anderson, director.
Roddy McDowall and Maria Schell co-starred.

This three-part TV miniseries, based on Ray Bradbury's science-fiction stories, was later released on tape. Rock played a father and husband on colonized Mars, simultaneously making contact with the ancient Martians and watching humanity blow itself up on Earth.

"The Star Marker," NBC (1981).
Channing-Debin-Locke Co., producer; Lou Antonio, director.
Suzanne Pleshette, Melanie Griffith, and Ed McMahon co-starred.

Rock played a big-time movie mogul in this casting-couch drama featuring a succession of submissive starlets.

"World War III," Telepictures Corp. (1982).
Bruce Landsbury, producer; David Greene, director.
David Soul, Brian Keith, and Cathy Lee Crosby co-starred.

In this topical doomsday thriller, Rock played a president-by-accident trying to avert a nuclear holocaust as the Russians tried to seize the Alaskan pipeline in retaliation for our grain embargo.

"Las Vegas Strip Wars," ITC Entertainment (1984).
George Englund, producer and director.
James Earl Jones, Pat Morita, and Sharon Stone co-starred.

This was Rock's last acting job before his "Dynasty" appearances. He played a hotel owner who tries to make his floundering enterprise the top attraction of Las Vegas.

INDEX

Hudson, Rock (*cont.*)
  stage fright experienced by, 44–45
  television career of, 134–54, 177, 180–82, 183–85, 190–91, 193, 194, 196–97, 202, 205–6
Hunt, Kimberly, 214, 215, 216
Hunter, Ross, 52, 78, 81, 171, 199, 220–21, 252–53, 274
Hunter, Tab, 23, 61, 274
Huston, John, 70

I Do! I Do!, 44, 154, 156, 176, 273
"I Dream of Jeannie," 174
"I Love Lucy," 134
International Pictures, 30
Iron Man, The, 42, 50

Jenner, Ed, 10–11
Jens, Salome, 89, 90, 94–98, 101, 154
John Brown's Body, 45–46
Jones, James Earl, 181
Jones, Jennifer, 70
Jones, Quincy, 208
Joy (RH's housekeeper), 115

Kane, Bruce, 174
Kanin, Garson, 78
Kasznar, Kurt, 74
Kaye, Danny, 11, 105, 191, 201–2
Kaye, Judy, 156, 158
Keaton, Diane, 136
Kennamer, Rex, 150, 153, 264, 266, 274
Kimble, Betty (RH's cousin), 7, 12, 13, 169–70
"King Show, Larry," 277
Klepfer, Arthur, 18–19
"Kraft Music Hall, The," 135
Kremins, Chris, xi–xii, 267–69

Ladd, Alan, 58
Lancaster, Burt, 250–51
LaRue, Danny, 128
"Las Vegas Strip Wars," 177, 180–83, 194–95

Latham, John, 252
Lauper, Cyndi, 250
Laurents, Arthur, 193
Laurie, Piper, 30, 32–36, 41–42, 44–45, 46, 52, 75, 106–7
Lawless Breed, The, 58
Lennon, John, xi, 267
Lewis, Ed, 91–92
Liberty (Christian's girlfriend), 161, 162, 163, 173, 275
Lloyd, Harold, 83
Lollobrigida, Gina, 85
Loos, Mary Anita, 76
Los Angeles Herald Examiner, 252
Los Angeles Times, 186
Lost Weekend, 65
Lover Come Back, 78, 79, 81, 83, 85
Luther, Lester, 26

"McCloud," 137
McDowall, Roddy, 196, 234, 245, 250, 274
MacGinnis, Marc Christian, *see* Christian, Marc
McGuire, Pat, 9–10, 11–18, 29, 108
MacLaine, Shirley, 250
McMahon, Ed, 148
"McMillan and Wife" (later renamed "McMillan"), 90, 120, 130, 131, 134, 135–44, 145, 147–48, 152, 154, 168, 183, 197, 236, 273–74
Madison, Guy, 23
Magnificent Obsession, 50–57, 82
Majors, Lee, 264
Maley, Ken, 140
Malone, Dorothy, 22, 67, 122, 195
Mammouth Films Inc., 152
Manchurian Candidate, The, 93
Manners, Dorothy, 34, 199
Man's Favorite Sport, 111
"Martian Chronicles," 147
Marvin, Lee, 242–43
Marx Brothers, 83
Matteoni, Gloria, 62, 63, 69, 86

ABOUT THE AUTHORS

JERRY OPPENHEIMER has been an editor and investigative reporter for the Washington *Star*, the Washington *Daily News*, the Philadelphia *Daily News*, and *United Press International News*, as well as a producer of several news programs and television documentaries.

JACK VITEK has been a reporter and editor for the *Wall Street Journal*, *Newsday*, and the Washington *Daily News*. He is co-author of *Moonstruck* and *The Defector's Mistress*.

BANTAM
SHOP-AT-HOME
CATALOG

Special Offer
Buy a Bantam Book
for only 50¢.

Now you can have Bantam's catalog filled with hundreds of titles plus take advantage of our unique and exciting bonus book offer. A special offer which gives you the opportunity to purchase a Bantam book for only 50¢. Here's how!

By ordering any five books at the regular price per order, you can also choose any other single book listed (up to a $4.95 value) for just 50¢. Some restrictions do apply, but for further details why not send for Bantam's catalog of titles today!

Just send us your name and address and we will send you a catalog!

BANTAM BOOKS, INC.
P.O. Box 1006, South Holland, Ill. 60473

Mr./Mrs./Miss/Ms. _____
(please print)

Address _____

City _____ State _____ Zip _____

FC(A)—11/86

Please allow four to six weeks for delivery.